D1108228

Living Adventures in Philosophy

Living Adventures in Philosophy

HENRY THOMAS
and
DANA LEE THOMAS

Hanover House

GARDEN CITY, NEW YORK

Library of Congress Catalog Card Number 54–5760

COPYRIGHT, 1954, BY DOUBLEDAY & COMPANY, INC.
ALL RIGHTS RESERVED
PRINTED IN THE UNITED STATES
AT
THE COUNTRY LIFE PRESS, GARDEN CITY, N.Y.
FIRST EDITION

Contents

INTRODUCTION   7

CHAPTER   I   *Empedocles, Who "Killed Himself to Prove Himself Divine"*   11

CHAPTER   II   *The Trial and Death of Socrates*   18

CHAPTER   III   *Plato's Crusade for Justice*   29

CHAPTER   IV   *Aristotle—the Philosopher Accused as a Spy*   39

CHAPTER   V   *Confucius—the Statesman in Search of a State*   49

CHAPTER   VI   *Diogenes—the Beggar-Philosopher*   57

CHAPTER   VII   *Epicurus and the Pursuit of Pleasure*   66

CHAPTER   VIII   *St. Paul, Who Saw When He Went Blind*   76

CHAPTER   IX   *Two Adventures in Courage—the Stoicism of Aurelius and Epictetus*   86

CHAPTER   X   *The Pilgrimage of Augustine—from Sinner to Saint*   95

CHAPTER   XI   *Maimonides, Who Discovered Wisdom in Disaster*   104

CHAPTER   XII   *Machiavelli—the Devil's Disciple*   114

CHAPTER   XIII   *More—the Philosopher Who Lost His Head*   123

CHAPTER   XIV   *Francis Bacon—the Philosopher Who Lived Like a Fool*   135

CHAPTER   XV   *John Locke's Bloodless Revolution*   145

CHAPTER   XVI   *Spinoza's "Expulsion" from the Human Race*   156

5

6 *Contents*

CHAPTER XVII *Rousseau—Father of the French Revolution* 165

CHAPTER XVIII *Voltaire's Adventure in Laughter* 174

CHAPTER XIX *Kant—the Hunchback Who Defied the King* 189

CHAPTER XX *An Adventure Toward the Light—the Philosophy of Goethe* 201

CHAPTER XXI *Schopenhauer's Struggle against Despair* 212

CHAPTER XXII *Auguste Comte's Journey from Suicide to Sanity* 222

CHAPTER XXIII *Thoreau's Adventure into the Simple Life* 230

CHAPTER XXIV *Nietzsche—Superman or Madman?* 240

CHAPTER XXV *Christ in Calcutta—the Vedanta Philosophy of Vivekananda* 248

CHAPTER XXVI *Havelock Ellis and the Dance of Life* 257

CHAPTER XXVII *William James, Who Brought Philosophy into Business* 268

CHAPTER XXVIII *Kropotkin's Progress from Riches to Rags* 278

CHAPTER XXIX *Croce—a Philosopher in an Earthquake* 291

CHAPTER XXX *John Dewey—the Architect of a Better World* 301

INDEX 313

Introduction

AMONG the living adventures in the world, as this book proposes to show, philosophy comes pretty close to holding the first place. There is no excursion so exciting as a trip to the summits of wisdom, no journey so thrilling as a philosophic flight.

To those of us who are fond of mystery stories, philosophy offers the greatest mystery of them all. Who are we, you and I? Who put us here? And why? But to all of us who have an open mind and an eager heart, this book is an invitation to the drama of the world's greatest thought.

And to the dramatic lives of the world's great thinkers. For the leading philosophers were no armchair heroes, no cap-and-gown warriors in an ivory tower. More often than not, they were daring pioneers, the vanguard soldiers in the battle for truth. Thus we shall observe how some of them were ready to endure poverty, ridicule, torture, oppression, exile, even death, in order that the truth might make men wise, and wisdom might make them free.

And so this book will deal not only with the general adventure of thought, but with the individual adventures of the thinkers. It will show how new ideas have been born, fresh horizons have been crossed, great mistakes have been corrected, spiritual victories have been won. While the emphasis will be upon the deed rather than the doer, the biographical element will play an important part in the story. Each chapter will present the dynamic picture of a great idea, put into the framework of the person who made it manifest to the world.

And, in the painting of these pictures, we shall attempt to show the shadows as well as the lights. For even the philosophers, though somewhat more than ordinary men, are somewhat less than angels. And at times their actions fail to measure up to the stature of their thoughts.

But for the greater part, as we shall see, the philosophers have tried to lead all of us to a saner human understanding. An adventure toward the love of wisdom and the wisdom of love.

Living Adventures in Philosophy

CHAPTER I

Empedocles, Who "Killed Himself to Prove Himself Divine"

[500?–430? B.C.]

THE DEATH of Empedocles was one of the sensations of the ancient world. He had taken his life, it was reported, by jumping into the crater of Mount Etna. For he had proclaimed himself as a god, and it was only fitting for a god to sacrifice himself for the sins of mankind.

This story of his death was generally accepted as true in his own day. "His mortal body has been consumed in the flames, and his immortal soul has been translated to the heavens in a chariot of fire."

Later generations, however, have come to regard the story of his sensational death not as an actual fact, but as a dramatic symbol. It is now believed that his disciples invented the strange story as a climax to the strangeness of his philosophy and his life.

For Empedocles was one of the most exciting personalities in history. His thoughts, as well as his actions, were like an erupting volcano. "Philosophy," as Plato has observed, "is a conversation in which the soul catches fire." It is the light of poetry illuminating the regions of thought. The earliest poets, like Homer and Aeschylus and the author of the Psalms, were philosophers. And Empedocles, one of the earliest philosophers, was a poet.

But he was also a religious teacher. And this was no accident. For philosophy is related not only to poetry, but to religion as well. Religion is the philosophy of the heart, while philosophy is the religion of the mind. The religious leader plunges confidently into the mystery of the world; the philosopher tries to find a path of reason through the darkness; and the poet illumines the scene with occasional flashes of lightning. These three are the pioneers in the great adventure of human thought.

Empedocles approached this adventure from all the three points. He was a prophet-philosopher who expressed his thought through the medium of a poem. Unfortunately we know little either of his life or of his poetry. But what we do know is enough to admit him into the circle of the world's great physical and spiritual adventurers.

II

Empedocles, a native of Sicily, was one of the fathers of democracy. He believed in the rights of the common man. He hated tyranny. One day he was invited to a feast. The host, an arrogant political leader, served wine to all the guests. But when some of them refused the wine, he dashed it over their heads. "If you don't drink it," he shouted, "you'll have to drown in it!"

Empedocles said nothing at the time. But the next day, at his insistence, the man was brought into court, tried, and condemned to death. "To compel others to do your will," declared Empedocles, "is the beginning of tyranny. And tyranny is a poisonous weed that must be rooted out."

The citizens offered to make him their king. But he refused. He preferred to remain their teacher. And their physician. He was the founder of a new school of medicine. He possessed, people believed, the healing touch. A number of miraculous cures were ascribed to him. On one occasion he was said to have brought back to life a woman who had been dead for thirty days. His followers began to regard him as a god. And he himself came to think that he was destined to lead mankind to a better life.

But his opponents, especially the powerful and the rich, denounced him as an enemy "to the established traditions of the state." They tried to put him to death; and failing in this, they brought about his exile.

Empedocles became a lonely adventurer of the mind. He was no longer interested in local politics. His chief concern now was the meaning of life—its cruelty and suffering, its destruction and creation, its apparently aimless drift between the opposing currents of Strife and Love.

But *was* this drifting aimless? Was there not some eternal law that governed the course of human existence? Empedocles believed that he had discovered such a law. And he proclaimed it in his philosophical poem on Nature.

III

Empedocles lived in the early-morning haze of philosophy (about four hundred and fifty years before Christ). Having no scientific instruments to help him, he saw the world rather indistinctly. Yet, in spite of this handicap, he caught many a glimpse of what is even today accepted as substantially true. Thus, he was among the first to hint at such "modern" ideas as the atomic theory, the chemical elements that go into the building of the world, the struggle for existence, the survival of the fittest, and the idea of evolution through nature's method of trial and error.

But let us briefly survey his philosophy.

The world, he said, consists of four elements: earth, air, fire, and water. These four elements are combined, in various proportions, into all sorts of things. The individual things keep changing all the time; they are born, they grow, they decay, they die. But the elements themselves are eternal. The real substance of a thing or a person, said Empedocles, can never be destroyed. What we call "death" is only a rearrangement of the elements of life.

Life, therefore, is eternal. It could never have sprung out of death, and it can never sink back into death. For life is a positive *something,* and death is a negative *nothing;* and it is impossible for something to emerge out of nothing, or to merge into nothing.

The end of a person's existence is not an annihilation, but a transition to another existence. Death is not a passing *away*, but a passing *on*.

Empedocles, like the Oriental philosophers, believed in the transmigration of souls. We are born, he said, again and again in the continual reshuffling of the elements that make up our existence. And the form we assume in a future life depends upon the character we develop in the present life. "He who has sinfully polluted his hands with blood . . . must wander thrice ten thousand seasons from the abodes of the blessed, being born throughout the time in all manners of mortal forms, changing one toilsome path of life for another."

These consecutive paths of existence will drive us on and on, as long as we prefer contentiousness to contentment, belligerence to peacefulness, hatred to love. For then our soul, migrating from body to body, will never be at rest. "The mighty air will drive it into the sea, and the sea will spew it out upon the earth; the earth will toss it into the blazing sun, and the sun will fling it back to the eddies of the air. Each will take the soul in turn, and all will reject it, one by one."

He himself, Empedocles believed, belonged to this category of restless souls. "I have been a boy and a girl, a bush and a bird, a beast and a fish in the sea . . . I am an exile from the gods, because I have put my trust in insensate strife."

IV

And this brings us to another important point in Empedocles' philosophy. All things, he declared, are governed by Strife and Love. Strife divides, Love unites. "Strife, called also by the name of Enmity, results in the devastation of war. Love, known also under the name of Friendship, leads to the constructiveness of peace."

Strife is centrifugal. It tends to tear us away from the center of life. But Love is centripetal. It helps to bring us back to the center.

And all history is a struggle between these two forces. For nations, like men, are living organisms. They are born out of harmony, or Love; and they live and flourish until discord, or Strife, tears them apart. And then Love reunites their elements into other nations which, like individuals, must submit to the eternal laws of birth, growth, decay, and transition into another form under a new birth.

And thus the innumerable units of the world—men, animals, cities, states, nations—are being constantly shuffled and divided and reunited into new forms as the two opponents, Strife and Love, play their eternal Game of Life. His own day, Empedocles declared, was a period of Strife. "But in the Golden Age, men worshiped only Love." And in that happy period, "there was no war, and no cruelty or hate. And the altar did not reek with blood, but this was held in the greatest abomination among men, to eat the limbs [of animals] after tearing out the life."

As to the ultimate triumph in the struggle between Strife and Love, Empedocles leaves us in some doubt. We must remember that the bulk of his writing has been lost. Today we have only a few fragments of his philosophical work. But these fragments seem to convey the idea that Love will be triumphant in the end. The Golden Age and the Perfect Man represent the philosophical theory as well as the prophetic dream of Empedocles.

Thus, for example, Empedocles had an instinctive idea of evolution. His theory anticipated Darwin's by almost twenty-five hundred years. It was therefore tentative, crude, and incomplete. Yet it definitely pointed to human progress through nature's experiments.

Nature made all sorts of animals, and incomplete parts of animals like heads without necks and arms without shoulders, and compelled them either to adapt themselves to their environment or to perish in the attempt. And only the fittest survived. Thus, as time went on, the parts of animals developed into whole animals, animals developed into men, and men are beginning to develop into gods. All this evolution is a process of adaptation—the survival of those creatures that are best able to adapt themselves to their environment.

Hence there is a progressive movement of Nature from the lower to the higher forms of life.

But the highest form of all is the life of the gods. And the principle that transforms a man into a god is the power of Love. As men gradually evolve from life to life, "they rise to the status of poets, physicians, philosophers and seers. And thence they rise up as gods exalted in honor, sharing the hearth and the table of the other gods, free from human woes, safe from destiny, and incapable of hurt."

This evolution—from the animal to the human and from the human to the divine—is a gradual purification. Purify yourself in your present existence. Cast out the divisive elements of your soul. Abstain from destructive emotions and revengeful thoughts. Refuse to hate or covet or kill. Don't touch the flesh of animals— "you may be eating your own ancestors." Turn away from Ares, the god of war, and pay honor to Cypris, the goddess of love. Be gentle to man and beast and bird. Prepare yourself to become— if not in this life, then in the next migration of your soul—"a man of rare knowledge, skilled in all manner of peaceful works, a man possessing wisdom, which is the greatest of all wealth." And thus purified, you will become endowed with foresight, the final step on the way to the divine. Your vision will no longer be confined to the little horizon of your sight. For then you will "see everything of all the things that are, in ten, yea twenty lifetimes of men."

And now, stepping out of the role of the philosopher and into that of the prophet, Empedocles declares: "My friends, I know that what I speak is true." He himself, he believes, has become purified at last. "In the course of my many lives, I have wept and wailed when I saw the unfamiliar land." But now, at last, he is on firm ground. He has cleansed himself of the merely human; he has finally attained to the divine. "I go about among you an immortal god, no mortal now." And wherever he appears, he tells us, his disciples greet him with reverence and love. "They go after me in countless throngs, asking me what they must do for the sickness of their body and the salvation of their soul."

V

And so he went about after he had been exiled—"a god among men"—healing people, inspiring them, scolding and teaching them in their ignorance—"I know my words will fall upon deaf ears when people are addicted to hate"—imploring them to cease from their slaughter—"See you not that you are devouring one another in the thoughtlessness of your hearts?"—and pointing out to them the way of escape from "the repetitious wheel of destiny" in order that they might come into the presence of the Eternal Guardian of mankind—"that sacred and unutterable Mind flashing through the world with rapid thoughts of Justice and Harmony and Hope."

This, in brief, is the teaching of the first philosopher-poet in Europe. The prophet of the new religion of democracy. For all of us, he declared, are essentially equal. Tossed about from migration to migration through the desire for war, we are nevertheless headed in the right direction through the power of peace. And the end of the journey is the same for all. The return to the source from which we have started—the all-embracing presence of God.

The reported suicide of Empedocles, therefore, was a religious parable. It brought home to the world, in a dramatic and picturesque lesson, the idea that salvation is born out of suffering, and that the ordeal of fire is the gateway to life. The exile of Empedocles, the persecution of the martyr and the crucifixion of the saint—all these are but the temporary gestures of hatred against the eternal triumph of Love.

CHAPTER II

The Trial and Death of Socrates

[469–399 B.C.]

IN HIS NOVEL, *The Time Machine*, H. G. Wells takes us upon a flight of the imagination into the distant future. Let us board this Time Machine for a similar flight into the past. Speeding over an arc of twenty-four centuries, we find ourselves on the streets of Athens, in 399 B.C.

We are on the way to the Court House, where Socrates is about to be tried for his life. The city is an amazing combination of beauty and squalor—golden statues and marble palaces and ankle-deep garbage and mud. And the people, like their city, have a psychology of violent contradictions. They take equal joy in creating and in destroying. They love harmony, and yet their political life is a life of continual discord. They converse with the gods and cheat their neighbors. They are a nation of precocious savages—precocious in their art, and savage in their dealings with one another. To model an imperfect finger on a statue is a grievous sin. To amputate the thumbs of their captured enemies is a noble and patriotic act.

Such are the people who are going to pass judgment upon the wisest man of his day. Brilliant minds and unstable hearts, these men of Athens, tossed about by their passions like flames in the wind. Only a few years earlier, we recall, they condemned their greatest sculptor, Phidias, to die in prison on a trumped-up charge. Genius in ancient Athens is a bitter and dangerous gift.

As we enter the Court House, the jurors are filing into their seats. There are five hundred of these jurors—an unwieldy number, more susceptible to mob hysteria than to mature deliberation.

And now the jurors are seated, and the three accusers are ready to begin. The prisoner is brought into the dock. There is a hubbub of excitement throughout the audience. Socrates alone remains calm.

The philosopher is by far the most striking personality in the Court House. Though seventy years old, he walks with the resilience of a man of forty. His face is tanned from his lifelong habit of teaching under the open sky. A strolling peddler of wisdom without pay. From his bald head to his bare feet, he looks like a squat bronze statue. Grizzled beard, round and bulbous nose, keen but compassionate eyes, and thick lips parted in a cynical yet friendly smile—he strikes you as half satyr and half saint.

His gaze travels over the audience. A disillusioned father looking at his wayward family. Foolish and excitable children, mature only in their grown-up capacity to do evil.

Yet he pities them as he observes their troubled faces. They have been through a harrowing period—a long and devastating war, a revolution followed by a dictatorship, and a counterrevolution degenerating into a government of selfish politicians rather than wise statesmen. No wonder everybody is suspicious of everybody else. There have been tragedies enough to unsettle the sanity of his people. It will be a hard day in court for any man who dares to think.

But hush, the trial is about to begin.

II

The clerk reads the indictment:

"Socrates is guilty of a crime against the state: first, for refusing to worship the gods whom the city worships; next, for corrupting the youth. The penalty due—is death."

A gasp of astonishment from a number of people. One young man whispers sarcastically to another: "They call Socrates an atheist because he believes in only one God."

But Socrates remains unperturbed. He will answer the indictment in due time. Let the accusers first have their say.

The leader of these accusers, Anytus, is a leather merchant. He harbors a personal grudge against Socrates. His son is one of the many disciples of the old philosopher. Anytus blames Socrates for having "seduced" the young man away from a "profitable career." He wants the "subversive teacher" removed in order to restore his son's affection for the conservative smells of the leather business.

But this isn't all. The other accusers, too, are anxious to have Socrates out of the way. He has been an irritating "gadfly" to the men in power. This objective on the part of the accusers becomes more and more obvious as the "evidence" is brought out against him. You get the distorted picture of an "agitator"—a man who has been spreading ideas that threaten the security of the old and the morals of the young.

Yet you also get the feeling that the Athenians are somewhat reluctant to insist upon the death penalty. Though the indictment specifically calls for this verdict, the accusers in their summary have left many loopholes for the philosopher's escape. It seems pretty obvious that they will be satisfied if he takes advantage of these loopholes. What they want is to curb his tongue rather than to take his life.

And, indeed, the Athenian law provides for just such an alternative. At the end of his speech, Anytus offers the jury a choice between his own demand for the extreme penalty and any reasonable suggestion for a lighter punishment that Socrates may care to make. This is strictly in accordance with the legal procedure of Athens.

So it is up to Socrates himself. His fate lies in his own hands. He can plead for exile instead of death. And the chances are that the jury will accept his plea.

What will Socrates do?

III

There is a recess now before Socrates begins his defense. While we speculate about the nature of this defense, it will be interesting to glance at some of the highlights of his life. His conduct in the past may give us a clue as to what he is going to say and how he will say it.

Several people in the audience, we note, are echoing our own thoughts. Let's listen to them.

"I served together with him in the war against Sparta," an old man is saying to a younger man. "His endurance was something to marvel at. It was in the dead of winter. The ground was all snow and ice. The rest of us had our feet bundled up in fleeces and felts. But Socrates marched barefoot. Wanted to feel Mother Earth under his soles, he said. And he sang as he marched!"

"Yes," replies the young man. "Nothing seems to faze him. Cold, hunger, fatigue, insults, threats—he takes it all with a shrug or a smile."

"And he can hold his wine, too," remarks a third. "I've never seen the like of it."

"I've heard about that famous Symposium." The speaker, to judge by his dress, is an Egyptian. "I mean the banquet where Socrates ate and drank and discussed love with his friends till the peep of dawn."

"You mean *Socrates* stayed awake till the peep of dawn," breaks in the old man. "All the other guests had fallen asleep. The wine was too strong for them. But Socrates drank a final toast to Apollo, the god of light, and went out to teach in the streets."

"I heard him that day," observes one of his pupils. "And, as usual, he was the only wide-awake man in the city."

A vigorous nod from one of the other spectators. "That's why he's on trial today. The politicians hate to be reminded that they're asleep, and that they keep chasing foolish prizes in their dreams instead of attending to the welfare of the state."

"In all his life," rejoins the first speaker, "he has never truckled to authority or failed to speak his mind."

"But what will he do at this trial, now that his life is at stake?" asks the Egyptian.

"The same as he has always done," replies the old man. "When we were in the Army together, he risked his neck again and again to save other soldiers. Whatever the crisis, you may be sure that Socrates will march straight ahead."

"Well, let's see."

The recess is almost ended. Socrates will soon be called upon to speak.

But he seems to be in some sort of trance. "It's one of his strange peculiarities," whispers the old man to his companions. "Once, in the Army, he stood on his feet all day and all night, buried in deep thought. I watched him for a long time. Not a single muscle moved."

"Just like now," observes the Egyptian. "Look at him. He seems to be in silent communion with someone."

"Maybe," ventures his pupil, "he's asking God what to do."

"This is exactly what he told me one day," nods the old man. "I jokingly remarked that he must have been receiving a message from Heaven during his trance. He smiled and said, 'You're quite right, my friend. I listen to the Divine Voice, and it tells me what to do—or, rather, what *not* to do.' "

"I wonder," whispers the pupil, "what the Voice is saying to him now?"

"We shall find out soon enough," replies the old man.

IV

The trance is over. The spectators who have left the room during the recess are back in their seats. The judge calls for order. He nods to Socrates. The philosopher rises to his feet. His head is held high, and his face is serene.

He speaks in a low but steady voice. No defiance in it, yet no uncertainty and no fear.

And his speech is one of the most exalted ever uttered by the lips of man. It is neither a defense of his conduct nor a plea for mercy, but rather a reaffirmation of his faith. Faith in the justice of his cause, and in the moral certainty that no evil can happen to a good man, either in life or after death.

But let us listen to him.

"Pay little attention to Socrates," he tells the judges and jury, "but much more to the truth. . . . My accusers have spoken so persuasively they almost made me forget who I was. And yet they have hardly uttered a word of truth. They have warned you not to be swayed by my eloquence. But you can see for yourselves that I am not a great speaker. I am neither a fiery orator nor a persuasive lawyer, but a simple man in search of justice. . . .

"So please bear with me if I cannot use the language of the courts. This is the first time in all my seventy years that I have had to appear before a judge. Just let me speak in my own way. Give heed not to the manner of my speech, but to the truth of my words. . . .

"And the truth is—that I am innocent of any of your charges against me. . . ."

Socrates now goes on to refute the charges, one by one. People call him an atheist. They claim that he considers himself too wise to believe in the gods. "But I am not wise at all. For I know that I know nothing. . . . Maybe *this* is what you call my superior wisdom. Most people don't even *know* that they don't know."

This is a subtle blow at the arrogance of his accusers. Socrates realizes that his words may endanger his life. But he is not trying to save his life; he is merely anxious to establish the truth. "This has been my only purpose in life. I go about telling the rulers that they ought to know something about the art of governing their state, just as the cobblers know the art of mending their shoes. . . . I have been quite absorbed in this occupation—call it, if you will, my service to God—and I have had no time to attend to any concern of my own. I am, as you know, in utter poverty because of my devotion to this work."

So much, then, for the first accusation. Socrates is not a disbeliever in the gods. On the contrary, he is the only true believer —he translates his devotion to God into the teaching of justice among men.

There is a restless murmur in the Court House, like the buzzing of bees who have been stirred by something strange in their hive. Socrates holds up his hand for silence, and the buzzing gradually dies down.

And now he is ready to answer the second accusation. He begins by calling one of his accusers to the witness stand. A dramatic situation, this—the prisoner cross-examining his judge.

This man is the poet Meletus. He, too, has a personal grudge against Socrates. For the philosopher has ridiculed him as a subtle weaver of words rather than a profound dispenser of wisdom.

And now Socrates entangles Meletus in the web of his own testimony. He gets the poet to assert that everybody in Athens is able to improve the youth and that Socrates alone is unable to do so. This, of course, is an absurdity—to think that the whole world is wise and Socrates alone is foolish. There is a ripple of laughter in the audience as Socrates goes on:

"I have said enough in answer to the charge of Meletus. But I know only too well how many enmities I have incurred, and that these enmities—due to my habit of freely speaking my mind —will most likely bring about my destruction. Not Meletus, nor yet Anytus will condemn me—if I am condemned—but the envy and the vilification of the world. This has been the death of many good men, and will be the death of many more. There's no danger of my being the last."

And thus Socrates has sealed his own doom. But he is not the least bit afraid. "A good man should not weigh his chances for life or death. He should only consider whether his actions are right or wrong. The one tragedy in the world is not death but disgrace."

Is it fearlessness, or mere bravado, that makes Socrates speak so nonchalantly about the death that stares him in the face? But let us listen. Perhaps he will answer our doubts: "No one knows whether death, which men fear as the greatest evil, may not in reality be the greatest good. . . . If you kill me, you will injure not Socrates but yourselves. For you who take away my life will suffer far more than I whose life is taken away. You will have removed from your midst the one man who dares to stir you into nobler action."

An involuntary shout of approval from many throats. But again Socrates asks for silence. "Please don't interrupt me until I am through. . . . As you know, my fellow Athenians, I have never shrunk from danger. I have held public office on two occasions—one under the dictatorship, and once during the democracy. On both occasions I criticized my superiors for their execution of some of our best citizens. No herdsman, as I pointed out, should take pride in his ability to diminish the number of his flock. . . .

"Men of Athens, this is about all I have to say. I will not ask for mercy. I am a creature not of wood and stone, but of flesh and blood. I have a family—a wife and three children. I will not bring them into court to arouse your pity. It is not pity I want, but justice. Don't be influenced by your feelings, but by your reason. Your duty is not to offer a present of my life, but to render a judgment in accordance with the law. For I believe in the laws of God, and in a sense perhaps higher than that which any of my accusers may entertain. And to you and to God I commit my cause, to be determined as is best for you and me."

V

The trial is finished. The jurors are casting their votes. There is a heated argument among the audience. What will the verdict be? Freedom, exile, life imprisonment, death?

We don't have to wait long. The vote has been counted, and

the judge calls out the result—220 votes for acquittal, *280 votes for death.*

How will Socrates take the verdict? In accordance with the Athenian law, he has the privilege of suggesting an alternative.

And this is precisely what he does when he stands up to speak again. But what an amazing speech! "Men of Athens, you propose death as the penalty; and there are many reasons why I am not grieved. But what shall I propose on my part? Clearly that which is my due. And what is my due after a lifetime of service in your behalf and at the sacrifice of my own interests? Maintenance at the public expense; so that, free from financial worries, I may devote the rest of my life to your instruction. This is the punishment I propose for my crime."

Pandemonium in the Court House. Cries of "Colossal effrontery!" "Sublime courage!" "The hemlock! The cup of hemlock!" "A god in our midst, and we slay him!" Insults hurled back and forth, blazing eyes, threatening fists. But Socrates begs once more for silence. "I have a few more words to say."

When the tumult has finally subsided, Socrates goes on. "I will not ask for exile; for wherever I go, I must insist upon speaking the truth. So if you cannot bear with me a few years longer, I am ready to die. . . .

"And why should I fear to die? Let us look death in the face— and what do we find? It is one of two things: a state of unconsciousness, a night of sweet sleep without a dream; or a journey to a new world, where you can meet the noblest and the wisest men of the past. In either case, I ask you to be of good cheer about death.

"And as for my accusers, they have done me no harm, although they have meant to do me no good. They have merely erred in their judgment; and for this I can forgive them, even as God forgives them. For their evil arises from their ignorance. . . .

"The hour of departure has arrived, and we go our different ways—I to die, and you to live. As to which is the better fate, God only knows."

VI

Socrates is led off to prison, to await his death. We shall stay in Athens until the end.

Just a few days before the execution, there is a strange rumor afloat. Socrates is going to escape. A number of his friends have arranged for it. And it is common knowledge that the judges and the jailers will shut their eyes at any attempt to rescue him.

But they have reckoned without their host. When his friend Crito comes to him with his plan, Socrates flatly refuses to go. "I have been condemned by the laws of the state, and I must abide by them. Otherwise I should be setting an example of lawlessness before my fellow men."

So the old philosopher-soldier is determined to march straight to the end.

And the end comes just a month after the trial. His friends have been with him in the prison all day. Earlier in the day he has sent his wife and his children home. "I don't want any wailing at the last minute."

Again, as in the Court House, Socrates is the least perturbed among all those present. He talks to them about the immortality of the soul—a testament of hope for the living uttered from the edge of the grave.

In this testament of hope, Socrates becomes the spiritual godfather of the Apostle Paul. His faith in the immortal soul is the basis for the Christian doctrine to be proclaimed four centuries later. The body is a prison, declares Socrates in his cell, and the soul is the prisoner waiting for his release.

The day is rapidly drawing to a close. The poison is to be given to him at sunset. Yet his words are confident, unhurried, serene. He turns his subject over and over, so that his friends may see it from every possible angle. The body is an instrument, and the soul is a song played upon it. If you break the instrument, you cannot destroy the song. Indeed, the soul becomes truly alive when it is purified from the imperfections of the body. So let us not grieve when the strings of our life are snapped. They were poor material at best. Let us rather rejoice that the soul is free at last to return to God. "Even the swans, when they are about to die, sing at their best. For they feel instinctively the call of Apollo, the god of music. Shall I, a philosopher, have less faith than the swans?"

And now the swan song of Socrates is ended. The hour of sunset is near. The jailer enters the cell. "Forgive me, Socrates, who in obedience to the authorities must give this cup of poison to the noblest and gentlest and best of all men." As the jailer turns away, he bursts into tears.

At this point, all the others break down—all but Socrates. "What is this strange outcry?" he asks. "I sent away the women in order to avoid this sort of scene. Be quiet, then, and have patience."

Ashamed at these words, his friends hold back their tears. Socrates drains the cup and begins to walk about the cell, with a heartening smile, a pat on the shoulder, and a word of comfort for each of his friends.

And now the poison has traveled up his legs. He can no longer walk. He lies down and covers his face. "When the poison reaches his heart," whispers Crito, "it will be over."

Suddenly Socrates uncovers his face. He has one more message for his friends. "Crito, I owe a cock to Asclepius. Will you remember to pay the debt?"

A final offer of gratitude to the god of healing. For Asclepius is about to release him from the fitful fever of life.

"The debt shall be paid," replies Crito. "Is there anything else?"

There is no answer. The poison has reached the heart. Crito closes his master's eyes and mouth. . . .

The tongue of Socrates is stilled. But his words live on. "Return pity for iniquity, forgiveness for hatred. Do not punish your enemies for their ignorance; teach them rather that they may know."

CHAPTER III

Plato's Crusade for Justice

[427–347 B.C.]

PLATO, like Socrates, pursued his philosophy in the stress of political turmoil and at the risk of his life. Let us follow him as he escapes from Athens at the time of his master's execution.

Socrates has been his teacher, his confessor, his guide. Yet Plato is too sick, in body and in mind, to visit this "gentlest and wisest of men" on his last day. And right after the execution he is warned that it is unsafe for him to remain in Athens.

He is twenty-eight years old. He is not afraid to die, but he has a message to deliver to the world. He must finish his master's unfinished work. He must put into living words Socrates' unwritten testament of truth.

And so he goes into voluntary exile—to seek further wisdom and to find time for the development of his central thought, the crusade for justice.

Fortunately, he is well equipped for his travels. A member of the aristocracy, he is blessed with a rich purse, a superb body, and a brilliant mind. He has served with distinction in the Army, and he has twice won prizes as a champion wrestler. His real name is Aristocles; but he is better known as Plato—a nickname his friends have given him because of his broad shoulders.

And so the sturdy athlete is ready for his adventure—to plunge into strange lands, to meet the greatest minds of the day, and to wrestle with the mysteries of life and the problems of human conduct.

But in all his travels, Socrates is to be his guiding star. "I thank God," he has declared, "that I have been born a Greek and not

a barbarian, a freeman and not a slave, a man and not a woman;
but above all, that I have been born in the age of Socrates."

II

For twelve years we lose track of him. But the various scenes
of his travels have left their stamp upon his mind. From the wide
horizon of his ideas we know that he must have journeyed to
Egypt, Sicily, Italy, and perhaps even to India and Judea. He is
less Athenian, and more cosmopolitan, upon his return. He shows
a wholesome respect for the old traditions of the Pharaohs as
well as for the political innovations of the Italians. And he has
also learned, it seems, about the Hebrew passion for justice and
the Hindu love for peace.

Indeed, his mind is a rich kaleidoscope of all the great thoughts
and problems that have occupied the philosophers and the statesmen throughout the world. Nothing has escaped him. The double
and single standards of morality, the public ownership of women,
of children, of wealth, free speech, free worship, free love, trial
marriage, eugenics, birth control, feminism, socialism, communism, democracy, the drama of the human struggle toward the
brotherhood of man—these are but a handful of the ideas that
have become part and parcel of his philosophical equipment.
And he is ready to weave all these ideas into a pattern for a new
Republic, a Kingdom of Heaven established on earth.

But his Republic is not meant merely as a theoretical treatise.
Plato is intrepid enough to translate it, if possible, into an actual
fact. Not far from Athens there is a city—Sparta—where some
of these ideas have been tried out. Visitors are not welcome in
Sparta; but Plato manages to gain admittance into the city,
where he can examine a crude prototype of his ideal Republic
at first hand.

And the result of the examination is not altogether satisfactory.
Plato's attitude toward the Spartan Government—an experiment

in Marxism 2,300 years before Karl Marx—is a mixture of admiration and disgust.

The Spartans, he observes, have a sort of communal life. The citizens eat in a common mess hall. For it is their ideal that no one in their city shall go hungry. Extreme wealth and extreme poverty are equally unknown. Everybody contributes to, and is supported by, the public fund. From each according to his ability, to each according to his needs. Nobody is permitted to own silver or gold or precious stones. The money is made out of iron—too heavy a metal to accumulate in a great mass.

And thus there is a certain degree of equality among the people. But it is the equality of brutes. Their sole business is to wage war. Only the sturdiest among their children are allowed to grow up. The rest are drowned in their infancy. Those who remain alive are educated in barracks instead of schools. They are taught to obey their officers and to fight the world.

The entire city, in short, is an armed camp. Every foreigner is a potential enemy. The Spartans will have no traffic with other states. They will enter no league for a United World or even a United Greece. They encourage no literature, no science, and no art save the art of military conquest. And so the city stands behind its iron curtain, with a chip upon the shoulder, always ready to instigate a quarrel with other nations in order to Spartanize the world.

Plato uses this city as a starting point for the building of his ideal Republic. He will adopt its good features and either modify or eliminate the faults. For his City of God must be not only strong enough to defend itself against its enemies, but noble enough to turn its enemies into friends.

III

We now find Plato back in his native city. There is a lull in his adventurous life. The passions aroused at the death of Socrates have subsided. It is now comparatively safe to think.

For a time, Plato will devote himself to teaching and writing. He will instruct his people, sharpen his mind against theirs, and lay down the blueprint for his philosophy—the perpetuation of justice and good will among men.

The period of his teaching is the calm before the storm. There is plenty of trouble ahead, but not for the present. He opens a school in a suburban garden called the Academy. And here, under the olive trees on the banks of a murmuring river, he tries to work out for himself, and to explain to his pupils, the diversified pattern of the world.

And this pattern, as he sees it, is a harmonizing of parts into a concordant unit. At times he refers to this harmony as *Beauty,* at other times as *Goodness.* But at all times he translates Beauty and Goodness into the simple word, *Justice.*

This is the basic word, the solid foundation upon which he builds his ideal Republic.

The *Republic* is the most important of Plato's works. His other books may be regarded as more or less elaborate sketches for this final master painting—The Commonwealth of Righteousness.

Shall we pay a visit to Plato's mythical Republic? This in itself will be a great intellectual adventure.

IV

Let us begin with one of its typical schools. The first thing that strikes us in this school is that all the children refer to all the other children either as brothers or as sisters. "Is this," we ask the teacher, "a peculiar custom among your people?"

'No," replies the teacher, "it is an actual fact. These children *are* all brothers and sisters."

And then, in reply to our look of astonishment, the teacher goes on to explain:

"All the children born in our Republic are the result of communal mating. Our best men are mated with the best women, our next best with the next best, and so on down the line. This, as you know, is the principle that farmers apply to their cattle. We try here to produce the best possible humans, just as the farmers try to produce the best possible livestock."

The teacher allows us to catch our breath and then goes on:

"There are no individual marriages in our Republic, and no private families. All the men and all the women possess all the children in common. As soon as the children are born, they are taken from their parents and placed in a public nursery. Thus the parents don't know their own children, or the children their own parents."

"But isn't this a heartless thing to do?"

"On the contrary," replies the teacher. "We find it quite humane. In this country there is no feeling of parental possessiveness so hurtful to the children of other countries. Nobody can boast that *his* children are wiser or better than *your* children. For all the adults are regarded as the parents of all the children in this city. And thus we have universal brotherhood not in theory but in truth."

"And what about the education in this 'universal brotherhood' of yours?"

"It is a system calculated to bring the best to the top. Up to the age of twenty, all our children receive the same education— gymnastics to strengthen the body, music to harmonize the mind, and religion to fortify the soul."

"And after that?"

"At twenty our children take the first great examination—or, as we prefer to call it, the weeding out. We subject them to all sorts of pains and toils and conflicts. Those who fail in the examination are relegated into the lowest rank—the merchants, the farmers, the factory workers, and the clerks. Our ranks, as you see, depend not upon inheritance or birth, but upon actual worth."

"And what about those who pass the examination?"

"They are allowed to continue their schooling up to the age of thirty. And then comes the second weeding out. Those who fail to pass this new test are put into the second lowest rank—the executive assistants, and the military officers for the defense of our state."

"And those that are left after these two difficult tests?"

"They are, as you will guess, but few in number. For five years they are taught philosophy—the meaning of the Ideas which serve as the models for the material things of the world. It's a difficult subject, this Platonic doctrine of Ideas. But I shall try to explain it, to some extent, in a few simple words. For we must go on to Plato's dominant purpose—the establishment of the Idea of Justice.

"The world, declares Plato, is an imperfect copy, or image, of God's perfect Idea. And every object on earth is the picture of an Idea in Heaven. The divine Idea of Manhood, for example, is the *real* thing, like the sun shining down upon the earth. But the individuals we call men and women are but the blurred images of the sun reflected in so many puddles. Dry up a puddle, and it no longer reflects the sun—that is, the individual man dies. But the Idea of his Manhood, the brightest and the best part of him, lives on.

"And thus the *things* of the world, perceived by the senses, are the fleeting shadows of time; but the *Ideas* of the world, discerned by the mind, are the solid substance of eternity.

"And these Ideas of God are woven into a harmony, like the notes of a song, which constitutes the pattern of life. And the name of this Ideal Harmony, in the character of the individual, in his attitude toward the world, and in the interdependence of human sympathies and cities and stars, is Justice.

"This, then, is the philosophy that is taught to the select circle —men and women alike—who survive the second test. It takes them five years to grasp the Ideal Harmony in all its ramifications, especially as it applies to our practical life."

"And then?"

"They are taken down from the heights of philosophy into the cavern of competitive life. They are thirty-five years old now. For the next fifteen years they are compelled to put their philosophy to the test—to beat their wings against the tempests of hatred and

ambition and jealousy and contentiousness and greed that keep
swirling over the hearts of men in their daily struggle to get ahead.

"And the few whose ethical standards remain unbroken in this
final test are automatically selected as the rulers of the state.

"For the Ideal Republic must be guided by men and women
with the sturdiest minds and the gentlest hearts. These highly
trained and severely tested philosopher-kings and philosopher-
queens are the only people in the world who can keep us at peace
with ourselves and in harmony with all mankind."

This is a strange sort of education we have just seen in Plato's
Republic. But let us glance at a few of the other peculiarities of
his state.

Wherever we go, we find adequate pay and a sense of fair play.
Business men abstain from amassing excessive profits. Workers
refrain from demanding unreasonable wages. Criminals are
treated like patients who are mentally sick. They are sent to
hospitals where they are kept out of mischief while they receive
treatment for their ills. And the length of their confinement depends, not upon the arbitrary decision of a judge, but upon the
scientific judgment of a physician. The criminals stay in the
"hospital" until they are cured.

There are no lawyers in the Republic, and not many laws.
"The more laws you enact," maintains Plato, "the more tempta-
tions you manufacture for lawbreakers." The people have been
taught to govern themselves instead of being restrained by the
police. And so every man is free to attend to his own business,
provided he does not interfere with the rights of other people.
This, declares Plato, is the true definition of Justice—a friendly
interweaving of mutual interests instead of a snarling warfare of
irreconcilable plots.

V

Such, then, is the quiet dream of Plato—a city of justice,
beauty, wisdom, brotherhood, and good will. But Plato is not

content to remain a dreamer. He wants to take an active part in the actual building of his Utopia. And so he leaves the shelter of his riverside academy to undertake the most dangerous of pioneering jobs. He secures an offer from Dionysius, the King of Syracuse (in Sicily), to establish a Republic of Peace in the jungle of our quarrelsome world.

He leaves Athens with no little misgiving. He is only too well acquainted with the fickleness of the human heart. Dionysius is in love with Truth in the abstract. But how will he take it when he comes face to face with it? The philosopher-king, Plato has declared in his *Republic,* must abandon all property beyond what is absolutely necessary. He must have no private house, no salary beyond his limited needs, no precious metal save that of a sterling character, and only such food and drink as will keep him physically and mentally fit. How will a king not trained in philosophy, or a philosopher not exercised in nobility, ever attain to such a high standard of regal power? In the mythical Republic, you will recall, it takes fifty years of rigorous training to produce only a handful of perfect statesmen. Certainly Dionysius, brought up from infancy in a palace, must be too fickle in his emotions and too arrogant in his power to fit into the framework of Plato's philosopher-king.

But, whatever the cost, Plato is willing to take the chance. He will try to tame the king into a philosopher even at the risk of his own life.

So let us see what happens. At first, Dionysius receives Plato with open arms. He finds it pleasant to have a wise old "counselor" at court. It gives him prestige among his subjects.

But after a while, the trouble begins. Dionysius has hired Plato as an approving commentator, but not as a critical guide. His desire for a Utopia has been an exciting fantasy to play with, nothing more. He definitely doesn't want a Republic in which he must give up any of his royal prerogatives. Or any of the advantages of his ministers, who are grafting upon the resources of the state. "I like your ideal," he tells Plato, "but I don't like your ideas."

And so, when Plato tells him to rebuild the state from the bottom up, he listens with a skeptical smile. When Plato advises him to "turn his courtiers inside out" and to shake their pockets free of their briberies and thefts, the king's smile turns into a frown. And finally, when the philosopher insists that even the king himself must submit to an examination in order to prove his fitness for the job, the frown turns into a snarl. "This is treason against the king!"

"And insubordination against the government!" comes the echo from the infuriated ministers. Before long, the entire populace takes up the cry. They listen the most, observed Plato, to those who shout the loudest.

Plato is arrested. Will there be another murder like that of the master? His disciple is ready for anything now. His *real* job is finished. He has given to the world the *Idea* of the perfect state. Others will carry it out. A little at a time, perhaps, but there it is—the blueprint for the brotherhood of man. Plato is resigned to his death.

But his punishment is worse than death. The king hits upon a simple plan that will tickle his humor and enrich his purse. He decides to sell the world's freest mind into servitude.

And thus Plato, the born aristocrat, becomes a slave.

VI

The man who bought Plato was, fortunately, less of a tyrant than Dionysius. He kept him for a time as the tutor of his children. He treated him not unkindly, but as an inferior assigned by the gods to a menial job.

And, perhaps, this is precisely what the gods had in mind. "Every life," said Plato, "has a pattern." To round out the pattern of his own life, he was compelled to break his bread at the table of the slaves as well as to drink his wine at the banquets of the king.

For in this way he realized the meaning of true justice—the

cultivation of what is good in the least of us, the elimination of what is bad in the best of us, and the adjustment of the ambitions of all of us into the harmony of ultimate peace.

VII

Plato was released from his bondage through the intercession of his friends. And he was able to end his days in the quiet memories of a stormy life. He sent out his pupils to the ends of the earth; and they, inspired by his wisdom, proclaimed a truth that lies at the basis of every great social and political reform:

"When the philosophers are the rulers, or the rulers have the spirit and the power of philosophy, only then will the human race emerge from its troubles and behold the light of day."

CHAPTER IV

Aristotle–the Philosopher Accused as a Spy

[384–322 B.C.]

WITHIN THREE successive generations, the Greeks produced the three wisest philosophers in the ancient world—Socrates, Plato, and Aristotle. And all three of them were repaid with torture for their thoughts. The great Greek poet, Aeschylus, had written that the human mind can learn only through suffering. He forgot to add that generally it is not the pupils but the teachers who suffer the most.

II

Aristotle was born (384 B.C.) in Stagira, a Greek colony about two hundred miles north of Athens. But he spent most of his boyhood at Pella, the capital of Macedonia—the "Wild West" of the ancient world. His father had been appointed court physician to King Amyntas, the father of Philip and grandfather of Alexander.

Aristotle and Philip often played together as children. Philip had the arrogance of a prince and the manners of a guttersnipe. And his passions were as untamed as those of the wild beasts that prowled in the forests of Macedonia. Aristotle learned to curb his temper in order to preserve his life. He saw too many people killed in street riots and court duels because of their too great propensity for heated arguments. The ability to hold yourself in check, concluded Aristotle, is the first mark of a gentleman. And the best insurance for a long life.

This lesson in practical ethics came home to him again and again throughout his career. For the philosophy of Aristotle, as we shall see, grew out of one of the stormiest periods in ancient history. It was an age in which it seemed that the entire world would be swept away in a deluge of blood.

But to return to Aristotle. At eighteen he left Macedonia to enter Plato's Academy in Athens. Here the master and the pupil conceived a great affection for each other. But it was a union not without its lovers' quarrels. A philosophical dispute, they observed, arouses a pleasant warmth without stirring up a consuming fire.

And so for a time they argued about wisdom and let the world go by. Plato was too old to get into the active "swim" of life, and Aristotle was too young. He remained at the Academy—as student and perhaps also as "graduate instructor"—for several years.

And then Plato died, and Aristotle found himself without a home. His friendship with Philip, who was now the King of Macedonia, made his further stay in Athens uncomfortable. For King Philip was threatening the liberty of all the Greek states. Aristotle, though innocent of any hostility against Athens, was obliged to leave the city.

But he had nowhere to go. Stagira, his native town, had been burned to the ground as one of the victims in the misfortunes of war. Perhaps, like his teacher before him, Aristotle might be able somewhere to find a king in search of a wise man.

And he did find this king in a former classmate, Hermias, the ruler of a small state in Asia Minor. He went to the court of Hermias, who, unlike Dionysius, treated his philosopher with respect. He even gave him his adopted daughter (or his sister), together with a bountiful dowry, in marriage. For about three years the course of Aristotle's philosophy and true love ran as smoothly as could be expected.

And then there came a change. King Philip remembered the thoughtful companion of his boyhood days. He heard of his brilliant career as a man. Aristotle might prove to be a good tamer for his savage whelp of a son, Alexander. He invited Aristotle to become Alexander's tutor. And the philosopher accepted the invitation.

III

Aristotle's second stay at the Macedonian court was even stormier than the first. The royal household was an unholy trinity of barbarian wildcats. King Philip, a genius in organizing empires, was unable to organize his own family. His wife, Queen Olympias, was a psychopath. In order to vex her husband, she told him that Alexander was not his son, but the offspring of a god who had visited her at night. And Alexander, a boy of thirteen, actually believed the fairy tale about his divinity. He treated both the king and the queen as his abject slaves.

And he looked upon his tutor, Aristotle, with as little regard. The philosopher was compelled, again and again, to serve as moderator in the tempestuous quarrels between the royal pupil and his parents. At one of the court banquets, when father and son were stupefied with drink, Philip tried to stab Alexander because the boy had insulted him. He was too unsteady on his feet, however, to make a perfect lunge. He fell to the ground, and Alexander was saved for future quarrels and debaucheries and wars.

This was the sort of atmosphere in which the philosopher had to teach and live. But it came to an end after only a few years. Philip was about to set out on a campaign against Persia, when he was assassinated—at the direct instigation of Olympias, it was said, and with the approval of Alexander. At Philip's burial, Olympias insisted that the murderer should receive the same honors as the murdered king.

With the death of Philip, Alexander assumed his father's scepter and sword. He dismissed Aristotle. He had no further time to think. From now on, he wanted to fight. "For my part," he wrote to his former teacher, "I had rather excel in the knowledge of right than in the extension of might." But that statement was sheer hypocrisy. He showed his real attitude toward philosophy in general, and toward his teacher in particular, by hanging Aristotle's nephew, Callisthenes, for his refusal to worship him as a god.

IV

But, in one respect, Alexander was helpful in the development of Aristotle's philosophy. He had lavished enormous sums of money upon his teacher. It was in general keeping with his unbridled passions and extravagant aims. In whatever he undertook, Alexander plunged himself to the hilt. He was determined to be the greatest conqueror, the most ruthless murderer, the most lavish giver, in all history.

Aristotle wisely took the money when he escaped with his life from the munificent madman. But he didn't pocket this money. He spent it all—the modern equivalent of about four million dollars—upon his scientific and philosophical research.

And now we see the pupil and the teacher engaged upon two stupendous adventures—Alexander's determination to spread death, and Aristotle's effort to understand life. The sentimental historians have devoted too much attention to Alexander, and too little to Aristotle. They have held the conqueror up as a model of all that is great and noble and virtuous in human life. They have called him a founder of cities, a tamer of savage races, and a uniter of nations and men. The historians make much of the few cities that he founded. What of the many cities that he burned down? It is not true that the wars of Alexander sowed the seeds of Greek culture in the ancient world. It was the wisdom of Aristotle that performed this miracle. Alexander paved the way between nation and nation with the skeletons of slaughtered men. Aristotle built the road of mutual understanding with the substance of living ideas. It is the philosophers and not the fighters who are the greatest adventurers. For it is they who explore the world without killing and try to bring it into a unity of knowledge without hate.

This, at any rate, was Aristotle's job. He hired a thousand men—soldiers of science—and sent them to the ends of the earth in search of the various specimens of the living world. They collected plants, animals, stories, ideas, fossils, and rocks; and Aristotle organized their contributions into the comprehensive encyclopedia of philosophy, literature, science, theology, and art. It was the first *co-operative* effort of the human intellect on a world-wide scale.

Aristotle founded a zoological garden and a museum of natural history, and opened a new school of philosophy in Athens. Here he remained for only about ten years. But within that single decade he produced a number of books which—to quote from Professor Fuller's *Life of Aristotle*—rank to this day as "one of the supreme achievements of the mind of man." These books, numbering nearly a thousand, covered practically every subject of artistic endeavor, metaphysical speculation, ethical conduct, and scientific research. We have at present but a handful of these books. But even this handful is almost a complete library of human thought.

Aristotle was a "walking encyclopedia" in a literal sense. He was always "on the go" as he lectured to his students or dictated his books. His school, situated in a park, was nicknamed *Peripatetic,* which means "walking about." Let us take a stroll with this restless philosopher and his students as they talk about the mystery of God and the morals of men.

Our host is a man of fifty—bald, keen-eyed, somewhat pot-bellied from his partiality to good food, and a little abrupt in his speech. For he has no patience with stupidity. He talks with a lisp—a congenital defect which shows us that this godlike philosopher is only human after all.

His clothes, too, display a human weakness for finery. This is the result of his early initiation into the splendors of the royal court.

But his voice is soft, and his manner urbane. He is the perfect gentleman teaching us to steer a middle course of wisdom in the tempest of the world's ambitions and jealousies and lusts. He is talking from personal experience. Even now he is steering his own middle course between the passions of the Macedonians, who distrust him as a Greek, and the suspicions of the Greeks, who misjudge him as a Macedonian.

Let us listen to him.

V

All life, from the lowest animal to the highest man, Aristotle tells us, is a striving toward greater growth. (This idea, we note by the way, is a foreshadowing of Darwin's theory of evolution.) Thus, the human egg grows toward the embryo; the embryo toward the child; the child toward the man; the man toward God.

Hence God is the goal of all growth, the fulfillment of every life, the source of every motion, the inspiration of every hope.

But just what, we ask, is the nature of God? Is He our Creator, our Judge, our stern Master, our loving Father, or what?

And Aristotle's answer is a bit startling. God, he declares, is none of these things. He is not the lover of men, but the object of their love. He is the Unmoved Mover of the world.

This is a rather vague description of God. But isn't it a pretty good description of Aristotle himself raised to divine stature? Most of the pictures of the divinity as given us by philosophers and theologians are glorified portraits of the authors themselves. If a triangle could talk, said Spinoza, it would define God as a perfect triangle. Perfection, as seen through the eyes of the storm-tossed Aristotle, was the power to contemplate the struggles of mankind without being hurt in the scuffle. Aristotle's conception of God is the consummation of his own heart's desire—the unmoved and undisturbed Mover of men to greater thoughts and nobler deeds. And the inducement to their motion is their love toward God, who is the Philosophical Observer of the perfect life.

And so Aristotle's God, like Aristotle's ideal picture of himself, is pure reason, fulfilled happiness in the contemplation of man's effort to bring himself closer to Heaven.

And man's progressive journey toward God, Aristotle tells us, can be hastened through the adoption of the Golden Mean. Here again Aristotle speaks out of his personal experience. He has seen the tragic consequences of the extreme passion of Philip, the extreme aggressiveness of Alexander, and the extreme apathy of a world waiting to be enslaved. None of these extremes, concludes Aristotle, is good for man. *Nothing too much.* The safety of individuals and of nations lies in the middle course.

Every human virtue, in other words, is a mean between two extremes. Courage, for example, is the golden mean between recklessness and cowardice; liberality, between extravagance and stinginess; reserve, between audacity and bashfulness; moderation, between self-indulgence and self-denial; friendliness, between adulation and strife.

This ideal of the Golden Mean, we must remember, is the utterance of a man who tried to bring sanity into an insane age. From time to time, Aristotle heard of the butcheries of Alexander. News traveled slowly in those days. But the refugees who came out of Asia brought back amazing tales about this Macedonian madman. His life was a furious whirlwind of illogical caprices. He would donate a kingdom to a friend, and then dash out the fellow's brains in a drunken fit. One of his officers died because he refused to follow the physician's orders. Alexander crucified the physician as a punishment for his officer's stupidity. And then, as an "atonement" for his own injustice, he slaughtered the inhabitants of an entire city. Once, when a dancing girl who had entertained him asked for a torch to light her way home, Alexander set fire to the palace of the Persian king. "This, my dear, will give you plenty of light," he said.

Such were the stories Aristotle heard about his former pupil, who wept, it was reported, because there was only one world for him to conquer. And Alexander, some of the refugees declared, had heard "unfavorable" stories about Aristotle. The philosopher was teaching "dangerous" ideas against aggression and in favor

of peace. Aristotle had analyzed all the various forms of government, and he had come to the conclusion that "of all these governments, dictatorships are the worst." This, believed Alexander,
was meant as a direct stab against himself. He had expressed his
determination, it was rumored, to "attend to Aristotle" as soon
as he got through with his conquests.

But Aristotle went right ahead with his teaching of the superior
government and the better life. The ideal government, he said,
is that in which the rulers aim at the contentment of the ruled.
It isn't the form of the government that matters, but the spirit
of the men at the head. Aristotle made a thorough study of 158
state constitutions, and he found that the chief trouble with most
of them was the absence of political vision. What we need, he
said, is an all-embracing consideration of all the different classes
and interests. Thus, for example, a plutocratic state is likely to
collapse because of the businessmen's indifference to the interests
of the workers, and a democratic state is liable to fail because
of the workers' indifference to the interests of the businessmen.
In short, a government is bad when the rulers try to advance
only themselves; it is good when they try to secure the greatest
happiness for the greatest number.

For the purpose of our existence, declared Aristotle, is not
aggressiveness but happiness. And the surest way to happiness is
to live a life of reason, to form the habit of self-control in all our
thoughts and deeds. To live, in other words, like gentlemen.
Seek, counseled Aristotle, for a modicum of wealth—not too
much, not too little. Form a few but true friendships. "A friend
is one soul in two bodies." And cultivate your mind. "In the quiet
exercise of the mind lies perfect happiness."

Happiness, therefore, is synonymous with gentlemanliness—
that is, *gentleness*. Aristotle's ideal man is eager to serve, yet
reluctant to be served. "To confer a kindness is a mark of superiority; to receive it is a mark of subservience." The superior man
never feels revengeful, and always forgets injuries. He is equally
unmoved by unjustified praise or unmerited blame. He is not
critical of others, except to their own face. He allows neither

exultation nor dejection to run away with him. He bears both his good and his bad fortune with dignity and grace. And he finds as much joy in other people's happiness as in his own.

To summarize Aristotle's ethics in a few words, "He who is hostile to others is his own worst enemy; but he who is friendly to others is his own best friend."

This ethical philosophy of Aristotle has been criticized as a "bouquet of fragrant platitudes." But to this criticism Aristotle might have answered, "So is a flower bed of violets—simple, obvious, commonplace, but *alive*. All the recurring phenomena of Nature are platitudes—the daily rising of the sun, the nightly miracle of the stars, the springtime resurrection of the earth, the warmth of human friendship in a world at war." What Aristotle did was to organize the laws of practical friendship into a moral code. This code in Aristotle's day was something new under the sun. And if by now his words sound trite, they are none the less true.

VI

In Aristotle's day his philosophy was considered so revolutionary that it brought about his undoing. His doctrine of the Golden Mean had placed him between two devastating fires. One of these fires—the hatred of Alexander—was suddenly quenched with the death of the conqueror as the result of a drunken debauch.

But the other fire—the suspicion of the Athenians—flared up more violently than ever. The Athenians accused him of sending secret information to Alexander's successor, Antipater. And when this accusation was proved to be false, they resorted to their old trick. They prepared to arrest him, like Socrates, for "blasphemy against the gods."

Aristotle eluded the arrest just in the nick of time. "I will not give Athens," he said, "a second chance to sin against philosophy." He escaped to the island of Euboea.

But he did not escape into safety. The world was too full of extremes—hatred, suspicion, jealousy, aggressiveness, greed. Here was a famous character in disgrace—an easy target for the unscrupulous hunters of the world. Whoever struck him down would win the acclaim of the mob.

The philosopher cheated them all of their prey. He drank a cup of hemlock only a few months after his departure from Athens. And in death, as in life, he chose the middle course of courage—equally free from ferocity or fear. "Since there is no further permission to teach, there is no further reason to live."

CHAPTER V

Confucius—the Statesman
in Search of a State

[551–479 B.C.]

THIS IS the story of a philosopher without a home, a vagabond who was hounded from city to city during his lifetime and who was glorified throughout the nation after his death. It is the story of one of the strangest characters in history—the irreligious founder of one of the world's great religions, an atheist who became a god.

A cynic has remarked that the history of China may be summarized in eight words: "From confusion to Confucius and back to confusion." "Before the wisdom of Confucius there was chaos; and now that his wisdom is forgotten, there is chaos again."

II

The Chinese believed in a crude form of evolution many centuries before Darwin. The world, they said, is several million years old; and the human race is a slow development from lice into men. This is what Confucius heard as a youngster. And when he read the history of China, he had reason to believe that there might be some ground for this unflattering theory about the origin of the human race. On almost every page he read about man's inhumanity to man. One emperor, for example, was said to have drowned three thousand rebels in an artificial lake of wine. Some of the other emperors compelled their prisoners to

hold fiery metals in their hands, or to walk upon greased tight-
ropes stretched over blazing pits of charcoal. And the rulers invited their guests to watch the "fried lice" as the victims fell into
the flames. One of the greatest philosophers of China, Teng Shih,
was decapitated for his daring to point out the difference between
right and wrong.

At the time of Teng Shih's death, Confucius was a young man.
Born in 551 B.C., he was the son of a general. He lost his father
when he was three years old, and he grew up with a hatred of
militarism. He was determined to be a teacher of the arts of
peace.

Perhaps he was unaware of the fact that as a teacher of peace
he would find himself in a battle against the world. He was only
twenty-two when he began to teach. By that time, he had already
married, begotten a son, and divorced his wife. For she had refused to bring up a family on his meager pay.

And so he continued his struggle alone. Unable to secure a
regular position, he traveled in an oxcart from town to town, and
picked up his pupils—rich or poor—wherever he could find them.
From those who could afford it, he took a small fee; from the
rest, a measure of rice, a piece of fried meat, or nothing at all.
In his spare moments, he amused himself with archery and music.
He was an accomplished flute player; and, like Plato, he found
in the harmony of a song a good pattern for the government of
a state.

But Confucius was a restless soul. He was not content with
teaching and playing the flute. He wanted to see a better world,
and to work for it with all his might. He went to Lao-tse, the
"wise old man" of China, and asked him for the secret of the
good life.

Lao-tse gave him the secret in a few words that sound almost
like a Chinese version of the *Sermon on the Mount:*

"Refrain from fighting, and nobody on earth will be able to
fight with you. . . . Repay an injury with kindness. . . . To
those who are good, I am good; and to those who are not good,
I am also good. In this way, all learn to be good. . . . To those

who are sincere, I am sincere; and to those who are not sincere, I am also sincere. In this way, all learn to be sincere. . . . The softest thing can overcome the hardest. There is nothing in the world softer than water; and yet for attacking things that are hard and strong, there is nothing more powerful in the long run."

Confucius, though a lover of peace, found this philosophy a little too tame. After all, he was the son of a soldier. He was anxious to be a spiritual if not a physical fighter. He saw too much injustice in the world. A quiet submission to tyranny, he felt, would never do. When he returned to his pupils, he declared that he admired Lao-tse but couldn't quite understand his unworldly point of view. "I know how birds can fly, fishes swim, and animals run. But the flier may be shot by the arrow, the swimmer hooked, and the runner snared. . . . I do not know how the dragon mounts on the wind through the clouds, and rises to Heaven . . . I can compare Lao-tse only to the dragon."

Confucius decided that his philosophy would be different from that of Lao-tse. It would deal with the practical problems of the earth rather than with the nebulous morality of Heaven. "Treat gentle people with kindness," said Confucius to his pupils, "but cruel people with justice." In other words, pay everybody according to his desserts.

III

Confucius was courting trouble when he refused to bow to cruelty "as the grasses bow before the wind." He entered politics, "to stem," as he said, "the course of injustice." The king of his native province of Lu had heard of his popularity among his followers. He made Confucius his minister of crime.

Confucius proved to be too honest for the job. The province of Lu was infested with gangsters and thieves. A delegation of businessmen asked Confucius what to do about the situation, and he replied: "The only way to put an end to stealing, is to put an end to profiteering. For the smaller your profits, the less things you can buy for others to steal."

The businessmen didn't like this sort of advice.

One day a father came to him with a complaint about his son's delinquency. Confucius ordered both the son and the father to be imprisoned for three months. "The father who fails to teach his son his duties," he declared, "is equally guilty with the son who neglects them."

On another occasion, a husband asked him what to do about his ill-tempered wife. "Sweeten her temper with honey," he said. "Don't answer bitter words with bitter words. If you do, you will only create two opposing tempests that will wreck your lives."

"But what if my wife injures me?"

"Punish the injury, and then forget it. A forgotten injury is like last year's snowstorm. It can no longer freeze your toes."

Again and again, when people came to him with complaints about others, he asked them to examine themselves. "The trouble with most of us," he said, "is that we expect our neighbor's conduct to be better than our own."

He insisted that the greatest sin is anger. "An angry man is full of poison that reacts against his own life."

It was a new kind of justice that Confucius was trying to administer. The King of Lu was unable to appreciate it. He preferred the old recipe for ruling his country—bribe, feast, and fight. He had just received a present of eighty "sing-song" girls. The king succumbed to beauty and dismissed virtue from his court.

Confucius became a homeless wanderer again. "I now live in the north, the south, the east, and the west. I am tossed about by every wind, but within me I find a haven of peace."

IV

Like Jesus, he wandered with his disciples from town to town, receiving stones for bread and spreading the gospel of joy wherever he went. A disciple described him as a "weather-beaten bell ringing out God's message to those who are willing to hear."

But Confucius himself was not concerned with the mystery of God. He was more interested in the morals of men. When his disciples asked him about Heaven, he told them to keep their eyes fixed upon the earth. "Never mind about serving God, whose desires you do not know. Serve your fellow men, whose desires and problems you do know."

The common people adored him. But those in power began to fear him. They hired assassins to kill him. But he went right ahead with his work. Several of his disciples, afraid for their own lives, deserted him. "His company is too dangerous for fellow travelers." One of them, who had become a hermit, advised Confucius to do likewise. "Disorder," said the hermit, "spreads over the world like a swelling flood. And who is there to stop it? Instead of withdrawing from state to state, why don't you withdraw completely from the haunts of men?"

But Confucius shook his head. "If I don't associate with men," he asked, "with whom then shall I associate?"

His business was neither with the animals nor with the angels, but with his own kind. He was still looking for a sick government that might be willing to be saved. But he found no such government. Everywhere the sickness had gone to the heads of the rulers. There was little justice anywhere on earth. Except, perhaps, in a few isolated spots. Once, as he was climbing over a rugged mountain with his disciples, he found an old woman weeping in a graveyard. When he asked the reason for her grief, she said: "My husband's father was killed by a tiger, and then my husband, and now my son."

"But why do you live in such a dangerous place?"

"Because," she replied, "there are no oppressive magistrates here."

"My children," said Confucius turning to his disciples, "remember this. An oppressive magistrate is crueler than a tiger."

And so Confucius went on with his adventure in wisdom, risking the attacks of animals and the fury of men, and describing himself with a shrewd and disarming frankness: "I am clever enough, perhaps, but not as good as I would like to be." He was not always above raising his stick against a sluggish pupil, or barking out a curt answer to a stupid question. Once, when he was lost in the wilderness, a traveler who met his disciples told them he had seen a "mountain of a man with the disconsolate appearance of a stray dog." When his pupils repeated these words to him, Confucius laughed aloud. "A perfect description!" he shouted. "Perfect!"

He regarded himself as a "homeless, harmless dog" whose bark of warning many people misjudged as a growl of anger. Yet he felt no anger against anyone. He never wasted any time attacking the views of other philosophers. "Arguments arouse tempers, and a man in a temper is unable to see the truth."

He harbored no grudges, in spite of his many nights without shelter and days without food. He was getting along in years, but he still retained the serenity of his youth. "Confucius," he wrote at this time, "is a man who in his eager pursuit of knowledge forgets to eat, who in his joy of attainment forgets his grief, and who in his love for living, does not perceive the approach of old age."

V

And yet, so far as worldly success was concerned, he considered himself a failure. "The kings are brutal, their subjects ignorant, and my words nothing but snowflakes falling upon a silent sea."

He was now in the winter of his life. Too old and sick for further traveling, too poor and hungry for complacent ease.

And too restless to wait patiently for death. It was only now, on the edge of the grave, that he entered upon the greatest adventure of his career. He undertook, at sixty-nine, to write a Bible for the generations to come.

In the preparation of this Bible, he aimed at no originality. "All the great things have already been said." What he tried to do was to select and edit the best thoughts of the past for the guidance of the future. But he made these thoughts his own with imaginary speeches and anecdotes which, like jewels, display the colors of the rainbow when you hold them up to the light.

He laid down a set of rules for the government of his people and a host of ceremonial duties for their self-discipline. Every act of life was subjected to the strict observance of an elaborate ritual. "Approach the poorest man with the dignity due to a king." Confucius taught his people to regard even the peasant's hut as a palace. He gave them the most precious of gifts—a sense of self-respect and a feeling of respect for others. "Be loyal to yourself and charitable to your neighbors"—this was the sum and substance of Confucius' teaching. Instead of an anemic selflessness, he implanted in them the ideal of a "co-operative selfishness." He defined this sort of intelligent selfishness as *reciprocity*—an idea which may be regarded as the negative aspect of the Golden Rule. "Do not unto others," said Confucius, "what you would not have others do unto you."

If people live by this rule for but a single century, said Confucius, all violence will disappear from the earth. And all resentment and discontent. "Multiply your good will toward others, and you lay up a capital of good will toward yourself." For, in the long run, all kindness is repaid with interest.

This, in brief, is the "democratic principle" that Confucius left as his legacy to the world. With the establishment of this principle, he said, "the whole world will become a Republic. . . . People will converse sincerely with one another and cultivate universal peace. . . . Every man will have his security, and every woman her rights. . . . Evil scheming will be repressed and will find no way to rise again. . . . Robbers, traitors, and thieves will no longer infest the earth. . . . This is the state of what I call the Great Understanding."

The Great Understanding between individuals and nations. "And when will this come about?" The master, recalling his exile from the kingdom of Lu, smiled and said: "When I have met with a king who loves Virtue as he loves Beauty."

VI

But he met with no such king. He finished his Bible, and "withered away, untended, like a plant." He died in obscure poverty, a defeated and disillusioned old man. Multitudes had listened to his words, but only a few had taken them to heart. And they, like the early Christians, were persecuted for their faith. One of the Chinese emperors had issued a decree to burn all the extant books of Confucius. A number of the faithful disciples concealed their copies. The king decided to burn the men in place of their books.

But Confucianism, like Christianity, lived on. It finally became a religion; and Confucius, the atheist, began to be worshiped as the Son of Heaven. Temples were built in his honor, and sacrifices were offered to him as a god. But those who offered the sacrifices revered the name and forgot the man. They split into sects and began to quarrel about the interpretation of his words. And the quarrels led to war, and more war, and the world today is no nearer to the Great Understanding than it was in the day of Confucius.

Has Confucius therefore failed? The answer to this question may best be given, perhaps, in the words of Bernard Shaw: "Neither Confucius nor Jesus has been a failure as yet. For nobody has ever been sane enough to try their way."

CHAPTER VI

Diogenes—the Beggar-Philosopher

[c. 412–323 B.C.]

A FEW YEARS after the death of Socrates, one of his disciples, Antisthenes, was lecturing to a class of students in Athens. Suddenly there was a commotion in the classroom. A disreputable young beggar stormed into the room and insisted upon becoming one of Antisthenes' pupils. He was greeted with shouts of anger and derision. "Get out, you mangy dog!" "No beggars allowed here!" "Put him where he belongs!" "Into the gutter with him!"

The teacher tried, gently but firmly, to dismiss the young beggar. But in vain. "They call me a dog. Very well, I snarl like a dog. But I've got a grip on philosophy, and I'm going to hold on!"

Again the teacher tried to remonstrate, and again the young beggar insisted upon his intellectual rights. "Go on, beat me as much as you like. There's no stick hard enough to drive me away!"

And so the young fellow stayed on. They called him the "dog-philosopher"—or "Cynic"—from his canine appearance and barking demeanor and biting tenacity against the conventions of the world.

This outspoken young cynic was Diogenes, the philosopher who "refused to be respectable because he wanted to be right."

II

There was much in common between Diogenes, his teacher Antisthenes, and Antisthenes' teacher, Socrates. All three believed in the doctrine that the beginning of wisdom is self-knowledge. But Antisthenes went a step beyond Socrates; and Diogenes, as we shall see, went several steps beyond Antisthenes.

Socrates had said, "Know yourself." And Antisthenes declared, "Learn to *master* yourself through the *knowledge* of yourself." This pagan apostle of self-mastery through self-knowledge was a Tolstoyan character. An aristocrat up to the time of Socrates' death, he became finally disgusted with the conventions of society and dedicated himself to a life of simple goodness. He dressed like a workingman, associated with the common people, and taught a philosophy that they could easily understand. A return to Nature—the Kingdom of Heaven on earth.

This Christian philosophy four centuries before Christ insisted upon the rejection of material wealth and the acceptance of the spiritual values of life. Nothing was to be owned in private. There were to be a community of possessions and a communion of souls. There were to be no masters or slaves, no luxury for the few and hunger for the many, and no laws favoring the strong at the expense of the weak.

It was therefore no difficult matter for Antisthenes to admit the ragged young philosopher into his classes. Though Diogenes was too outspoken at times, his teacher was not altogether displeased to see his own ideas expressed in his pupil's blunter terms. And even his fellow students learned to enjoy the observations of their cynical classmate. He had no use for literature, he told them. "Why waste your time on the sufferings of Odysseus and neglect your own suffering?" He made sport of their love for music. "You waste your time stringing your lyre when you ought to spend it harmonizing your soul." And he ridiculed the pretensions of the orators. "They condemn in others the injustices that they perpetrate themselves."

Above all, he insisted upon a transvaluation of values. He used a picturesque image to express this idea. "Let's change the currency of the world." Abolish the false coinage of human prejudice. Erase the stampings of your social conventions—"the men stamped as generals and kings, the ideas stamped as honor and wisdom and happiness and riches." All these are base metal, useless and false.

III

Diogenes had reason to feel sensitive about counterfeit coins. His own father, a banker, had been imprisoned for "defacing the coinage." And he himself had been exiled from his native city of Sinope, on the Black Sea, as a suspected accessory in the crime.

The suspicion was probably groundless. For Diogenes looked upon money, as well as upon the comforts it could buy, with the utmost contempt. He was not at all sorry to leave the shelter of his city. When the authorities condemned him "to depart from Sinope," he retorted, "And I condemn you to remain in Sinope."

He became a vagabond citizen of the world. He had lost his social standing. But he had found a number of things that he prized much more—leisurely walks, undisturbed slumber, and freedom from the fear of thieves because he had nothing worth stealing. Above all, he had gained his independence. "Aristotle," he said, "breakfasts when it pleases the King; Diogenes, when it pleases Diogenes."

He wrapped himself up in a shabby cloak. "When I meet a man who is elegantly dressed, it is *my* eyes and not *his* that get the richer feast. For I see his splendor, and he sees my rags." One night he observed a mouse running about "with no need of a sleeping place or fear of the dark." He decided to live like the mouse. "Until he and I are caught in the trap of fate, we shall be content to scurry unhampered over the world." And so, leaving the burden of possessions to those who "wanted to be burdened with cares," he slung a knapsack over his shoulders—"that I may carry my home about with me"—and entered upon the carefree adventure of exchanging his philosophy for his food. "Call me a beggar, if you will. But I pay with a word of wisdom for every crust of bread."

He slept outdoors when the weather was good. "What better

roof do I need than the sky, what softer pillow than a bundle of rushes, and what richer ornaments than the flowers and the trees?" When the weather was inclement, he crept "like a snail" into an empty watercask. "For this shelter I need no furniture, and no lock or key."

Though he traveled a good deal—on foot—he made his headquarters at Athens. Here he lectured in the streets to idlers who came to scoff and remained to think. He was very fond of company, and was often seen conversing with the crowds on the way to the theater or the games. On one such occasion, a man asked him derisively whether he was going as a spectator.

"No," he replied, "I am going as a contestant."

"A contestant against whom?" laughed his interlocutor.

"My pleasures and pains. I find it very exciting to wrestle against my passions and to pin them down to the earth." The greatest pleasure, he declared, is to despise all pleasure.

On another occasion, when asked how a man could get the better of an enemy, he replied, "By treating him as a friend. For friendliness, you know, is contagious."

The ragged clothes and satirical tongue of Diogenes concealed one of the warmest hearts in the ancient world.

IV

Diogenes was so bitter against folly because he felt so tender toward the fools. He wanted mankind to find greater happiness through superior wisdom. A life lived under the guidance of wisdom, he said, will result in security, liberty, and simplicity.

Security. "You can lighten the blows of fate by preparing yourself in advance." The less you expect of life, the fewer the disappointments. And the smaller your possessions, the lighter your losses. In the words of Porgy—how Diogenes would have loved that character!—"I got plenty o' nothin, an' nothin is plenty for me." Real security consists not in having much but in being satisfied with little. Ask little, and the chances are you will get it. Ask much, and your hunger will never be stilled. In this philosophy, Diogenes is at one with the writers of the Old Testament. "He has the most who is most content with the least."

Contentment is the shortest way to security. And discontent is the long and painful way that has no ending. The grass is always greener on the other side of the fence. But when you get across the fence, you find the spot as dreary as the one you have just left. And beyond *this* fence there are other spots to lure you on and on —always agitated and hungry and fearful, never satisfied or secure.

"Hence we should not endeavor to alter circumstances, but to adapt ourselves to things as they are. If we meet our hardships with a courageous heart, we can stand secure amidst a falling world."

Liberty. For then we shall be free from self-inflicted suffering. All suffering, declared Diogenes, is a state of mind. It is not your misfortune but your self-pity that causes your pain. If you have lost a loved one, you are sorry not for the departed but for yourself. The departed can not miss you, it is you who miss the departed.

So you can liberate yourself from the vicissitudes of fate by casting out your fears. Don't become a slave to your anxiety about the future or to your regret about the past. What has been, has been; what will be, will be. Assert your independence—in the face of your fate and in the presence of all men. One day Alexander the Great came to visit Diogenes as he was taking a bath in the sun. There was an interesting conversation between the would-be conqueror of the world and the conqueror of his own soul.

Diogenes: What, Your Majesty is your greatest desire at the present time?

Alexander: To subjugate Greece.

Diogenes: And after you have subjugated Greece?

Alexander: I shall subjugate Asia Minor.

Diogenes: And after that?

Alexander: I shall subjugate the world.

Diogenes: And after that?

Alexander: I shall relax and enjoy myself.

Diogenes: Then why don't you relax and enjoy yourself right now?

Alexander is said to have thanked Diogenes for his advice. "Is there anything I can do for you?" he asked.

"Yes," replied Diogenes. "Remove your shadow that stands between me and the sun."

Whereupon the king laughed and said: "If I were not Alexander, I would rather be Diogenes than any other man."

"And if I were not Diogenes," retorted the philosopher, "I would rather be any other man than Alexander."

Diogenes was so fearless because he had nothing to lose but his life. "And my life has been forfeit from the day I was born. So what difference does it make whether I pay the debt now or later on?"

It was his sense of security from the fear of the future that gave Diogenes his liberty. "The wise man will be independent of physical goods and secure in the possession of the goods of the mind— virtue, contentment, and freedom from the conventions of the world." Even Socrates, as an ancient biographer of Diogenes observed, submitted to the injustice of the Athenian courts. "I obey the law," said Socrates, "and I go willingly to my death." This was an act of slavery—an acceptance of the temporary laws of Athens as against the eternal laws of God. "But Diogenes, unlike the demagogue, the orator, the sea captain, the general, the king, and even unlike Socrates, was absolutely free. For these other men were the slaves of their own passions or fortunes. But Diogenes attained to the highest mastery of all—the complete mastery of himself." This self-mastery, he said, is the only liberty worth while.

Simplicity. The shortest way to happiness, declared Diogenes, is the simple way of security and liberty. Security through contentment, and liberty through renunciation. Diogenes not only preached this doctrine, but proved it by his daily practice. Happiness, he said, lies in the fulfillment of desire. And the simpler your desires, the more likely they are to be fulfilled.

An adherence to the simple life is healthy not only for your body but for your soul. For it will enable you to face the world with justice and truth. "Why should I lie? To gain money, applause, glory? But I have no need of these counterfeit coins."

And thus he went about the streets of Athens, begging his bread and rebuking the mighty and telling the truth. One day he was arrested as a disturber of the peace. "Who are you?" asked the judge. "A spy," answered Diogenes. And then he explained his strange answer. "I spy upon the dishonest stupidities of the world." Sometimes, in broad daylight, he walked about with a lighted lamp. When asked to explain what he was looking for, he said, "An honest man."

Often he went hungry. But even this he took with a smile. "Dogs and philosophers do the greatest good, and get the least reward." Once he was observed begging of a statue. "What is the meaning of this?" asked someone. "I am learning to meet with hearts of stone," he said.

His cynical simplicity was not merely a pose. It was the practical teaching of a man "so gentle and philanthropic"—to quote Epictetus—"that he cheerfully took poverty upon himself for the common good of mankind." Excessive comfort, he believed, is man's greatest curse. In the old Greek legend, God punished Prometheus for bringing fire to mankind. And the punishment was just. For the use of fire brings luxury and laziness and all the other woes of civilized life. When some one argued that men, unlike beasts, were "tender and naked and needed artificial warmth, Diogenes retorted that frogs, who had less hair than men, could live comfortably in the coldest water." It is all a matter of habit, he declared.

Like the Yankee Diogenes of the nineteenth century, Henry Thoreau, Diogenes came to his hardihood through his hardship. "This saintly Cynic," said Epictetus, "found himself happiest under the discipline of poverty."

Blessed are the poor, for they shall inherit the earth. One of the stories told about Diogenes sounds almost like a parable out of the Bible. "I weighed the gifts of those who offered me bread," said Diogenes, "and from those who had profited (by my teaching) I accepted, while the others I refused. For I thought it unfair to accept from those who had received nothing. And I did not dine with everybody, but only with those who needed my service as a healer. . . . On one occasion I went to the house of a very rich young man, and was received on a couch in a room hung all over with pictures and decked out with gold. I showed, by my demeanor, that I had no respect either for the person or for his possessions. . . . 'Your attitude,' he said, 'seems to indicate that I am an uneducated boor. But I will show you that I am on your side.' And in fact, on the very next day, he disposed of all his property to his family, put on the Cynic's knapsack, folded his cloak, and followed me. . . .'"

V

This is how Diogenes gathered his disciples and united them to Lady Poverty. The early Cynics renounced all family ties. Diogenes himself had no wife or children. "The true Cynic is parent of all men, has all men for his sons, all women for his daughters. . . . He is a servant of God who is Father of all."

A servant of God and none other. In the course of his wanderings he was captured by pirates. When put up for sale in the slave market, he greeted his would-be purchasers with the cry, "Come, slaves, buy a master!"

It was said that the pirates were so enchanted with his words that they took him down from the slave block and carried him off to their haunts. For a time he remained their teacher. "It is all the same to me whether I teach the pirates of the sea or the parasites of society." Finally his captors gave him his liberty in exchange for his wisdom.

He returned to Athens where he continued for many years to mint the "new coinage" of his cynical philosophy. He seemed to thrive upon the winds of ridicule and the ravages of the weather. For he lived to the age of eighty-nine.

He died on the same day, tradition said, as Alexander.

Legend has it that the two met as they were crossing the River Styx. After an exchange of greetings, Alexander said: "So we meet again, the conqueror and the slave."

And Diogenes replied: "Yes, we meet again—Diogenes the conqueror and Alexander the slave. For you were the slave of your passion for conquest. But I was the master who conquered my passions."

And, as they entered into the presence of the immortals, concludes the legend, it was Diogenes who led the way.

CHAPTER VII

Epicurus and the Pursuit of Pleasure

[c. 342–270 B.C.]

P LEASURE," observes the French writer, Remy de Gourmont,
"is a delicate art to which only a few are apt." The philosophic
quest of Epicurus was to make this art available to all mankind.
It is on earth, and not in the skies, declared Epicurus, that Heaven
can be found. And he launched the human mind upon an adventure to discover this Heaven on earth. Epicurus was a pagan philosopher whom many Christian writers have regarded as a saint.

And yet many others have pointed to him as a devil of debauchery. The adjective *epicurean* is synonymous with *sensual, voluptu-
ous, unrestrained.* The early Church Fathers condemned the philosophy of Epicurus as "an invitation to the pigsty." Among the
pious Jews an Epicurus—or Epikouros—is an atheist, a scoundrel,
and a clown. And even among many of his adherents today, the
refined pleasures of Epicurus are confounded with the "belly lusts"
of the material world.

Who was this man, so widely followed, so little understood—
the least Epicurean of the entire Epicurean sect?

II

Epicurus grew up in a generation which, like our own generation, seemed to be headed toward a tragic fall. Impelled by the
ambition of Alexander, the world was being engulfed in a whirlpool of blood. The young men had become disillusioned about life
as a result of the wars of Alexander, just as the young men are

disillusioned today as a result of the two world wars. The schools of philosophy had reached a low ebb of despair. The Skeptics questioned the ways of the gods and the values of life. The Cynics derided all human ambition as a mere chasing after dissolving clouds and vanishing rainbows. The Pessimists went a step farther. They said that even at its happiest, life is a bitter dream between a sleep and a sleep; and that the sooner the dream is terminated, the better. One of the pessimistic philosophers, Hegesias, spent all his life demonstrating to his students that the best thing for a young man to do was to commit suicide. He himself, it is interesting to note, died a natural death at the age of eighty. When asked to explain why he refused to practice what he preached, he replied that he had to live in order that he might teach others how good it was to die.

In contrast to these rejecters of life, there was a group of philosophers, called the Hedonists, who accepted life as an orgy of intoxication through sensual indulgence. Eat, drink, and be merry, was their motto, for tomorrow another Alexander may call upon you to die.

It was in this atmosphere of intellectual confusion that Epicurus passed his early years. The apostles of pain and the high priests of pleasure were trying to advise people how to adapt themselves to a world which nobody understood. The minds of the young men, unsettled by the wars of Alexander and the fears of other wars to come, were like rubber balls tossed about between apathetic resignation on the one hand, and hysterical sensuality on the other. Humanity was without a religion. The old gods had betrayed it, and no other gods had been found worthy of worship and trust.

Epicurus, like other thoughtful young men of his day, tried to rebuild the shattered world and to fill the heavens with new gods. He came to this task out of a home which had its private little turmoils amidst the larger turmoils of the Alexandrian age. He was a native of Samos, a Greek island in the Aegean Sea. His father was a schoolteacher; and his mother, a quack doctor of the soul who pretended to cure people with amulets and charms. And thus Epicurus found himself, from his early childhood, caught between the opposing currents of rational discipline and religious superstition.

Above all, he grew up with a horror of war. He was eighteen years old at the death of Alexander (323 B.C.). Together with his parents and three brothers, he was turned out of Samos as a part of the human displacement that followed Alexander's conquests. He became a refugee, drifting from country to country in search of a guiding star.

He found it at last, at the age of thirty-five, in Athens. He bought a little house and garden, invited a group of his friends to live with him, and showed them how to remain at peace in a war-crazed world.

As time went on, the Brotherhood grew in numbers, and every member contributed whatever he could afford to the general fund. It was one of the world's first adventures in co-operative living. They added more land to their modest estate, which came to be known as the Garden of Epicurus. It was a little island of tranquillity—single people as well as entire families—untouched by the tempests of life. The enemies of Epicurus began to wag their tongues about the Brotherhood. They referred to it facetiously as the "Brothelhood"—and they spread all sorts of stories about the "dissipations" of Epicurus and his friends.

There wasn't the slightest truth to any of these stories. Actually the members of the Brotherhood were the most temperate of people. They adhered to a code of plain living, high thinking, and mutual assistance without jealousy or hate. "A kindness rendered to another," Epicurus taught them, "is a kindness to yourself. . . . What you do for your neighbor today, your neighbor will do for you tomorrow."

But the main business of the Brotherhood was the pursuit of pleasure. It was this word—*pleasure*—that gave rise to the evil reputation of the Epicureans. To the world at large there was no distinction between the temporary pleasures of the flesh and the permanent happiness of the soul. It was this important distinction that lay at the core of the Epicurean philosophy.

Let us look at this philosophy a little more closely.

III

Epicurus was one of those mental adventurers who dreamed out his action instead of acting out his dream. Most of our trouble, he declared, comes out of our aimless activity. Be a spectator, rather than an actor, in the drama of life. Learn to laugh at your own sufferings. Try to calm the turmoil in your soul. And thus, to the Epicurean, the pursuit of pleasure becomes a flight from the world.

For the world, Epicurus pointed out, contains more evil than good. The human race is more closely attuned to sorrow than to joy. As Epicurus put it, our bodies have more openings to pain than to pleasure. And the paroxysm of our pain is more intense than the rhapsody of our pleasure.

The thing for us to do, therefore, is to strike a balance—to avoid the one extreme and to moderate the other. Epicurus called this balance *ataraxia*—a word which, translated into English, means *imperturbability*. "Let your mind, like our Garden, be an island of peace amidst the turbulence of your life."

This was the ultimate aim of the Epicurean philosophy as practiced in his monastery of pleasure. Walt Whitman has well expressed this idea in one of his poems:

"Me imperturbe, standing at ease in Nature, master of all or mistress of all, aplomb in the midst of irrational things . . . finding my occupation, poverty, notoriety, foibles, crimes, less important than I thought . . . me wherever my life is lived, O to be self-balanced for contingencies, to confront night, storms, hunger, ridicule, accidents, rebuffs as the trees and animals do."

Epicurus might have found just one objection to this poetical summary of his philosophical creed. Let me meet life, he said, not with the insensitiveness of an animal or a tree, but with the sensibility of a rational human being.

And this rational outlook on life reveals to us that the greatest of pleasures is the recovery from pain. "Today's joy lies in the memory of yesterday's sorrow." The harbor of safety is pleasantest to those who have just escaped from a storm. The true Garden of Epicurus, therefore, exists not in the body but in the mind.

We have a vivid picture of this mental Garden of Epicurus in the famous poem of Lucretius, *On the Nature of Things.* The Epicurean philosophy, as outlined in this poem, is—in the words of George Santayana—"perhaps the greatest thought that mankind has ever hit upon." This thought, briefly summarized, is a philosophic escape from pain, through a contemplation of Nature, to an emancipation from terror about our ultimate fate.

Most pain, especially when it is severe, is brief. And even if the pain is protracted, it can be lessened by the discipline of your mind. Remember that all suffering, however bitter, is followed by a sweet sleep. And you can always avoid much of your suffering by "lying concealed" from the cruelties of the world. Don't waste your strength in a battle against the waves and the winds. It is so much wiser to observe, from the shelter of the shore, the struggles of the victims who have been caught in the storm.

But don't be merely a disinterested observer. Try to make your own shelter a haven for those who have been saved from the wreckage. Inspire them with a "longing for the quiet beauty of the sequestered life."

Live quietly, eat and drink moderately, and enjoy the cheerful company of your friends. "It is more important to know *with whom* you are to eat and drink than *what* you are to eat and drink." This abstemious and friendly sort of existence will bring you not only physical but spiritual health. For "it is not possible to live pleasantly without living wisely and fairly and justly, or to live wisely and fairly and justly without living pleasantly."

And thus the Epicurean life of pleasure was not merely a selfish escape from the world. It was rather a concerted effort to calm the world's fever and to lessen the world's pain. Epicurus often spoke of his order as "our holy body." The membership was devoted to the holiness of shared sympathy and the continual rejoicing in one another's joy.

But, declared Epicurus, there can be no joy where there is fear. Hence the first requisite for a life of pleasure is to abolish the fear of death. The end of life, as taught in the religion of his day, is the beginning of real suffering. The superstition about the punishment of the soul in the afterworld is, to Epicurus, the greatest enemy of mankind. Like Dante's Inferno, the Hades of the ancient Greeks was a horrible nightmare. The myths of the agonies in Hell, mere fairy tales to the readers of today, were to the contemporaries of Epicurus actual forebodings of tortures to come.

To all those who suffered from such forebodings, Epicurus said: "Be of good cheer. There is no future life. Your soul will not continue to suffer after your body is dissolved. Death is the end of your nightmares, your terrors, your pains."

But what of the great terror that still remains? This present thought of our future annihilation, the presentiment of sinking into an "abyss of nothingness," isn't this in itself the cause of our greatest distress?

Not in the least, replies Epicurus. "Why feel distress over a dead body which can feel nothing at all?" Are you terrified at your nonexistence before you were born? Why then be terrified at your nonexistence after you die? Your life is the dream of a moment in the midst of an eternal sleep. And the dreamless sleep is always sweeter than the dream.

Moreover, even the longest sleep is but a moment in duration. Have you ever awakened after a sound sleep of several hours with the feeling that you had just barely closed your eyes? In the sleep of death, this fleeting moment of insensibility is the measurement of a million years as well as of a single night.

And, in this eternal instant of death, you are not even aware of your identity. That which has no personal awareness is nothing to you. Your dead self has no relation to your living self. Then why worry about it?

Enjoy your life, then, as a fascinating day-dance between a sleep and a sleep. Indeed, the whole universe is a dance of Nature over the infinitude of space. The dance of the atoms.

And this brings us to the most interesting part of the Epicurean philosophy—the atomic theory which Epicurus had borrowed from the great Greek scientist, Democritus.

This theory of a materialistic universe—of a world of stars and planets growing out of the "perpetual fertility" of the atoms—is what Santayana had particularly in mind when he referred to the philosophy of Epicurus as perhaps the greatest thought in all history.

The entire universe, said Epicurus, is a rhythmical whirlwind of atoms; the stars are dancing flames in the heavens; and our life is but a fleeting figure in the choreography of the world.

And what causes these multitudinous configurations in the earth and the heavens and the innumerable creatures that inhabit them? What causes the very creation and destruction of these stars and planets, clouds and cataracts and oceans, beasts and birds and fishes and men? The collision of the atoms as they move eternally over the aisles of space. These atoms are the tiniest possible particles of matter—the word *atom* comes from the Greek *atomos,* which means something so small that it cannot be cut or divided. The universe, Epicurus tells us, and modern science seems to corroborate him, consists of an infinite void with an infinite number of atoms streaming continually over it.

But these atoms are not streaming all in a single direction. They have a tendency, "at uncertain times and uncertain places," to push themselves from their course. This swerving of the atoms is what causes the dance of the universe—the collision of matter with matter to form the infinite variety of Nature.

For all Nature, declares Epicurus, is material. Even the human soul is material. The atoms of the soul are finer, lighter, less solid than the atoms of the body. But the soul, like the body, dissolves at death. The individual atoms remain—all matter is indestructible—but the configurations of these atoms known as you and I are scattered over the void to combine into other units and other forms.

All these units and forms are thrown out by Nature in an infinite variety, but without any previous design. The choreography has no Choreographer—declares Epicurus—the created world has no Creator. How then, he asks himself, can we explain the uniform pattern of life—the movement from inferior to superior forms, from imperfection toward perfection? In his effort to answer this question, Epicurus anticipated Darwinism two thousand years before Darwin. The emergence of our human species, declared Epicurus, is a result of evolution. The repeated collision of the atoms throughout the centuries has, by sheer accident, produced all sorts of living forms. The forms that were fitted to their environment survived; those that were unfitted perished. Just how life originated, Epicurus doesn't tell us. Nor does he tell us what it was that fitted or unfitted a species to its environment. These gaps in the philosophy of Epicurus are due to the fact that he refused to admit a governing intelligence into his materialistic conception of the world.

But to return to his theory of evolution. At first, he declares, the earth was stark and lifeless. And then, gradually, it began to put forth grass and shrubs and flowers, just as animals and birds put forth hair and feathers. Next came life—how and why? Some of the living creatures were born with defective sight or hearing; they were the freaks of Nature in the accidental process of trial and error. Unable to fight against the animals that were better equipped for the struggle, they died out.

And, finally, the fortuitous dance of the atoms developed into the figures of men. Crude and savage and afraid, they lived like the other animals in fields and caves and woods. But they were endowed with one characteristic that enabled them to advance beyond the rest. A soul that gave them speech and thought and compassion, and the faint first conception of Heaven.

And here the atheist philosopher found himself in need of the gods. He had tried to depict a world without a divine plan. But he couldn't live in a world without divine friends. At bottom, Epicurus was a very religious man. He tried to direct his life into an imitation of the life of the gods.

But how did the gods fit into his purely materialistic scheme? Simply enough, according to his own conception of the world.

The gods, too, he said, are the result of the atomic dance. They are made of subtler atoms than those of the human soul. They pursue a blessed existence in the heavens—a sort of celestial Garden of Epicurus. They are enlarged portraits of humanity at its best—enjoying a divine tranquillity of mutual friendliness untroubled by the follies and the foibles and the misfortunes of mankind. "No sound of human sorrow mounts to mar their sacred, everlasting calm."

IV

This was the goal of the Epicurean adventure in philosophy. A Garden of Sacred Friendship in an unfriendly world. A life of serene pleasure can best be attained in a society of unselfish friends. "Friendship cannot be divorced from pleasure, nor pleasure from friendship."

Epicurus returned again and again to his idea of "kindly comradeship" as a shield against the onslaughts of fate. "Cultivate the genius of friendship. Make a religion of it. Worship it. For friendship is a sweet and beautiful and holy thing. The sympathy of true friendship is the only certain gift we possess in this world of doubtful worth. If the sufferings of life can reconcile us to death, then the joys of friendship can reconcile us to life."

Epicurus spent much of his time writing letters to his friends, and especially to their children. He wanted them to grow up in a world of "enlightened selfishness"—of giving their love that they might be repaid with gratitude. His own life was a long series of gentle words and generous deeds. His was the supreme pleasure of giving and receiving in kind.

The knowledge that he was surrounded with kindness sustained him through all his sufferings. He died of a painful disease. Yet just before his death he wrote to one of his friends: "I am now passing this last and blessed day of my life. Strangury—a disease of the bladder—has laid hold of me; and I am wracked with torments which the body can no longer endure. But over against all this I set my joy in the memory of our thoughts and words together in the past."

Joyful thoughts of the past, and no fear for the future. After a lifelong banquet of simple food and tender affection, he was ready to depart quietly to an untroubled sleep.

CHAPTER VIII

St. Paul, Who Saw When He Went Blind

[c. 3–68 A.D.]

THE STORY in this chapter begins with one of the most dramatic journeys in history. The leading character in the drama is Saul of Tarsus, the fanatical young rabbi who has been commissioned by the authorities in Jerusalem to persecute the followers of Jesus in Damascus. Saul is determined to uproot "the poisonous weed of the false Messiah," and to destroy the seeds wherever he may find them.

It has been a long and exhausting journey from Jerusalem to Damascus. Saul and his fellow fanatics have traveled most of the way on foot. Saul's eyes are red from sleepless nights and the sandstorms of the desert. As he approaches Damascus, the noonday sun beats down upon his head. His body, emaciated by repeated attacks of malaria, is ready to succumb to the heat and the sweat and the sand. His eyes, his nostrils, his mouth, his very lungs are choked with dust.

Yet his spirit drives him on. He has a mission to perform—to free the Holy Land from the "perversions" of the Nazarene creed.

And so he travels on through the rain of sand and fire, until he reaches the gates of Damascus. He has now crossed the desert and finds himself in one of the most enchanting regions of Asia. The Garden of Eden—the world's first meeting place between the human and the divine.

And here, suddenly, a great darkness descends upon Saul. He falls to the ground. His companions bend over him in terror. His sightless eyes are wide open, and his lips move as if in earnest conversation with someone.

It is several minutes before he recovers sufficiently to hear his companions.

"What has happened to you, Saul?"

"I have seen him."

"Seen whom?"

"The Messiah."

"The false one?"

"No, the true one. Jesus of Nazareth."

"The man must be out of his mind!" whispers one of his companions to another.

But Saul overhears these words. "No, my friend. I have just come *into* my right mind."

But he tells them no more about his vision. They probably wouldn't believe him if he did. The whole thing has been so utterly beyond his own comprehension. A great light out of the darkness —and in the midst, a rabbi dressed in white as for the Sabbath. A radiant face with sorrowful eyes. And the rabbi has held out his hands to him. "Saul, Saul, why persecutest thou me?"

"Who art thou, Lord?"

"I am Jesus of Nazareth."

"And what am I to do?"

"Go into the city, and there it shall be revealed to thee what thou must do."

Still shaken by the vision, Saul lies trembling on the ground. His companions try to help him to his feet. "His eyes are still blind," whispers one of them.

Again Saul overhears the words, and shakes his head. "Now for the first time I can really see."

There has been a great deal of controversy as to the actual nature of the vision before Damascus. But all such controversy is useless. Whether the vision was an objective reality or the subjective fantasy of an exhausted mind, it was to Saul a matter of the most vital significance. To him, therefore, it was a true vision. For it transformed an extreme hater of men into a supreme lover of mankind.

II

Saul was his given name at birth. But his Gentile playmates at Tarsus called him *Paul,* the Latin word for *little fellow.* He was a delicate child with a brilliant mind. His father, a Roman citizen and pious Jew, encouraged his boy to study the pagan philosophers as well as the Hebrew prophets. Saul wanted to be a teacher. But following the advice of the rabbis—"Seek no earning through your learning"—he apprenticed himself to a tentmaker. Like the holy men of Palestine, he preferred to work with his hands for a living and to give his thoughts freely to the world.

Tarsus, a city in Asia Minor, was a trading center of ideas and goods. It was here that Cicero had lived while Governor of Cilicia, and Anthony had invited Cleopatra to sail down the Cydnus in a gilded barge with silver oars. The writers called this city "the gateway between the East and the West." A meeting place of poetry, philosophy, science, religion, and art. Saul absorbed the sights and the sounds and the thoughts of this city throughout his formative years.

But his main interest was in the teaching of the Torah—"the inspiration of the prophets of the past, and the hope of the Messiah to come." At fifteen he went to Jerusalem; and here, in the temple courts, he sat at the feet of Gamaliel. It is possible that the young student of fifteen may have heard of a little boy of Nazareth who had confounded the rabbis of the temple with his questions.

But Jesus and Saul never met in the flesh. After some years in Jerusalem, Saul returned to Tarsus, where he continued his studies at the university. And then, his education completed, he was ready for his life's work—a body subject to the "thorns" of disease but a heart overflowing "like a volcano" with devotion to God.

This devotion led him into strange paths before he found his way. The more fanatical among the Jews had banded themselves against the followers of Jesus. Saul joined this band. He was present at the martyrdom of Stephen. Some of those who were stoning him to death had asked Saul to watch their cloaks. He saw the martyr's face, with "God's glory raining down upon it." He heard the martyr's voice saying, "Master, lay not this sin to their charge."

He left the place of the stoning with mingled emotions. The Nazarenes, he believed, were heretics. Their teaching was false. Hence they must be destroyed. But what was there about them that made them so utterly resigned to die, so passionately eager to forgive? Could falsehood breed such goodness in the human heart?

The more he thought of it the more perplexed he became, and the more frightened at his perplexity. It was therefore to drive away his own doubts that he volunteered to persecute the Nazarenes. He castigated his own conscience by whipping the followers of Christ.

This was his state of mind when he started upon his journey to Damascus. He had taken several subordinates along with him, and he had offered to arrest and to bring back to Jerusalem the leaders of the Nazarene sect.

But at the gates of Damascus he had come to the parting of the ways. He had found his vision in the blinding of his eyes. From now on, he had no further doubts about the mission of Christ.

But what was to be his own mission in the days to come? "In the city it shall be revealed to thee what thou must do."

His companions brought him into the city, where he lay blind and helpless for several days. He was nursed back to health by the very people he had come to persecute. "Why are you so kind to me?" he asks.

"The Lord has taught us to return good for evil."

Good for evil! Was not this also the teaching of Rabbi Gamaliel? And was not his own suffering meant as a sign for him to spread this Gospel throughout the world?

His physician, Ananias, answered his question. "You are right, my son. You can repay our services to you by offering yourself as a servant to the Lord."

III

Saul went back into the desert, to commune alone with God. And he came out of the desert determined to turn his weakness into "a tower of strength." His adventures as the ambassador of the Lord carried him over tens of thousands of miles, and plunged him into almost incredible hardships. On five different occasions he received "thirty-nine lashes" from a leather thong. On three occasions he was beaten with rods. Once he was stoned and left for dead. At least four times he was shipwrecked. During one of these shipwrecks he remained in the water, clinging to a plank, for over twenty-four hours. And throughout his career, he was repeatedly cast into prison, where he lay, shackled to the wall of his cell, for months at a time. Added to all this, he suffered hunger and thirst and sickness and cold, as well as the buffetings and the jeers of those he tried to teach. Yet he endured all this suffering as a "labor of love"—the wages of his love for God.

For he was a soldier of Christ engaged upon a lifelong battle of peace. Within a single century the world witnessed two great conquerors—Caesar and Saul. Caesar had started a torrent of blood flowing eastward from Europe to Asia; and Saul, retracing the course, opened a river of love flowing westward from Asia to Europe. The arrogant warrior on horseback, the humble Apostle on foot.

Saul's pilgrimage of love—he changed his name to Paul at about this time—began in Damascus, where he returned after his sojourn in the desert. And at once the hunter became the hunted. He barely escaped with his life when his friends concealed him in a basket and lowered him from the city wall at night.

And then on to Antioch, where the Nazarenes first called themselves Christians; to Cyprus, where he began to preach Christianity as a religion embracing all mankind, Gentile as well as Jew; to Lystra, where the people started to worship him as a pagan god and ended by stoning him when he told them that he was only a man; to Ephesus, where the tradesmen mobbed him because he spoiled their market for the images and the amulets of the goddess Diana; to many other cities of Asia and Europe and the islands of the Mediterranean. And everywhere he carried bread for the body and comfort for the soul. Again and again he was thwarted by his illness and hooted down when he tried to speak. Even his enemies were amazed at his persistence and his growing success.

Yet he cared for no personal triumph. He received no pay for his preaching, and he expected no thanks for his charity. He was completely dedicated to his work. When he had the time, he attended to his tentmaking for his simple needs. When his disciples asked him how he could endure his hardships, he answered simply: "I am merely making up what was lacking in the sufferings of Christ."

IV

And so he went on, hounded as a revolutionist, stoned as an outcast, arrested as a spy, yet radiant in the thought that he was Christ's ambassador to the world. Often, when he was unable to come to the Christians in person, he sent them a letter of faith and comfort and hope. Sometimes he scolded them for their quarrels, but always he ended with words that softened their sorrows and brought them peace of mind.

These letters of Paul—his beautiful poems of pity—explain the basic philosophy of the New Testament. Paul's philosophy is a blending of Greek and Hebrew thought. It is founded upon three ideas united into one—the Father, the Son, and the Holy Ghost. Translated into popular terms, these ideas mean (1) the Fatherhood of God and the Brotherhood of Man, (2) the Transcendent Power of Love, and (3) the Immortality of the Soul.

1. *The Fatherhood of God and the Brotherhood of Man.* The Hebrews had always regarded themselves as the Children of God. But Paul widened the family by including the entire human race into the divine relationship. Paul was one of the first internationalists in history. In his *Epistle to the Romans* he writes: "Is he the God of the Jews only? Is he not also the God of the Gentiles?" All of us—Jew and Gentile, black and white, master and slave—"are the joint heirs of God."

Let no man therefore think himself higher or lower than any other man. For we are members of one body. We have been brought into this world—like the eyes, the ears, the hands, the feet—to perform our different functions in the common business of life. We need every organ, every function, every man, for the healthy existence of the body of mankind.

The Greeks referred to this idea as *harmony;* the Hebrews called it *comradeship;* Paul raised it to the status of *human brotherhood.* "Be kindly affectioned to one another like the brothers of a single family." And, between brothers, "It is more blessed to give than to receive." Those of us who are strong should bear the infirmities of the weak. Let us therefore be slow to injure, but quick to forget an injury. For thus, and thus only, can we "follow after the things which make for peace."

2. *The Transcendent Power of Love.* Paul offered to the world the bread of peace with the leavening of love. Here again Paul combines the Greek and the Hebrew ideas into a philosophy of his own. His Canticle to Love—Chapter 13 of his *First Epistle to the Corinthians*—is one of the high peaks in the literature of the world:

"Though I speak with the tongues of men and of angels, and have not love, I am become as sounding brass, or a tinkling cymbal.

"And though I have the gift of prophecy, and understand all mysteries, and all knowledge; and though I have all faith so that I could move mountains, and have not love, I am nothing.

"And though I bestow all my goods to feed the poor, and

though I give my body to be burned, and have not love, it profiteth me nothing."

The word *love* in this chapter has often been translated as *charity*. But the original Greek equivalent of this word means more than *charity*. It means not only *giving* but *forgiving;* it means gentleness, courage, understanding, humility, compassion —complete forgetfulness of self in the devotion to serve others. The rest of the chapter shows clearly that Paul had this wider meaning in mind when he wrote:

"Love suffereth long, and is kind; love envieth not; love vaunteth not itself, is not puffed up,

"Doth not behave itself unseemly, seeketh not her own, is not easily provoked, thinketh no evil. . . .

"Beareth all things, believeth all things, hopeth all things, endureth all things. . . ."

And this brings us to the climax of the chapter—the quintessence of the Apostle's philosophy:

"And now abideth [the Gospel of] faith, hope, love, these three; but the greatest of these is love."

3. *The Immortality of the Soul.* Love, declared Paul, is the common heritage of our immortal souls. Once again, Paul based his philosophy upon the beliefs of the Socratic and the Hebraic teachers. Each one of us, he said, is not only a *physical* member of the universal *body* of mankind, but a *spiritual* member of the universal *soul* of mankind.

The disbelief in immortality, according to Paul, may be regarded as a worm's-eye view of the world. A worm, burrowing under the earth, sees a seed rotting in the darkness. This, concludes the worm, is the end of the seed's life. The worm has no conception of the new life of the seed—the bud, the stem, the flower—that grows out of the "dead" body under the surface of the earth. "Some man will ask, 'How are the dead raised up? And with what body do they come?'

"Thou fool, that which thou sowest is not quickened unless

it die . . . So also is the resurrection of the dead. It is sown
in corruption; it is raised in incorruption:

"It is sown in dishonour; it is raised in glory: it is sown in
weakness; it is raised in power:

"It is sown a physical body; it is raised a spiritual body. . . .
The first body is of the earth, earthy: the second is from heaven.
. . .

"And as we have borne the image of the earthy, we shall also
bear the image of the heavenly. . . .

"Behold, I show you a mystery; We shall not all sleep, but we
shall all be changed. . . .

. . . "For this corruptible must put on incorruption, and this
mortal must put on immortality. . . .'"

Have no fear, then, about your last day on earth. The day of
your death is the birthday of your immortality. Your final journey
is but a passage through a tunnel of darkness into a greater light.

And thus life is triumphant, eternal, and assured—the loving
heritage of God to all His children on earth. "O death, where is
thy sting? O grave, where is thy victory?"

This idea was for Paul not a mere speculation. It was the
mature conviction of a mind that had gone through a great deal
of suffering and thought. "When I was a child, I spoke as a child,
I understood as a child, I thought as a child. But when I became
a man, I put away childish things." And therefore, he declares,
he knows what he is talking about. "Now, in this life, we see
through a glass, darkly; but then, in the life to come, we shall
see face to face. Now I know in part; but then shall I know even
as also I am known."

V

And what is the sum and substance of this knowledge? The
promise of eternal life, in loving communion between man and
man, under the universal Fatherhood of God.

Buttressed by this faith and hope and love, Paul continued

through his almost unendurable hardships to the end. Arrested in Jerusalem and handed over to the Roman governor of Judea, he appealed as a Roman citizen to be sent to the emperor.

It was a case of passing from the frying pan into the fire. The emperor of Rome was Nero—still young at the time and somewhat under the influence of his tutor, the philosopher Seneca. The beast had not as yet emerged from under the mask. He posed as a patron of art and student of philosophy and religion. For a few years he allowed Paul, under "protective custody," to preach the Gospel in Rome.

And then Nero's evil nature came to the surface. Like several of the other Roman emperors, he was hopelessly insane. He ordered his mother to be strangled, kicked his wife to death, compelled his tutor Seneca to take his life, and finally perpetrated one of the most atrocious crimes in history. Believing that he was an inspired poet, he set fire to Rome in order to get the material for an epic "greater than Homer's *Burning of Troy.*"

But he had to find a scapegoat for the fire; and so he pinned the crime upon the Christians. He declared a Roman holiday for their wholesale execution. Many of them he fed to the lions in the arena, while the audience shouted "Hail Caesar!" and the victims sang "The Lord is my shepherd, I shall not want." Some of them he crucified and lighted as torches for his triumphal procession through the Roman streets. "A poem of fire," he gloated, "an artistic creation such as the world has never seen!"

Paul had noted the growing madness of Nero. He knew that his own days were numbered. But he was not afraid. "I have fought the good fight," he wrote, "I have finished the course, I have kept the faith."

As a concession to his Roman citizenship, Nero treated him with "special mercy." He neither threw him to the lions nor nailed him to a cross. He merely ordered his head to be chopped off.

"An end to Christianity!" exulted Nero. But the ending of Paul's life was the beginning of the Christian Church.

CHAPTER IX

Two Adventures in Courage—
the Stoicism of Aurelius and Epictetus

$$\begin{bmatrix} \text{Aurelius, 121–180 A.D.} \\ \text{Epictetus, 60?–120? A.D.} \end{bmatrix}$$

THE TWO GREATEST exponents of Stoicism—the philosophy of a courageous acceptance of fate—were Marcus Aurelius the emperor, and Epictetus the slave. And both of them, starting from the opposite poles of human fortune, arrived at the selfsame conclusion: We can be chained to our happiness, and we can be happy in our chains.

The emperor, looking down from the heights of his glory, saw the pain that subsists at the heart of all pleasure. And the slave, looking up from the depths of his degradation, saw the pleasure that is possible even in the midst of pain. But the wise man, both of them agreed, is above the vicissitudes of glory and degradation and pleasure and pain. He finds his peace of mind in a quiet resignation to the pattern of his life.

Yet it was the emperor, and not the slave, who had the greater need of the tranquillity of Stoicism. For Aurelius was compelled to teach men how to kill, but Epictetus was able to instruct them how to live. Two Stoic adventurers—the unhappy master of men, and the happy master of himself.

II

Marcus Aurelius was bound to a career for which he had no taste. A prince who hated war, he ruled over a nation of fighting men. From early boyhood he had wanted to be a philosopher. Fired by the example of Socrates and the Cynics—those intrepid philosophers who preferred righteousness to riches—he had dressed himself in a shabby cloak and slept on a hard couch. At eighteen he was torn away from his philosophy to become the adopted heir of his uncle, the Roman emperor Antoninus. When the emperor died (161 A.D.), Aurelius inherited unwanted riches and an unrighteous war.

From now on, his throne was the saddle; and his palace, a tent on the battlefield. It was here, by the fitful light of an oil lamp, that he wrote his *Meditations* on life and death. Flickering shadows of wisdom, interspersed with his plans for the next day's slaughter. "All life," he wrote from his own bitter experience, "is a warfare and a journey in a strange land."

He hated his job, but he was chained to it by the necessity of his royal heritage. Like a faithful Stoic, he submitted to his dignity as an emperor and to his cruelty as a soldier, though by nature he was simple and kind. It was only in the pages of his book that he was able to look into his heart. And there he found peace in the midst of the gladiators and the murderers and the thieves that made up the bulk of his army.

A peaceful sailor in a stormy sea. Some of the more ambitious Romans, realizing that he had no heart for the fight, thought it would be an easy matter to overthrow him. They started a revolt, with one of his own generals, Avidius Cassius, at the head. "Avidius," it was said facetiously, "is avid to replace Aurelius on the throne."

"As well as in his bed," added some of the more outspoken gossips.

The ugly rumor had finally reached the emperor's ears. A tottering throne, an unfaithful wife. How would a Stoic react to this crisis? Especially when the conspirators had spread the falsehood that the emperor was dead, and many of the legions were ready to enthrone Avidius in his place.

Marcus Aurelius rose to the occasion. "Accept your fate," the Stoics had taught him. "Follow the pattern of your life; be true to your nature." Very well, this was the pattern of *his* life—to act, at all times, like a king. With foresight and firmness, but without malice or hate. He called his soldiers together and addressed them as follows:

"Men, I am told that my best friend is plotting to overthrow me. I am therefore compelled to take the field against him . . . There is only one thing I fear—and that is, that Avidius Cassius may kill himself in a moment of shame, or that someone else may kill him in a fit of rashness. In that case, I shall be robbed of the greatest prize possible to any conqueror—to forgive the man who has wronged me, to remain a friend to him who has broken his friendship with me."

Just as he had feared, Aurelius was robbed of his prize. One of his hotheaded followers assassinated his rival, Avidius. The emperor's soldiers were ready to throw themselves upon all the other conspirators. But Aurelius nipped the plan in the bud. "Let the banished come home. Let the dispossessed take back their property. I wish that I could recall from the dead the poor victims who have already suffered the penalty."

And then he set out, together with his wife, on a personal visit to the rebellious provinces. He wanted to pour the oil of mercy upon the stormy waters of sedition. It was in the course of this journey that he suffered one of his deepest sorrows—the death of his wife.

In spite of the rumors about her infidelity—and he had reason to believe these rumors—he had loved Faustina devotedly throughout their married life. And this devotion persisted even after her death. He built a golden statue in her likeness, and he took it along with him on his journeys. He founded a home for destitute women in her memory. And he offered a daily prayer to her image.

Yet, true to his Stoicism, he tried to master his own grief. "Let us remain indifferent to pain and pleasure, and unmoved by the scandals of the wicked and the gossip of the fools."

As for Faustina, "she is better now that she has awakened from the misty dream of her life."

And so he went back to his battles, and killed innocent strangers for his kingdom, and tried to find a meaning for his own "misty dream." In this strange nightmare of a philosopher turned king, he uttered wisdom and perpetrated folly with the illogical sequence of a mind just stirring out of its sleep. "All of us," he said, "are brothers in sorrow. I cannot be angry with my brothers, or sever myself from them. For we are made by nature to help one another, like the feet, the hands, the eyelids, the upper and the lower rows of teeth."

Yet he was far from helpful toward those of his "brothers" known as Christians. They believed in a "strange kingdom of Heaven"—a dangerous challenge, he thought, to the Roman kingdom on earth. In the advance of this new doctrine he foresaw a struggle between Christian idealism and Roman imperialism. And in his own soul, too, he sensed a similar struggle. His Stoicism was on the side of the Christians; his ambition, on the side of Rome.

And his ambition won out in the end. He ordered the Christian leaders to be crucified.

This was the darkest stain on his character. And the greatest tragedy of his life. It was just as hard for the emperor as for the rich man to enter into the Kingdom of Heaven.

III

But not so hard for the slave. Epictetus was more fortunate than Aurelius. For Epictetus found it easier to maintain a free soul in the slavery of his body. "I have nothing to lose," he said, "but my life." And he valued his life less than Aurelius valued his throne.

We know very little about the story of Epictetus. But what we do know reveals him as a man who belonged to himself. He was a cripple as well as a slave, yet he seems to have been one of the happiest of men. For his sick body was sustained by a healthy soul. He had learned to follow the guidance of his reason rather than the goading of his flesh. "If you cannot raise your achievement to the level of your ambition, lower your ambition to the level of your achievement."

And so he accepted his lowly station in life with a shrug and a smile. He had learned, as a good actor, to suffer in the drama of life. But he had also learned, as an amused spectator, to laugh at his own suffering. His master was a cruel upstart who took delight in tormenting his servants. One day he subjected Epictetus to physical torture. "You had better stop," Epictetus said calmly, "or you will break my leg." And when the leg was broken, the philosopher continued in his calm voice, "I told you it would happen."

Misfortune followed him wherever he went. Freed from his slavery at his master's death, he settled down to teach philosophy in Rome. But the emperor Domitian expelled him from the city, along with several other philosophers. At that period, tyranny and wisdom were unable to live together. Epictetus opened a school in Greece, became famous but remained poor, and accepted his fame as well as his poverty with his usual Stoic indifference.

One day his lamp was stolen, but Epictetus made no effort to punish the thief. "He has already paid for it more than I. This lamp has cost me only a few pennies. It has cost him his soul."

To Epictetus, the greatest thing in the world was the freedom of the soul. "You can chain my body, you can starve it, you can even kill it, but you cannot harm me—that is, the immortal part of myself."

And thus Epictetus, with his tortured body, found solace in the freedom of his soul. In order to maintain his free soul, he never married.

But he didn't live alone. He adopted a child that he had rescued when its parents, unable to support it, were about to put it to death. And he hired a nurse, whom he took into his household, to take care of the child.

And thus he lived his life of Stoic simplicity—a pagan practitioner of Christianity although he had never heard of Christ. "The truth, like the sunlight, comes to us through many windows —at different times, in different places, and by different words. But the meaning is always the same—the Fatherhood of God, the brotherhood of man, and the universal commandment to give and to forgive. Give unstintingly of yourself, and forgive those who are unable to do likewise."

Above all, and unlike Aurelius, Epictetus was a man of peace. "Life is indeed a warfare," he said. "But it is a warfare against enmity, and not against an enemy." Destroy your enemies by turning them into friends. Epictetus illustrated this idea with an interesting story: "Lycurgus, the lawgiver of Sparta, was attacked during an uprising of the mob and blinded in one eye." The assailant was captured and handed over to him for an appropriate punishment. Lycurgus spared the young man and accepted him as a pupil. Several months later he took him to the theater. When the Spartans expressed their amazement, Lycurgus said: "My punishment of this young man has been logical and just. I have received him from you as a ruffian; I return him to you as a gentleman."

This characteristic story about Lycurgus is in keeping with the character of Epictetus himself. He repaid his ill-treatment at the hands of ruffians by trying to convert them into gentle men.

IV

And thus Aurelius and Epictetus arrived at Stoicism by different roads and saw it from different points of view. The philosophy of the emperor was negative—don't grieve for what you haven't got. But the philosophy of the slave was positive—rejoice in what you have. Aurelius tried to shut his eyes to the evils of the world. "Is the cucumber bitter? Throw it away. Are there briars in your path? Turn aside from them. This is enough. Do not ask, 'And why were such things ever created?'" But Epictetus accepted evil as a necessary part of life. "It is only by contrast to the bitter that the sweet is so good. It is the emergence out of the darkness that makes the sunrise so splendid."

This difference in their attitude appears throughout the philosophy of Aurelius and Epictetus. Aurelius has emptied the cup of glory, and he cautions us against the dregs at the bottom. "Camillus, Scipio, Cato, Caesar, Augustus, Hadrian, Antoninus—all are forgotten. All things hasten to an end, shall speedily seem old fables, to be mouthed for an instant and then to be buried in oblivion." But Epictetus has had his fill of misery, and he heartens us with the hope of something better to come. "Be content. What God has chosen for you is greater than what you choose for yourself. Rest assured that tomorrow, like today, He will give you what is best for your soul."

The Stoic philosophy, therefore, has a double appeal. It tempers the arrogance of the rich, and it fortifies the humility of the poor. It enables all of us to find a middle ground of reliance upon the rightness of Nature and the goodness of life. On this point Aurelius and Epictetus agree. Riches or poverty, success or failure, mastery or servitude, pleasure or pain—all these are of minor account. The important thing is that all men are equal in the end. The Stoics were the first democratic party in history. All of us, declared Aurelius and Epictetus, are subject to the selfsame destiny. Men are born to different fortunes, but in death they experience a common fate. Death takes away more from the rich and less from the poor, but the balance in all cases is the same—an immortal soul.

Let us, therefore, accept our fate. For we know that it is good. "Take me up and cast me where you will," writes Aurelius. "I shall have serene within me my own divinity." And Epictetus, in a similar vein, declares: "I rest content in this thought—that God has given my soul to myself and has put my will in obedience to my own divine power."

You possess within yourself, therefore, your own best friend. Or, if you are not careful, your own worst enemy. Many of us, unfortunately, are little souls carrying big bodies. And the strain is too much for us. Let us measure our capacities, and live accordingly. Let us be temperate, in our actions, our emotions, our thoughts. Too much ambition, like too much wine, is dangerous. The first cup leads to pleasure; the second, to intoxication; the third, to violence.

Avoid any stimulant, whether physical or mental, that will lead to blurred vision and violent action. Retain a firm grip upon yourself. Accept whatever comes to you, whether it seems good or bad, with a quiet mind. Be assured that your Father knows best. Live, therefore, in conformity with His plan—that is, with the current of nature as it carries your life to its destined end. Your apparent misfortune may in reality be an obstacle put into your path to exercise your soul. Rely upon the judgment and the goodness and the parental love of God. Whatever is, is right. Even death is for your good, just as birth is for your good. Each of these events is a summons for your entrance upon a stage that God has prepared for you in advance. And your entrance cue— make no mistake about it—has been accurately and intelligently timed.

And your role upon the stage of life is that of an interrelated actor. Learn to speak your lines, and to suit your actions, in harmony with your fellow men. Study your own nature, and act accordingly. "The gods," observes Epictetus, "have given us two ears and one tongue, that we may hear twice as much as we talk."

Two ears to hear, one tongue to talk, and two hands to do good. Be ready to hear and to help your brother's sorrow. But don't complain about your own.

Live, therefore, as a courageous, helpful, and hopeful member of your society—the society of the human race. The political as well as the moral outlook of the Stoics was cosmopolitan. "So far as I am Marcus Aurelius," wrote the emperor, "my city is Rome. But so far as I am a man, my country is the world." And Epictetus, writing in the same spirit, declared: "Live in accordance with reason—not merely as a member of your family, your city, or your state, but as a compatriot of all mankind."

For only thus can you live in harmony with God—transforming your passion into compassion, and your hatred into love.

Both Aurelius and Epictetus insist upon our human collaboration to a common end. In summarizing their philosophy, the two Stoics employ the selfsame figure of speech. They compare the organized human body to the organization of the world. "Consider nothing as if it were detached from the community and belonged to you alone. Act as your hand or foot would act, if they had reason to understand their relationship to your head and your heart."

Significantly enough, we find this same figure of Stoic philosophy expressed in the Christian doctrine of St. Paul. "Many as we are," writes St. Paul, "we are members of one universal body . . . and we are interrelated parts of one another." The light of truth, an Oriental poet has observed, is variously reflected in the thoughts of men. The reflections are many, the light is one.

V

This, then, is the composite picture of Stoicism—which, in its ethical content, is not far from Christianity. And Stoicism, like Christianity, is a philosophy that can fit all sorts of men. It is quite logical that the two supreme teachers of this philosophy came, respectively, from the highest and the lowest ranks. And it is one of the revealing lessons of history that the Stoic pessimist was the child of fortune, while the Stoic optimist was the stepchild of want. It's a pretty sorry world, observed Aurelius, even though you are a king. But, countered Epictetus, it's a pretty jolly world even though you are a slave.

And both of them, perhaps, were right.

CHAPTER X

The Pilgrimage of Augustine—
from Sinner to Saint

[354–430]

THE CHARACTER of St. Augustine was somewhat similar to that of Tolstoy. Both of them were passionate in their youth. Both gave in to their passions, sinned and suffered and instinctively felt their way toward the light. And then, when they had found it in their old age, they advised all the young people to live sinlessly and serenely like themselves.

But both of them had forgotten an important psychological fact. Clear thinking and tranquil living are very difficult when the emotions are strong. It was when their own fires were almost extinguished that they were able to subdue them with the composure of philosophy. It is hardly fitting for the old to preach abstinence to the young. Especially when they themselves have been unable to practice this abstinence in their own youth.

And so the preaching of St. Augustine, like that of Tolstoy, lacks conviction. But the story of St. Augustine's sins, and his conversion to sainthood. is one of the world's most fascinating spiritual adventures.

II

The entire early life of Augustine may be summarized in his own prayer: "Give me chastity and continence—but not yet." He hated the forbidden fruits that he enjoyed. Or, rather, he enjoyed the forbidden fruits that he hated. Born (354 A.D.) of a pagan father and a Christian mother, he was from infancy subjected to conflicting influences. His father wanted him to be a teacher; his mother, a priest.

At the beginning, his father had his way. He studied philosophy and rhetoric—"the tongue-science that praises falsehood in elegant words." His boyhood had its average admixture of work, study, and sport. At one time he joined other boys in robbing a neighbor's pear tree. But so morbid was the shame aroused by this youthful escapade that he later devoted several chapters to the confession of his "black sin." His stealing of the fruit had been motivated by no hunger, he said. His parents had better pears at home. "It was a wicked crime, O God, and I loved it. I loved to perish, I loved my own fault—not because I hungered for the pears, but the sin itself I loved."

It was in this mood of mischief and morbidity that he spent the years of his early manhood. Like Goethe's Faust, he kept sinning and repenting and sinning again, and "forever groping blindly" toward the light. As an adolescent, he was—to quote his own confession—"a liar, a bully, and a cheat." And he was all too ready, he tells us, to yield to the lusts of the flesh. "I boiled over in my passions, and I lost myself in a multiplicity of sins."

This, too, we must take with a grain of salt. Augustine suffered not so much from an overwhelming wickedness, as from an overdeveloped conscience. Throughout his confession we see a gentle, sensitive, and brilliant young man who suffers because he is not better than Nature intended him to be. He referred to the exuberance of his youth as a "wallowing through the mire of Babylon," and to his love for the theater as a "heaping of fuel upon the fires of my lust."

He underrated his virtues and exaggerated his faults. He spoke disparagingly of his success as a professor of rhetoric, and he flagellated himself unmercifully for cohabiting with a woman out of wedlock. "For several years we lived, seducing and seduced." They had an illegitimate child—Adeodatus. Augustine loved the boy—and felt ashamed of his love. "For the child had been begotten in sin." He wrote several books "on the fair and fit" in our human existence—and repudiated the books later on.

He called himself "a soul astray in a sea of mud." His father had died when Augustine was seventeen. His mother, a devout Christian, prayed for her son. But for several years "her prayers failed to reach my heart." He scorned her advice "not to commit fornication, and especially never to defile another man's wife." He kept sailing always away from the light—"in search of something, but I knew not what it was."

In the course of his wanderings to find his own soul, he left his native Africa and came to Rome. And from Rome he went to Milan. Here he continued his profession as a teacher of rhetoric. But the teacher still had need to be taught. He was hungry for promotion, profit, praise. But to what end?

And then came his first lesson in humility. He had delivered a public eulogy on the Roman emperor. The speech, punctuated by "many a lie, was applauded by those who knew I lied." Puffed up with his success, he was walking with some friends through the streets of Milan. They were accosted by a beggar who, "enjoying a full belly at the moment, greeted us with a jest and a song."

The episode made a deep impression upon Augustine. "What the beggar had obtained by means of his unearned pennies, I was plotting to attain by means of my unearned praise. . . . The beggar rejoiced in his drunkenness, and I rejoiced in my glory. Where was the difference between us?"

From that time on, Augustine decided that he would no longer be a beggar for glory. He was well on the way to finding his soul. A man's happiness, he realized, depends upon the nature of his joy. The only kind that is worth while is "the joy of a faithful hope."

Faith in the goodness of God, and hope for the salvation of your soul.

III

But Augustine was not yet at the end of his pilgrim's progress. "I had overcome my pride, but I was still pursued by my lust." He had organized a communist society for those of his friends who, like himself, detested the "turmoils of life" and "the business and the bustle of men." They moved into a single household and united all their possessions into a common fund. But the womenfolk spoiled it all. As a result of their jealousies, the community fell apart.

At this time of his life, it was always a woman who thwarted the "salvation" of his soul. "I delayed to turn to the Lord . . . because I thought I should be too miserable unless folded in a woman's arms." In an effort to moderate his passion, his mother tried to have him married. He dismissed his mistress, whom he deeply loved, and became engaged to a "respectable" girl. But he had to wait for the wedding, since the girl was "two years under the fit age." This was too long an abstinence for the "impetuous hunger" of his flesh. He took another mistress, enjoyed her embraces, and castigated himself for remaining "an abject slave to lust."

In the end, he didn't marry at all. For he became, at his conversion, a celibate for life.

The conversion came about as a result of his mother's solicitations. As he grew older, he had become "fed up" with his "sins." The devotee of the flesh had turned into a disciple of the soul. He gave up his revelry for religion. And the scene of his renunciation is one of the most poignant passages in his *Confessions*.

He was sitting with an intimate friend in his garden. His mind, "poised on the threshold of decision," was visibly agitated. "Two conflicting wills were struggling for the possession of my soul." The boisterous call of the flesh, and the still, small voice of God. His friend watched his agitation in silence.

Finally, overcome by his emotion, Augustine burst into tears.

Ashamed to be seen "weeping like a woman," he left his friend and went into a deep recess of the garden. And there, under a fig tree, he cast himself on the ground and gave vent to his feelings.

In the midst of his weeping, he heard a voice—as of a child—chanting the words: "Take up and read, take up and read." Regarding this as a "command from God," he opened at random a "volume of the Apostle—St. Paul."

And this is what he read: "Not in rioting and drunkenness, not in chambering and wantonness, not in strife and envying, but in the Lord is thy trust."

He read no further; he had no need to read any further, he tells us. "For instantly, at the end of this sentence, by a light, as it were, of serenity infused into my heart, all the darkness of doubt vanished away."

His prayer up to that point had been: "Give me chastity and continence—but not yet." But now he said to himself: "How long tomorrow and tomorrow? Why not at this very hour an end to the uncleanliness of my life?"

And thus at last the adventure of his soul had turned "fromward Satan and toward God."

IV

The philosophy that grew out of his soul's quest "deserves"—in the words of Bertrand Russell—"a high place" in the world's great thought. Though he wrote in the so-called "Dark Ages," St. Augustine enlightened many a modern mind. He gave Descartes a starting point for his argument about the existence of God. He helped Spinoza to paint his picture of the world against the background of eternity. And he was the first to hint at a theory which is now being widely accepted in scientific and philosophical circles—the relativity of time.

St. Augustine, in other words, delved deeply into three of the greatest mysteries of the world and came up with many a nugget of precious thought. Let us try to catch some of the color of these thoughts as we hold them up to the light of the present day.

1. *The Mystery of God.* In spite of our infinite ignorance, declares St. Augustine, there are two things we know for certain: we *exist,* and we *think.* And the fact of our existence and our thought leads us to one other certainty—the existence of God, the Source of every living creature endowed with a living body and a thinking mind.

But God himself is not a material Body. He is a Spirit unconfined by the limits of time and space. He created time and space, the sun and the stars, and all the concrete objects and creatures of the earth as a stage for the development of our human spirit during our journey through this life.

The human spirit, therefore, is a "pilgrim on earth and a citizen of Heaven." This spirit of ours, a pupil for a time in the school of eternity, is provided with the entire universe for our textbook, and with all the objects of the earth—including our mortal clay— as the instruments of our learning. When this state of our education is over, we shall put aside the textbook and the tools of our present life—for our spirit will no longer need them—and we shall be ready for the next stage. Whatever form that next stage may assume, we can be sure of one thing. It will be for the best. Everything is for the best in God's good plan.

And the ultimate purpose of this plan is for the human spirit to advance in its education from the City of the Earth to the City of God.

2. *The Riddle of Eternity.* The City of the Earth exists in time. The City of God lives on in eternity.

But what is eternity? It is not, declares Augustine, a summation of all the points of time. Indeed, it has nothing to do with time. Time is a *material extension,* from the past to the future. It has had a beginning, and it will have an ending. But eternity is a *spiritual infinitude,* a perpetual and all-pervading present. It has often been asked, observes St. Augustine, "What did God do *before* He created the earth?" But in eternity there is no such thing as *before* and *after*. In other words, there can be no time without a created being to measure it. And therefore it is meaningless to speak of a time before the Creation—that is, *before there was any time.*

For God created time when He created the world. This idea, admits St. Augustine, is hard to explain because of the poverty of our human language. We are at a loss when we try to express an infinite thought in our finite words. The world of our senses, we must remember, is a limited world—consisting of the textbook and the tools of our workaday classroom. But the world of our spirit is an unlimited world. It soars above and beyond the little schoolhouse of our present existence. We get a glimpse of this unlimited world—this eternity of our human spirit as allied to the Spirit of God—when we think of such ideas as *faith, devotion, love*. We cannot *plumb* the depths of *faith,* or *measure* the heights of *devotion,* or *encircle* the boundaries of *love*.

These ideas are to us the "divinely dropped hints" about the infinity of our spirit, the eternity of our life. St. Augustine conceives of the visible world as a finite sponge, and of the spiritual world—or the thought of God—as a surrounding ocean of infinity. But, in spite of the beauty of this figure, we must be careful not to accept it too literally. For both the sponge and the ocean exist within the material boundaries of the world. But the infinite and eternal Spirit of God is forever free from the limits of space and time.

And thus the spirit is the soul of the body, and eternity is the soul of time. The body is born, lives for a little while, and dies. But the soul is eternally alive.

3. *The Meaning of Time.* The world of our physical existence is a mechanical world of space and time. But this physical world is not the ultimate reality of life—a theory that is receiving corroborative evidence in the findings of modern science. "The universe," writes Sir James Jeans, "begins to look more like a great thought than like a great machine." And the eternal thought is the creator of the temporal machine.

Time, therefore, is one of the measuring rods of our mechanical universe. And it is a relative rather than an absolute measure.

For example, there are many different time clocks in the universe. The relation of the earth to the sun gives us our days and our years. But the relation between other planets and their suns would give us an entirely different computation of days and years.

Time, therefore, is an artificial way of computing duration between what we call the past, through the present, and into the future. Actually, however, there is only one kind of real time—and that is, *the present*. The so-called *past* is our *present memory* of yesterday. And the so-called *future* is our *present expectation* of tomorrow.

And thus the only reality is an *eternal present*. Our human mind, which is spiritual, can grasp this idea in all its dimensions. But our human brain, which is material and therefore imprisoned within its limitations, can follow it only in a straight line.

To illustrate this point in modern terms, let us assume that the mind imprisoned in the brain is like a traveler confined in an airplane. The plane, let us imagine, is traveling from Washington to Boston. At this moment it is over New York, the present. Behind it is Washington, the past. Ahead of it is Boston, the future. It is wrong to say that Washington *was,* New York *is,* and Boston *will be.* All three of them at the very same moment *are.* It is only our limited vision that prevents us from seeing them all *at once.*

The same, Augustine would say, is true of time. It is wrong to say that yesterday *was,* today *is,* and tomorrow *will be.* These three periods—*all* periods of time—*are.* They exist *simultaneously.*

Material time, therefore, is the finite image of an infinite and spiritual eternity. And the City of Man is the imperfect copy of the perfect City of God. Let no one grieve over the destruction of his temporary home. For his permanent home is ready and waiting for his arrival. There is no expiration to the good man's lease on Heaven. Have you lost your loved ones, your savings, your life? Never mind. You have not lost your soul. For your soul is indestructible.

In any event, and under all conditions, rely upon the guidance of God. Try to submerge the material part of yourself that the spiritual part may emerge. Control your body for the salvation of your soul. For your soul is ever trying to return to the divine from which it came.

V

When Augustine was giving his thoughts to the world, Rome—the City of Man—was sacked by the Goths. It was a time when life was held cheap and hope had given way to despair. Added to the universal turmoil was his own great loss—the death of his son. But in spite of his own suffering, he led his fellow sufferers back to the heights from which they could see eternity through the mirror of time. "What though thy city is destroyed and the whole world is threatened with death? Go on with thy business in meekness and hope, so shalt thou be beloved by men and acceptable in the eyes of God."

CHAPTER XI

Maimonides, Who Discovered Wisdom in Disaster

[1135-1204]

THE CENTURY of Maimonides was one of the most turbulent periods in history. It produced three of the greatest fighters in the world. Two of them—Saladin the Magnificent and Richard the Lion-Hearted—were soldiers of war. The third—Maimonides —was a soldier of peace.

The story of Maimonides—the name *Maimonides* means the *son of Maimon*—has been overlooked in the blare and the splendor of the Crusades. Many legends have sprung up about the chivalry of the two rival leaders—Richard and Saladin. When Richard was sick, Saladin sent him peaches preserved in snow. And Richard, not to be outdone in gallantry, proposed a marriage between his own sister, Joan, and Saladin's brother, El-Adil. But the chivalry of these two heroes toward each other was but a romantic background for their cruelty toward each other's soldiers. On one occasion, owing to a "slight misunderstanding," Saladin massacred twenty-five hundred of his Christian prisoners. And Richard retaliated by slaughtering twenty-five hundred of his Moslem prisoners. The misunderstanding was explained afterwards. Saladin and Richard most generously apologized to each other. But the murdered prisoners had no opportunity to applaud the generosity of their leaders.

Such was the period of chivalry and barbarity in which Maimonides pursued his own adventure toward a saner world.

And the fruits of his quiet adventure produced a greater effect upon the world than the battles of the noisy Crusades.

Maimonides was the intellect of the twelfth century just as St. Francis was the soul of the thirteenth.

II

Two philosophers were once discussing the history of mankind. Said the first, who was a pessimist, "All history may be summarized in four words—*man's inhumanity to man.*" But the second, who was an optimist, retorted, "No, my friend. The four words that summarize history are these—*from suffering to wisdom.*"

The story of Maimonides shows that both these philosophers were right. As a child he learned a bitter truth. Men love to torture their fellow men. And out of this bitterness grew a wise and tender and beautiful system of thought.

He was only thirteen (in 1148), when his family was expelled from his native Spanish city of Cordova. Whoever is in the saddle, he noticed, takes delight in trampling upon those who are on foot. The Jewish kings of Palestine had killed their prophets. The Christian bishops of Europe had persecuted the Jews. And now the Mohammedan rulers of Spain were driving both the Jews and the Christians out of Cordova.

This expulsion was the beginning of a stormy adventure for Maimonides—a lifelong quest for physical security and peace of mind, not only for himself but for the entire world.

III

The life of Maimonides was a battle against danger, privation, ill-health, the violence of nature, and the hatred of men. For nine years after the expulsion from Cordova, his family was tossed about from country to country, only to be told everywhere—Not

Wanted. His father Maimon, a Hebrew scholar, astronomer, and mathematician, was his only teacher. And his only library was his own retentive mind, since the scanty baggage of the refugees had little room for books.

And thus he studied the Scriptures and the Talmud and the Greek philosophers, as well as mathematics and medicine, throughout the years of his wandering by ship, by camel and on foot. A journey through the wilderness, with no Promised Land in sight. How he managed to grow into one of the greatest intellects in history, amidst all these distractions and dangers, is one of the mysteries of the human mind.

Yet, at the age of twenty-three, this brilliant refugee was the author of two books—one on astronomy, and the other on logic. He had learned to know and love the stars in his lonely nights at sea. And, in his contacts with all sorts of people in all sorts of countries, he had learned to understand the workings of the human mind.

IV

By this time (1165) he had settled in Fez, the capital of Morocco. But it was only for a breathing spell. The Mohammedan inquisitors were about to arrest and to execute him for his Judaism. Warned by a Mohammedan friend, he barely managed to escape in the darkness of night.

Another crowding into a rickety vessel, a month of hardships, tempests, and the danger of shipwreck, and finally he arrived in Palestine.

But the Holy Land of his ancestors had little to offer him in the way of mental stimulation. Devastated by the Crusades, it was a wasteland of scattered, impoverished, and disorganized villages. He decided to seek a better field for his energies, and took ship to Egypt.

Here, in the city of Cairo, he found an end to his wanderings. But no end to his troubles. In order to support him in his studies, his brother David had become a trader in jewels. During one of his business trips, David lost his life in a shipwreck.

It was a long time before Maimonides recovered from this blow —"the heaviest evil," he writes, "that has ever befallen me. His little daughter and his widow were left with me. For a full year I lay on my couch, stricken with fever and despair. . . . David grew up on my knees, he was my brother, my pupil. . . . He went abroad to trade that I might remain at home and study. . . . My one joy was to see him. He has gone to his eternal home, and has left me confounded in a strange land. . . . I should have died in my affliction but for the Bible, which is my delight, and but for philosophy, which makes me forget to moan."

For a livelihood, now that his brother was gone, Maimonides took up the practice of medicine. This meant a long struggle against obscurity and want. But finally his extraordinary skill came to the attention of Alfadel, Saladin's prime minister. Alfadel invited the philosopher to become the court physician.

Yet even now there was no peace for Maimonides. In one of the minor skirmishes of the Crusades, the city of Fostat, where Maimonides had made his home, was set on fire. The conflagration lasted almost two months; and when the flames had subsided, the city was swept by a plague.

During this tragic period, Maimonides was busy attending to his patients, allaying the fears of his scattered nation with a number of heartening letters, and putting the finishing touches to one of his philosophical works—*The Light*.

V

The philosophy of Maimonides was designed as a light for those who are wandering in the darkness, a signpost toward a haven of peace, a guide for the perplexed. Maimonides himself used this phrase—*A Guide for the Perplexed*—as the title of his last, and greatest work.

His aim as a guide out of our material and spiritual darkness

was to combine the ethics of the Hebrew prophets and the speculations of the Greek philosophers. Like the Hebrew prophets, he
proclaimed the supremacy of Justice. And like the Greek philosophers, he maintained the importance of Harmony. Indeed, he declared, Justice *is* Harmony. If you lead a harmonious life—that is,
a life in which your own rights are attuned to the rights of other
people—you are a just man. Life is a symphony in which every
one of us must play his proper tune, neither too softly nor too
loudly. And those of us who play our part right are not only *just*
but temperate. For we possess the power of what the Greeks called
self-control. And thus the ideal of Maimonides, like that of the
Greek philosophers, is a life of justice, of harmony, of temperance,
of self-control. In a word, it is the Hebrew prophetic ideal of
Righteousness.

In Maimonides, therefore, we find the wisdom of the ancient
Greeks proclaimed with a Hebrew accent. His philosophy is closely
akin to that of Aristotle. It is equally close to the philosophy of
Isaiah, or of St. Paul. Indeed, the Jew of Cordova and the Jew of
Tarsus believed in an ethic based upon the selfsame Christian
principles of Faith and Hope and Charity.

First of all, declared Maimonides, we must have faith. We
must believe in a Creator—not as a physical personality of superhuman proportions, like Jupiter, but as a spiritual Power, a
Wielder of Justice and Weaver of Harmony. The wisdom of God
created us, and the goodness of God sustains us. God is the purpose, the plan, the *eternal law* of life. He is the music out of which
symphonies are made, the stuff out of which dreams are fashioned,
the design in accordance with which a universe is created. His is
the spirit that consecrates the prophets, and the will that moves
them to reveal the truth. And the gist of this truth, of which the
prophets are the messengers, is that all things have life, and that all
life is eternal. Nothing dies.

And this leads us to the second principle of Maimonides' philosophy. In addition to faith, we must have hope. We must look
forward to a continuation of life after death. Maimonides refines
our conception of immortality just as he refines our ideas about

God. Immortality, he tells us, does not mean a sensuous fulfillment of our personal desires, but rather a merging of the individual mind into the universal consciousness of God. Every living creature is a visible thought in God's Poem of Creation, imprinted upon the pages of time. When the page containing your own life is destroyed, the *visible form* of God's thought known as your individual self has disappeared. But the *essence of the thought* has not died.

Let us, for illustration, take the idea contained in any passage from the Bible—say the Twenty-third Psalm. When a book containing this psalm is torn, it is not the essence of the psalm but its visible impression that has perished. The poems of the Psalmist are imprinted upon many pages. You may destroy all the pages, but you cannot destroy the thoughts. "The body dies, but the spirit lives on."

To change the metaphor, each of us is a bit of colored glass in the kaleidoscope of life. When the glass is broken, the color is not lost, but melts into the white radiance of immortality.

To use still another figure, the human body is a puddle of mud; and the soul, a reflection of the sunlight that gives it its brightness. When the puddle dries up—that is, when the body dies—the reflection of the light has disappeared from it. But the sun itself shines on as brightly as ever before.

Life after death, therefore, is an *ecstasy*—a *standing away from* the individual and a *merging into* the universal. We get occasional hints of this sort of *ecstasy* in those moments when we experience the expansion of our little selves into something beyond the envelopes of our skins—when we read a beautiful poem, or hear an inspiring song, or see a gorgeous sunrise, or utter an unselfish prayer, or identify our own happiness with that of our fellow men through the performance of an act of charity.

Which brings us to the third principle of Maimonides' philosophy. Faith and hope lead to charity; and, to reverse the process, charity strengthens our faith and hope. We are in greatest harmony with the universal spirit of life when we best sympathize with the needs of our neighbors. Maimonides is not only a philosopher, he is a practical man. Our belief in God and our hope for a future life, he maintains, are worthless to us if we have no fellow-feeling for those who suffer. The good life is more than a passive aspiration; it is an active motion—a reaching out for nobility. "The good man is ever on the ascent toward heaven over the Eight Golden Steps in the Ladder of Charity."

These eight degrees of charity, as elaborated by Maimonides, are as vital a power today as they were eight hundred years ago.

"*The first* and lowest degree," declares Maimonides, "is to give, but with reluctance or regret. This is the gift of the hand but not of the heart.

"*The second* degree is to give cheerfully, but not proportionately to the distress of the sufferer.

"*The third* is to give cheerfully and proportionately, but not until solicited.

"*The fourth* is to give cheerfully, proportionately, and even unsolicited, but to put it in the poor man's hand, thereby exciting in him the painful emotion of shame.

"*The fifth* is to give charity in such a way that the distressed may receive the bounty, and know their benefactor, without their being known to him. Such was the conduct of some of our ancestors, who used to tie up money in the corners of their cloaks, so that the poor might take it unperceived.

"*The sixth,* which rises still higher, is to know the objects of our bounty but to remain unknown to them. Such was the conduct of those of our ancestors who used to convey their charitable gifts into poor people's dwellings, taking care that their own persons and names should remain unknown.

"*The seventh* is still more meritorious, namely, to bestow charity in such a way that the benefactor may not know the relieved persons, nor they the names of their benefactor, as was done by our charitable forefathers during the existence of the Temple. For there was in that holy building a place called the Chamber of the Silent, wherein the good deposited secretly whatever their generous hearts suggested, and from which the poor were maintained with equal secrecy.

"Lastly, the eighth, and the most meritorious of all, is to *anticipate charity by preventing poverty.* . . . This is the highest step and summit of charity's Golden Ladder."

Maimonides was one of the founders of the philosophy known today as social science.

VI

Maimonides devoted the last twenty years of his life to the social and the physical needs of the sick and the poor. His was perhaps one of the busiest careers in history. Physician, philosopher, rabbi, and corresponding ambassador of the comforting word to his "neighbors" throughout the world, he frequently crowded the work of an entire week into a single day.

We get a vivid picture of his daily activities—and he was far from a well man—in one of the letters he wrote to a translator of his works.

"With regard to your wish to come here to me, I would anticipate our meeting with even greater eagerness than yourself. Yet I must advise you not to expose yourself to the perils of the voyage, for you would derive very little advantage from the visit."

Maimonides then proceeds to explain his reason for this statement. His time is too crowded for entertainment:

"I live at Fostat and the Sultan lives at Cairo. These two cities are about a mile and a half distant from each other. My duties to the Sultan are very exacting. I am obliged to visit him every day, early in the morning. If he or any of his children, or any of the members of the harem, are indisposed, I am compelled to spend the greater part of the day in the palace. Then, too, it frequently happens that some of his courtiers fall sick, and I must attend to their healing. Hence, as a rule, I find it necessary to stay in Cairo till late in the afternoon. When I return to Fostat, I am about dead with hunger. (For, as you know, I will not eat of the Sultan's food.)

"On my arrival, I find the waiting-rooms of my home filled with people, both Jews and Gentiles, rich and poor, judges and bailiffs, friends and foes—a mixed multitude, who wait to consult me about their illness.

"I dismount from my animal, wash my hands, go forth to my patients, and entreat them to bear with me while I partake of some slight refreshment. Then I examine my patients and write their prescriptions.

"My patients," he continues, "keep coming and going until sunset, and sometimes even two hours and more after dark. I talk with them and prescribe for them while lying down from sheer fatigue; and when the last patient has gone, I am so exhausted that I can scarcely speak. . . ."

Someone has described genius as "an infinite capacity for taking pains." In the case of Maimonides, the quotation may be revised somewhat as follows—"an infinite capacity for work *in spite of* his pains." In his letter to his translator, he makes no mention of his medical and philosophical researches, his voluminous books, and his thousands of written messages dealing with philosophy, religion, medicine, and practical advice.

Yet, in spite of his labors and his pains, he ends his letter upon two characteristic notes—his courtesy and his modesty. "If you still persist in your desire to visit me, you may come as soon as you have finished the translation. I promise you that I shall derive great pleasure from you, but I warn you that you will learn nothing from me."

VII

He ended his career, as he had begun it, in doing good without fanfare or pomp. His life was well summarized in a couplet written by a medieval poet:

> He gave his days to peaceful labor;
> He served his God, and loved his neighbor.

And, within the horizon of his neighborly gentleness, he included not only Jews, but Christians and Mohammedans as well. His

Gentile as well as his Jewish contemporaries called him "the Doctor and Teacher of Mankind." He identified medicine with morality. "There are," he said, "three requisites for good health—a moderate diet, sufficient exercise, and a tolerant attitude toward the world." And his philosophy, like his medicine, was designed as an alleviation for the bickerings and the sufferings of men.

Three soldiers of the Crusades—Richard, Saladin, Maimonides. The first two looked to the past, and aggravated the world's quarrels by force of arms. The third looked toward the future, and mitigated the world's animosities with the power of good will.

There is a dramatic legend that emphasizes the power of Maimonides' good will toward men. When he died (at seventy), his body was carried from Egypt to Palestine. For he had requested to be buried in the Holy Land.

As the funeral procession was passing through the desert, it was attacked by a band of Bedouins. But as soon as the robbers were told that it was Maimonides' body which they were about to desecrate, they hung their heads in shame. Forming a protective circle around the casket, they guided the funeral cortege all the way safely to the burial place.

For Maimonides was a man whom they all revered. Many a time he had treated their families in their illness. And always without pay. "I practice medicine," he had said, "not to get rich, but to heal the sick."

CHAPTER XII

Machiavelli—the Devil's Disciple

[1469–1527]

IN 1498, Savonarola was burned at the stake for his honest convictions. One of the witnesses of the execution was Machiavelli. Honesty, he decided, is the worst policy. This idea became rooted in his mind, and later grew into one of the most vicious doctrines in the history of human thought. Dishonesty, declared Machiavelli, is the shortest way to glory.

The teaching of Machiavelli is a manual of tyranny and oppression and fraud. To this day he is the inspiration of the political adventurers who believe that the end justifies the means—however mean. He was a typical product of his time. It was the age of Caesar Borgia, master of hypocrisy and virtuoso in the art of killing. Through the murder of his brother, his brother-in-law, and other relatives and friends who stood in his way, Borgia had become the Duke of Central Italy and one of the leading potentates of Europe. He was a monster capable of stabbing his friends as he embraced them and poisoning his guests as they sat and broke bread at his table.

Yet Caesar Borgia was not an isolated case. On the contrary, he was fairly representative of the leaders of his day. Directing the attention of the common people to the good things of Heaven, they plundered them of the good things of the earth. They had no interest in justice or in mercy. They cared only for power and wealth. They pretended that they believed in the word of God, but what they really listened to was the voice of greed. They regarded the Bible as a gospel for slaves. Its commandments would never do for those who expected to get ahead. Leadership, and nothing else, was to them the final goal of human aspiration. They believed in government without a heart.

This, in general, was the ideal of the ambitious Europeans at the time of Machiavelli. There were, of course, exceptions to this rule. But these exceptions were swept aside as the scum of the earth. The only individuals regarded as worth while were the ruthless climbers—the diabolical Mediterranean ancestors of what Nietzsche was later to sanctify as the Nordic "blond beast."

These savage individuals realized—although they were too hypocritical to admit it—that the philosophy of Plato and the ethics of the Bible were too "unworldly" for their ambitious aims. They needed a more realistic code of ethics, a manual that would tell them how to cheat and rob and slay in order to get to the top. They wanted a new philosophy—a textbook for scoundrels and thieves.

And Machiavelli supplied the want. He, too, was anxious to get ahead. In order to curry the favor of the rulers of his day, he gave them a code of misconduct that would enable them to climb to the heights over the bodies of their fellow men.

Machiavelli's system of ethics is a new decalogue of brutality, an adventure in hatred and fraud. Instead of the Golden Rule, he formulated a rule of iron. "Do others before they can do you." He rejected the Sermon on the Mount as an impractical dream. In its place, he preached the sermon of deceit. "Blessed are the scoundrels, for they shall inherit the earth."

It was to inherit his own little portion of the earth that Machiavelli became a traitor to his own better thoughts. In one of his books entitled *Discourses,* he approved of the old Latin proverb, *vox populi vox Dei*—the voice of the people is the voice of God. But in his major work, *The Prince,* he advocated the diametrically opposite doctrine—the voice of the people be damned; let the tyrant alone be heard.

Unfortunately for Machiavelli, he failed in his personal objective. He had written his book in an effort to become one of the favorites of the prince. But he had taught the prince his lesson. Machiavelli, too, belonged to the scum of the earth. The prince accepted the flattery, and rejected the flatterer. Machiavelli remained poor and obscure.

But unfortunately for the world, Machiavelli's philosophy found a ready acceptance in a fertile soil. The Devil's disciple is to this day regarded, in some circles, as the unfailing guide to the more practical life.

But let us look a little more closely at the man and his work.

II

Born in Florence (1469), Machiavelli received his training as a diplomat in various courts of Europe. For ten years, from 1502 to 1512, he was the right-hand man of Soderini, the lifelong President of Florence. He therefore had an opportunity to see what was going on behind the scenes in the European drama. He reorganized the Florentine Army, he wrote Soderini's speeches, and he was most likely responsible for many of Soderini's acts.

When Soderini was overthrown by his rivals, Machiavelli was tortured and then exiled to a country estate at a distance of about twelve miles from Florence. Here he was near enough to observe the trend of affairs in his native city, and yet too far away to interfere with the policy of the new rulers. Unable thus to take an active part in politics himself, Machiavelli spent his time in teaching others how to become successful politicians. He wrote a number of books on statecraft (note the word *statecraft;* a man had to be *crafty* in order to be a *statesman*), seven books on the art of war, a satire on marriage, a diabolical play or two, and several realistic stories with a decidedly salacious flavor. He turned morality upside down—in private as well as in public life. He looked upon political chivalry as a fatal weakness, and upon honest warfare as a stupid farce. In politics and war, he said, nothing is honest and everything is fair. If you *must* stab your enemy, be sensible about it and stab him in the back.

Machiavelli's ideas are most clearly brought out in *The Prince.* This book is a gospel of greed. Machiavelli was an ardent admirer of Caesar Borgia, and in *The Prince* he uses this tyrant as a model of greatness. He advises the new prince of Florence, Lorenzo de Medici, and all other princes, to employ the methods of Borgia if they want to seize the government of a new state and to retain their mastery over it. He is not at all interested in the welfare of the subjects. His chief concern is for the advancement of the prince. This book is an excellent, though unintentional, commentary on the state of morality in Europe during the fifteenth and sixteenth centuries.

In order to present a clear picture of *The Prince,* we shall condense its doctrines into a Machiavellian creed of ten savage commandments:

1. Look out for your own interests.
2. Honor nobody but yourself.
3. Do evil, but pretend to do good.
4. Covet, and get, whatever you can.
5. Be miserly.
6. Be brutal.
7. Cheat whenever you get the chance.
8. Kill your enemies, and, if necessary, your friends.
9. Use force, rather than kindness, in dealing with other people.
10. Think of nothing but war.

Let us examine each of these commandments in turn.

1. *Look out for your own interests.* Machiavelli was morally blind. He failed to see the world as a unit. Humanity, to him, was not a closely knit family of brothers in sorrow, but a scattered horde of brutes and simpletons. He believed that it was the business of the brutes to use the simpletons for their own ends. The best way to use them, he thought, was to oppress them. For, according to the laws of the jungle, if you do not oppress others, others will oppress you. Might is right. Therefore, he said, the strong must always assert their strength and make laws for their own protection against the weak. The duty of the weak is to

serve the strong, and the privilege of the strong is to serve themselves.

2. *Honor nobody but yourself.* "He who is the cause of others' greatness," wrote Machiavelli, "is himself undone." Advance the interests of others so long as you can make good use of them. But the moment they threaten to become popular, kill them. For an ambitious man can afford to have no rivals. A successful nation, in the opinion of Machiavelli, should have but a single master. All the rest must be slaves. A prince should receive, but not confer, benefits.

3. *Do evil, but pretend to do good.* Machiavelli sincerely believed in the value of insincerity. He frankly advised the statesman never to be frank. To be good, he said, is harmful; but to *appear* to be good is useful. "He who proposes to himself to act up to a perfect standard of goodness among all men alike, must be ruined among so many who are not good." In order to preserve his power—and plunder—it is often necessary, said Machiavelli, for a prince to act in opposition to justice, charity, humanity, and good faith. Yet his subjects must not be aware of this. They must be fooled into thinking that he is noble, compassionate, pious, and just. In other words, a successful ruler of men should make his subjects believe that he is protecting them at the very moment when he is crushing them. Let mercy be on your tongue, he admonished his prince, and evil in your heart.

4. *Covet, and get, whatever you can.* A prince, according to the brutal code of Machiavelli, should consider nothing but his own desires. He should have no regard for the rights of others. Plunder all you can, he said, and silence those who make complaints. But try to appear to be liberal. Don't go too far in your avarice—not because it is wrong, but because it is dangerous to acquire too much. It is better to plunder foreigners, who are too weak to retaliate, than to tax your own citizens, who may rise in their anger and overthrow you. In other words, rob the weak

and beware of the strong, and in this way you will become a great man.

5. *Be miserly.* Machiavelli goes on with his barbarian code of ethics by advising his prince to save his own money and to spend the money of other people. It is unwise for a prince to be too lavish in entertaining his subjects. At first, to be sure, he will get a reputation for generosity. But before long his funds will be exhausted, and then he will be obliged to increase the taxes of his people in order to entertain them. In this way the liberal prince is always ruined in the end—that is, if he is liberal with the money raised in his own country. "What injures you is to give away what is your own." With money plundered from foreigners in war, however, it is well for a prince to be as lavish as possible. For in this way his subjects will not only praise him for his generosity, but they will be ready to fight and to die for him.

6. *Be brutal.* A prince, whose business it is to enslave everybody, can never afford to be gentle. Machiavelli points out the fact that Caesar Borgia surpassed all other contemporary princes in glory because he surpassed them in cruelty. (But he fails to note that the glory of Caesar Borgia finally *collapsed* because of his cruelty.) Another man whose "pious cruelty" Machiavelli greatly admired was King Ferdinand of Spain. Only a brute, writes Machiavelli, can succeed as a king. Lovers of justice, enemies of cruelty, human and kindly emperors come to a bad end. Goodness never pays. A prince, in order to retain the obedience of his subjects and the respect of his soldiers, should stifle the man in him and develop the beast.

7. *Cheat whenever you get the chance.* Machiavelli insists again and again that in order to crush his competitors, a man must deliberately turn into a brute. He tells his prince to cultivate the ferociousness of the lion and the cunning of the fox. "He who has best known to play the fox has had the best success." Force, he maintains, is greater than justice, and fraud more power-

ful than truth. Do not, he advises his prince, ever bother about keeping your word, for nobody does. "If all men were good, this would not be good advice; but since they are wicked and do not keep faith with you, you, in return, need not keep faith with them." It is easy, he says, for a ruler to break his promise. "No prince need ever be at a loss for plausible reasons to cloak a breach of faith." For most men are stupid. *Mundus vult decipi*—the world is always ready to be fleeced.

8. *Kill your enemies, and, if necessary, your friends.* The age in which Machiavelli lived was almost devoid of humanity. Among the leading sports of the sixteenth century were the hunting of animals and the burning of heretics. One of the emperors of that period, desiring to study the digestive process of food in the human body, had two living men dissected in his presence just as a medical student might dissect a couple of frogs. Centuries of almost continual warfare had hardened the feelings and cheapened the lives of men. Murder was but an incident, and the betrayal of a friend an accepted rule, in the game of life as played in those days. Machiavelli's readers were thus perfectly able to follow his argument, and they were now ready to accept the next link in the chain of his diabolical logic.

9. *Use force, rather than kindness, in dealing with other people.* Machiavelli set it down as a general rule that it is better to be feared than to be loved. When you have driven a rival prince out of his possessions, make a thorough job of it and destroy the entire root of his family. Otherwise some relative of his will spring up to avenge the wrong you have done him. An ambitious man cannot afford to be only partially cruel. You must either be an absolute cad, or else you must give up your ambition. Yet there must be a method, even though there is no measure, to your cruelty. When you have seized a state, or robbed a man, you must inflict all your injuries at once, so that they will soon be forgotten. On the other hand, if you ever *must* confer benefits, confer them little by little, so that they will be long remembered.

But still better, try to avoid conferring benefits altogether. For a tyrant should maintain himself by force, and not by good will.

And this brings us to the last, and from the standpoint of the savage, the most important, of Machiavelli's commandments:

10. *Think of nothing but war.* War is to be the chief business of the Machiavellian superbrute. A prince, writes Machiavelli, should devote himself exclusively to the art of killing. "For war is the sole art looked for in one who rules." A prince ought never to allow his attention to be diverted from military pursuits. In time of peace he should always prepare himself for war. His conversation, his studies, his games, his reading, his most serious meditations, should be centered on the one question of how to conquer his fellow men.

III

In the Machiavellian philosophy, all roads lead to war. And perhaps one of the reasons why war is so prevalent to this day is that too many countries are governed, or rather misgoverned, by the disciples of Machiavelli. His ethics are the ethics of the militarist and the self-seeking politician the world over. Life to them is a warfare in the jungle, and the only right is might. They do not understand the compassion that distinguishes the true nobility of gentle men.

Machiavelli is the ideal philosopher for an aristocracy of "affable wolves." Yet his disciples have been found not only among leading soldiers, but among statesmen and writers as well. Lord Bacon, that strange contradiction of wisdom and wickedness, recommended to all rulers the Machiavellian formula of a maximum of hypocrisy and a minimum of honesty. Thomas Cromwell, the minister of Henry VIII of England, regarded *The Prince* as "the quintessence of political wisdom." Macaulay, one of the most famous historians of the nineteenth century, found in the writings of Machiavelli "much elevation of sentiment." And Nietzsche drank most of his inspiration from the poisoned well of Machiavelli's diabolical creed.

In the political field, the leading disciples of Machiavelli included such men as Napoleon, Kaiser Wilhelm, Hitler, and Mussolini—aggressors whose hunger for power almost destroyed civilization.

And today, the savage doctrines of Machiavelli are still regarded as the gospel of the warrior, the dictator, the imperialist, and all the other indecent oppressors of the human race.

CHAPTER XIII

More–the Philosopher Who Lost His Head

[1478–1535]

IN 1499 there was a dinner given by the Lord Mayor of London. Among the invited guests were two young men who had not been introduced to each other. When they sat down at table, they began to converse in Latin—the common language used among the scholars of the day. After a few sallies which enabled them to recognize their kindred spirits, one of them exclaimed: "Either you are More or you are nobody." Whereupon the other retorted: "Either you are Erasmus or you are the Devil."

This was the beginning of a lifelong friendship between two of the most brilliant men of their day. "The Dutch devil and the British saint."

II

Several years later, Erasmus described Thomas More in a letter which he wrote to a friend. "He is a man of medium height . . . with a faint flush of pink under the whiteness of his skin, and with dark brown hair. . . . His features are better framed for gladness than for gravity . . . and an air of joy surrounds him at all times. . . . There is nothing from which he does not extract enjoyment. . . . His eyes are alive with laughter . . . and his talk, especially with women, is full of banter and jests. . . ."

And no wonder. He was a favorite child of fortune—the most successful lawyer in England, and a bosom friend of the king. "A glitter of glory surrounded him wherever he went." Yet nobody but his daughter knew that under his glittering clothes Sir Thomas wore a hairy shirt.

A strange personality, this philosopher with the courtly demeanor and the ascetic soul. Born in 1478, he came of "honest and solid stock." His father was a judge who trained him to follow in his footsteps. As a babe, we are told, he was being carried across a ford by his nurse—Mother Maude. The current was so strong that both the nurse and the child were in danger of being swept away. To save the babe, Mother Maude threw him over a hedge that skirted the river. And when she got to the bank, she was astonished to find him smiling and unhurt. "God must be saving him for something great," she said.

At school, Thomas More outdistanced all the other pupils. In those days, Latin was "flogged in at the bottom as well as crammed in at the top." But, in the case of young Thomas, the rod was spared without spoiling the child.

His attractive manners and brilliant mind brought him to the attention of Archbishop Morton, the lord chancellor of England. He became a page at the archbishop's palace, where he served for two years. Here, standing behind Sir Morton's chair, the youngster was all eyes and ears for the glitter of learning and the gossip of the court. A fascinating place, this world that opened up before him—beautiful and adventurous and gay, yet at times dishonest and treacherous and full of spite.

At fourteen, he left the archbishop's service to enter Oxford. This was in 1492, the year in which Columbus discovered the New World. A period of widening horizons, restless explorations, inquiring minds. The age of the Renaissance—the reawakening of the human spirit to past beauty and future hope.

More was caught up in the spirit of the Renaissance. Much to his father's disgust, he plunged into the "New Learning" of the day, studying the philosophy of Greece as well as the jurisprudence of Rome. His father wanted him to be an expert in the law, and not "a dabbler in pagan thought." But More, with the quiet determination that was to mark his later struggles against two kings, persisted in selecting his own mental fare.

And mental fare was literally almost the only food allowed to the Oxford students of those days. College life was almost as austere as prison life. Four students were crowded together into one room; and each student was allowed the equivalent of twenty-five cents a day for all living expenses. The young men attended mass at five in the morning, studied till ten, ate their dinner—their first meal of the day—a piece of coarse corned beef and a cup of broth, studied again until ten at night, and then, "being without fire in their rooms," they had to "walk or run up and down half an hour to get heat on their feet" before going to bed. A good training, no doubt, for a man who was to embrace a philosopher's life and a martyr's death.

At any rate, he came out of his education ready to cope with all the exigencies of life. Though at the beginning his road was rather smooth, he was prepared for anything he might find around the bend.

For a time, he was unable to decide between an active or a passive career. Before he became a lawyer, he entertained the idea of becoming a monk. For four years he lived in a monastery and seriously considered joining the Carthusian order of "perpetual silence." But finally his love for social intercourse won him over to a life of worldly success.

But he took out of the monastery a symbol of his struggle between the spirit and the flesh. It was at this time that he assumed the hairy shirt of asceticism under the outward splendor of success.

And his life from now on—at least in the eyes of the world—was a pageant of triumphant achievement. Yet More realized only too well that all this pageantry was a hollow sham.

III

At twenty-seven he married. Five years later, his wife died and left him with four small children on his hands. A month after her death, he married again—to get a mother for his children as well as a companion for himself.

His legal practice, in the meantime, had succeeded beyond his dreams. Everybody admired him—that is, everybody but himself. "Man at best," he observed, "is a god in ruins." He had his own career in mind when he wrote this. He looked upon his fame at its true value, neither with too great a pride nor with too deep a disgust. The main tragedy of life, he observed, is that a man sets out to be a saint and ends up by being merely a success.

So he took his triumph in a genuine spirit of humility. And in climbing the ladder to the top, he avoided stepping upon the fingers of others who were holding desperately on to the rungs below. He refused to defend the strong against the weak, or to take fees for defending the poor against the rich.

His scrupulous sense of fair play extended even to his dealings with royalty. He was a member of Parliament when Henry VII asked for an appropriation of ninety thousand pounds to defray the expenses of Princess Margaret's wedding to the Scottish king. More was the only one who dared to oppose this excessive burden upon the people. He fought for a smaller sum, and won. The appropriation that the king actually received was scaled down from ninety thousand pounds to less than forty thousand. At this insult to his majesty, King Henry was so incensed that he threw More's father into the Tower. He didn't dare to imprison the "culprit" himself because More was too popular with the masses.

And then Henry VII died, and Henry VIII came to the throne. The coronation of the new king was greeted as the dawning of a new day for England. "Heaven laughs," wrote a contemporary enthusiast, "and the earth rejoices. Avarice has fled the country. Our King is not after gold, or gems, or precious metals, but virtue, glory, immortality."

Such were the hopes held out for a king who was destined to perpetrate the worst tyranny in the history of England. At first, however, Henry was disarmingly pleasant. Tall, golden-haired, "angelic," slender—it was only in after years that he came to resemble a bearded and bloated satyr—he made it his initial business to surround himself with scholars. "Without them," he said, "life would be hardly life." And he meant it at the time. His later passion for cruelty was equaled only by his earlier hunger for learning.

And one of the learned men to whom he took a particular fancy was Thomas More. He offered him an annual pension—"to relieve you of your private duties that you may devote yourself to the service of your King." But More refused the offer, and requested that the money be paid to Erasmus. For the Dutch scholar was now living in More's house, and depending upon More's bounty. It was here that Erasmus wrote his famous testament of common sense, *In Praise of Folly*.

Yet Erasmus advised More against his own folly in disregarding the king's demand for his services. And finally More yielded— not for his own but for his country's sake. England needed a man who could see both sides of a case with equal impartiality.

This sense of fair play had a dramatic illustration in the "May Day Riots" of 1521. On that day, a crowd of workingmen tried to mob the foreigners who lived in London. More, at the risk of his life, tried to restore order among the rioters. At first they threw "stones and bricks and hot water" against him. But finally he persuaded them to return quietly to their homes.

A few days later, about forty of the rioters were hanged by the order of King Henry. A great many more would have been executed but for the eloquent plea of Thomas More. "I pray you be a good and gracious Lord unto them, and to accept them now being sorrowful and heavy." The king accepted the plea and redoubled his efforts—this time, successfully—to bring the fair-minded "advocate of peace" into his personal service. "At last," wrote Erasmus to a friend, "the King has dragged More into the Court." And then, for emphasis, Erasmus repeated, *"dragged* is the word."

Knighted by the king, More entered the court with great misgiving. He promised the king "the last limit of loyalty short of my duty to God." To this promise Henry graciously replied that his own duty to God would never permit him to disregard the advice of his faithful friend. But More knew that these were empty words. "If King Henry could buy a castle in France with my head, he wouldn't hesitate to pay the price."

For, even now, More could see the evil heart behind Henry's angelic mask. He understood the ways of the world and the wiles of the king. For years he had dreamed about a world of wiser rulers and nobler men. And he set down the results of this dream in his philosophical romance, *Utopia* (1518).

IV

Utopia is an imaginary island where everything is done for the best interests of all the people. This story of ideal perfection is really a satire on the England of More's day—or, for that matter, on the entire world of the present day. More adds a semblance of truth to the story by telling it in the form of a dialogue between himself and a sailor named Raphael Hythlodaye. This sailor, More informs his readers, accidentally found the island, lived there for five years, and returned to England to bring home the good news about the perfect state.

To make the story all the more plausible, More declared that he approved of some of the reported customs of Utopia while he disapproved of some of the others. One of the customs he called "fond and foolish," for example, was the requirement for prospective brides and grooms to see one another naked, so that there would be no later cause for complaint on the ground of unsuspected physical defects. The entire story was written with such sincerity and conviction that many of the readers believed it to be true.

Because they *wanted* it to be true. For, in many respects, Utopia was an answer to their own dream. In Utopia, declared More, there was no conspiracy of the rich to defraud the poor, no hatred, no intolerance, and no "princess and mother of all mischief"— excessive pride. "All things are held in common"; for private property is inconsistent with the public good, and without a communion of interests there can be no equality of justice for all.

What More had in mind when he made this observation was the communism of early Christianity—the religious spirit of share and share alike in the common gifts of God. More was a devout Catholic; and it was his devotion, as we shall see, that brought about his untimely death. His Utopia, like his entire life, was dedicated to the idea of bringing Heaven closer to earth.

In this picture of Heaven-on-earth, as painted in *Utopia,* there are fifty-four towns, all built upon the selfsame plan of equal comfort for all. The streets are of equal breadth; and the houses are built alike, with one door opening upon the street and the other upon a garden. The doors are always unlocked, and any one may enter any house at any time. For everyone has enough goods to satisfy his needs, so that the temptation for stealing is reduced to a minimum.

The houses are not privately owned, but are rented to the tenants by the government. And every tenth year, the tenants exchange houses—to prevent the feeling of exclusive possession on the part of any man.

In Utopia there are no exploitation, no cruelty, no hunting, no gambling, no cheating, and no need for lawyers or jails. As for the religion of the Utopians, observed More with tongue in cheek, the priests are expected to be "of exceeding holiness, and therefore they are very few." Throughout his life, More insisted upon the ordaining of "fewer and better men" to the priesthood in England. His picture of a superior devotion in Utopia was but an outgrowth of his desire for a devotional house cleaning in his own country. More had the greatest admiration for the humbler clergy of England—the shepherds who refused to fatten themselves at the expense of the flock. But he had an equally great aversion for some of their leaders—the dignitaries of the Church who, like Cardinal Wolsey, confused their divine mission with their human ambition. More could see no affinity between God and gold. "Let us have a priesthood with lighter pockets and purer hearts."

As for the rest of the people in Utopia, they get the highest pay for the least amount of labor compatible with the production of the necessities of life. All the people—men and women alike—

work six hours a day. And they spend their leisure time in study and sport. A six-hour working day is enough, since everybody is employed and nobody wastes his time producing luxuries for the rich. When there is an oversupply of goods, nobody loses his job. Instead, a shorter working day is proclaimed for all until the demand has caught up with the supply.

The magistrates who govern this country are elected by the people. And they are chosen not for their political cunning or economic success, but for their wisdom and honesty and devotion to peace. The Utopians have little occasion for war because they have little desire for wealth. Their contempt for gold is so deep that they use it only for chamber pots and garbage cans. Their money is neither gold nor silver, but iron—a metal so heavy that nobody cares to amass it into a sizable pile. Pearls and diamonds are used as trinkets for children but not as adornments for adults. The chief aim in the life of the Utopians, in short, is the friendly co-operation of equals, without rancor or jealousy or greed.

This friendly attitude applies to their relationship not only toward one another but toward all foreign countries. The Utopians never start a war against another nation. But if another nation starts a war against them, they hire mercenaries who are willing to die instead of conscripting young men who are anxious to live. And their fight is not against the *people* of the aggressive country but against their *princes*. They offer large rewards for killing the belligerent prince, and even larger rewards for capturing him alive. As for the rank and file in the enemy's country, the Utopians pity them, "knowing that they are driven and enforced to war against their wills by the furious madness of their princes and heads."

In this Utopian nation of tolerant understanding, there is complete freedom of religious practice as well as of political thought. Everybody is permitted to worship and to vote as he pleases. Even the atheists are allowed to live unmolested in their midst. "Let us endure them in this world, and leave their punishment to the judgment of God in the next."

Many of the Utopians, however, are Christians. Their conversion took place when they learned that Jesus was opposed to the private ownership of wealth.

More's *Utopia* was meant as a model for what is now called *Christian socialism*—a social democracy based upon the life of Christ. This form of government, as Shaw has somewhere observed, has not as yet been tried. "We have socialism without Christianity, and Christianity without socialism, but nowhere a combination of the two." When More painted his picture of the "ideal" state, he translated the parables of the Gospel into the language of his own day. He castigated the conditions under which a "lumpish blockhead churl" could lord it over the wise and the good simply "because he hath a great heap of gold." He emphasized the idealism of the early Christians when he spoke of the accumulation of riches as "the thing by which . . . all nobility, magnificence, worship, honour and majesty . . . of a commonwealth are utterly overthrown and destroyed."

More's *Utopia,* in short, was an attempt to bring Christianity nearer to the teaching of Christ.

V

Shortly before the publication of *Utopia,* Machiavelli had produced *The Prince.* The public applauded More, but the king adopted Machiavelli. He took *The Prince,* rather than *Utopia,* as the model for his tyrannical government. And England became engulfed in a deluge of murder, injustice, and greed.

For a time, however, More's personal fortune continued on the upswing. Henry VIII appointed him lord chancellor—the highest judicial office under the crown. He attended the king's banquets— a gracious, friendly figure with a somewhat satirical glint in his eyes—nibbled at the capons and peacocks set before him, and barely touched with his lips the golden goblets of wine. He accepted his honors with a shrug, and he waited for his downfall— he knew it would come sooner or later—with a mind at peace. Why worry about the time and the manner of your end? "All of

us are prisoners under sentence of death." Whether today, or tomorrow, or twenty years hence, the ax is sure to fall on every
head.

So hold up your head while it is still on your shoulders, and
meet the world with an honest face. Above all, More was determined to remain honest with the king. No matter how much the
king might be displeased. He pointed out Henry's transgressions
to him, and the king nodded with a hypocritical smile.

But, little by little, the smile on the king's face wore off. His
chancellor had become more than an adviser. He sounded too
much now like the voice of Henry's own conscience. Especially
when More admonished him against the annulment of his marriage to Katherine of Aragon.

The king was anxious to get rid of Katherine so that he might
be free to marry Anne Boleyn (pronounced Bullin). But the Pope
was opposed to the annulment, and More agreed with the Pope.

This opposition on the part of the lord chancellor aroused the
fury of Anne Boleyn. She worked upon Henry's fickle temper
and engineered the downfall of "the man who stood against her
love." And so, as the king's jester remarked, "Chancellor More
became chancellor no more."

But the final blow was yet to fall. After Henry's divorce from
Katherine and his marriage to Anne, More was invited to the
coronation of the new queen. He refused to come. Though he
knew the consequence of this refusal, he passed it off with a characteristic joke. A Roman emperor, he said, had decreed that a
certain offense be punishable by death—unless the offender happened to be a virgin. And strangely enough, the very first offender
proved to be a virgin. This circumstance put the emperor into a
dilemma. But one of his counselors—"a good, plain man—made
the happy suggestion: 'First let her be deflowered, and then she
may be devoured.'

"As for myself," concluded More, "they may devour me; but
God being my good Lord, I will provide that they shall never
deflower me."

More realized that Anne would not rest now until she got her complete revenge. He called his family together, and prepared them for the almost certain end. "If my wife and children were to encourage me to die in a good cause, it would so comfort me that, for very joy thereof, it would make me merrily run to death."

One of his closest friends, the Duke of Norfolk, cautioned him to "bend his stubborn neck." It is dangerous to struggle against princes, said Norfolk, "and therefore I would wish you somewhat to incline to the King's pleasure." Whereupon More retorted: "Is that all, my Lord? Then in good faith there is no more difference between Your Grace and me, but that I shall die today, and you tomorrow."

Meanwhile, the fury of Anne kept stirring up the tempest against the philosopher. But the immediate cause of his arrest was his unwillingness to take the "oath of supremacy." In 1534, the king had induced Parliament to declare that he, and not the Pope, was the head of the Church of England. Every Englishman was compelled to take the oath that acknowledged this "spiritual supremacy" of Henry VIII. When More refused to take the oath, he was committed to the Tower and sentenced to death.

On the way to the Tower he whispered to his son-in-law, who was rowing him down the Thames, "I thank God the field is won." He had gained his victory over the temptation to prolong his life at the expense of his self-respect.

VI

While waiting for his death, More produced the most cheerful of his works, *A Dialogue of Comfort against Tribulation*. It is a vivid picture of the psychology of a martyr. All of us are martyrs in this world—an idea to which More returns again and again in his philosophy. It is painful to die, he concedes, and he has always been afraid of pain. But natural death may be even more agonizing than martyrdom. "For the sharp pang of martyrdom is swiftly over," while the protracted suffering of illness may continue for weeks and months.

Moreover, the martyr is upheld by the faith that he is dying for a noble cause, whereas the ordinary death seems to be a tragedy without reason or rhyme. Should he save his life, as so many of his friends are urging him, by yielding to the king? But by doing so, he would only be saving the worst part of himself and killing the best. He would drag out his days as the most contemptible of creatures—a living body with a dead soul.

And so he rejects the easy way to "the lust of an old fool's life, to sit well and warm with a cup and a roasted crab, and drivel and drink and talk." Better to go now [at fifty-seven] to "the glory of death for the faith of Christ."

And it was with Christlike sublimity that he spoke to his judges after they had pronounced sentence against him. "St. Paul consented to the stoning of St. Stephen, and yet be they both twain holy saints in Heaven. . . . So I verily trust, and shall therefore right heartily pray, that though your Lordships have now on earth been my judges to my condemnation, we may yet hereafter in Heaven merrily all meet together, to our everlasting salvation."

The judges had imposed a most horrible sentence—that the prisoner be "hanged, drawn, and quartered, with the bowels ripped out while he is still alive." But the king commuted the sentence to one of "simple beheading." And, in return for his "clemency," Henry requested "that Master More refrain from making a speech on the scaffold." The king was afraid of the philosopher's eloquence to the very end.

As he approached the scaffold, More turned to his guard with a smile. "I pray you, Master Lieutenant, see me safe up. As for my coming down, let me shift for myself." And a few moments later, when the headsman appeared nervous, More tried to cheer him up. "Pluck up thy spirits, man. I am not afraid; therefore be not thou afraid."

As the ax was about to descend, the philosopher had a parting jest for the world. "Pray let me remove my beard from the block. For surely this beard hath committed no treason against the king."

CHAPTER XIV

Francis Bacon—the Philosopher Who Lived Like a Fool

[1561–1626]

IN 1621 there was a sensational crime investigation in London. A number of high officials had been suspected of bribery and extortion. As a result of the investigation, the leading extortionist turned out to be none other than Francis Bacon—the Lord Chancellor of England and the greatest philosopher of his day.

Who was this Dr. Jekyll and Mr. Hyde of the seventeenth century?

II

Francis Bacon was an amazing type of adventurer. His mind was aflame with the light of the stars, but his body hungered after the fleshpots of the earth. As Shakespeare reminds us, it is much harder to *do* than to *know* what is right. The story of Francis Bacon is a living proof of this truth. It is very difficult for a philosopher-politician to live in harmony with himself.

Francis Bacon tried this and failed. And thus he proved the wisdom of his teaching, not by his *conduct* but by his *misconduct*. He warns us by the wrong things he did, as well as by the right things he said.

For Bacon was a man at war with himself. Throughout his career, he was torn between two emotions—a love for wisdom, and a passion for wealth. A precocious youngster—he entered college at twelve—he declared that he was "fitted for nothing so well as for the study of truth." But his father had been a successful politician, and young Francis was anxious to emulate him. "My birth, my rearing, my education . . . all pointed toward politics." So he set out upon a double course—to become the greatest philosopher and the most powerful courtier of his day. He tried to serve God and Mammon at the same time.

And he learned, too late for his own salvation, that it couldn't be done. He had drowned his soul in the whirlpool of his greed.

III

He started upon his incongruous career early in life. At thirty-one he declared, "I have taken all knowledge to be my province." And he took, or tried to take, all England to be his private hunting ground. He wrote exquisite epigrams about the beauty of an independent mind. And at the same time, he penned groveling notes to influential people who might advance him in the eyes of Queen Elizabeth I. In a letter which he sent to the Earl of Essex —the Queen's favorite at the moment—he expressed his willingness to "serve the Queen in any particular," and his desire to advance his own fortune through any possible means. "I lean to Thales' opinion," he admitted, "that a philosopher may be rich if he will."

He was quite unphilosophical in his anxiety for wealth. His expenses ran always a couple of laps ahead of his income. On several occasions he was sent to a debtor's prison; and as time went on, his letters for financial help and political advancement became more and more abject.

Yet he had a way with people that impelled them to like him in spite of his faults. Essex tried again and again to advance him at court. "I will spend all in my power, might, authority, and amity," he wrote, "and with tooth and nail I will procure the Queen's favor for Francis against whomsoever."

But, in spite of his efforts, the queen was slow to recognize the philosopher. And Essex, to assuage the disappointment of his "dearest friend," presented him with an estate.

In a letter of gratitude to Essex, Bacon declared himself as "more beholding to your Lordship than to any other man."

And then he proceeded, in true Baconian fashion, to prove the extent of his "beholdingness" to his benefactor. The treatment of Essex at the hands of Bacon is a striking example of man's inhumanity to man. Essex had incurred the enmity of the queen. She ordered his arrest on the charge of treason. And—of all ironies—she selected Bacon as her queen's attorney to prepare the prosecution against his own best friend.

It was a ticklish job for Bacon. On the one hand, he had a genuine affection for Essex. Moreover, he believed—at least, theoretically—in the sanctity of friendship. A friendly servant, he had said, gains a generous master; and a friendly master gains a devoted servant. But, on the other hand, his friendship for Essex stood in the way of his own advancement. His ambition, he declared, was like the sun "which passeth through pollutions and itself remains as pure as before."

And so he weighed his ambition against his friendship and repaid the generosity of Essex with a vigorous prosecution that sent his benefactor to the block.

It was over the body of Essex that "the wisest and meanest of mankind"—to quote the words of Alexander Pope—took his first definite step toward the heights.

And, as we shall see, toward his ultimate disgrace.

IV

Bacon received considerably more than thirty pieces of silver for the betrayal of his friend. The actual amount was twelve hundred pounds—about six thousand dollars. Yet he complained that it was not enough. His capacity for avarice, as well as for eloquence, was almost infinite.

His rise after the Essex episode was steady. But he was too

much of a philosopher to be too greatly elated over his success. He felt instinctively that his pride was but the prelude to his fall. His treatment of Essex had gained him many enemies who were only waiting for the chance to overthrow him. As for the few powerful friends he had made, he realized that with them it was a case of dog eat dog. Every one of them was interested in himself alone. "Wisdom for a man's self," observed Bacon, "is the wisdom of rats, that will be sure to leave a house . . . before it falls."

And so he went on building his house upon a shaky foundation. He married—for money and not for love. Indeed, he had no deep capacity for love. "Great spirits," he wrote with more bitterness than truth, "do keep out this weak passion." He surrounded himself with many of the luxuries of wealth, but failed to find the most important of them all—contentment. He had a Machiavellian formula for success: Surround yourself with obedient cronies; truckle to the powers above you; and treat everybody, as does the bee, with honey that contains a sting.

With this formula he advanced step by step, and—to paraphrase his own words—"rose by his indignities to all his dignities." First under Queen Elizabeth, and then under King James, he begged and flattered his way to the positions of solicitor-general, attorney-general, privy councillor, and lord keeper of the royal seal. And finally he climbed to the highest office in England next to the king. He was appointed lord chancellor.

His ambition was now fulfilled. He had become not only the greatest, but perhaps also the richest, man in his country. He owned several city and country estates. On the grounds surrounding one of his country palaces, he built a lake and studded it with islands. The centermost island contained a magnificent summer house with a marble colonnade and a gallery for musicians. After the concerts at the summer house, dozens of servants regaled the guests with the choicest meats and wines. And in the midst of all this luxury stalked the beruffled little man with the grandiose dreams.

Altogether he had several hundred servants to do his bidding, and several thousand retainers waiting to trip him up. And the Viscount St. Albans—this was now his official title—was well aware of the dangerous road he was traveling as the king's favorite. "The footing," he wrote, "is slippery, and the regress is either a downfall or at least an eclipse." In spite of his good fortune, he suffered—as he confessed—from a "disposition to melancholy and distaste."

He had good reason for his melancholy forebodings. For the blow fell at the very summit of his fame.

V

This is how it happened:

Bacon had just celebrated his sixtieth birthday with a great banquet. His London residence, York House, was crowded with guests. Ben Jonson recited an ode which he had written especially for the occasion. A troupe of actors presented a pageant extolling the exploits of St. Albans. On every side, congratulations to the pompous little chancellor with the chestnut beard and the lively hazel eyes—"eyes," his enemies said, "that looked like a viper's." A guest proposed a toast to the "most honored, most fortunate subject of the King."

In the midst of the toast, one of his retainers whispered a few words in Bacon's ear. The chancellor's face turned pallid. An ominous message from the Parliament. The members had decided to investigate his conduct as the highest judicial officer of the crown.

The investigation was swift, and it brought out the most amazing facts. Francis Bacon was involved in a "gigantic swindle." Though exaggerated through the too eager testimony of his enemies, the story in brief was that he had extorted money from businessmen by means of promises and threats, and that he had taken bribes from indicted criminals in return for a favorable verdict.

At first, Bacon tried to brazen it out. "Your Lordship," he wrote to Buckingham, one of his influential friends, "I know I have clean hands and a clean heart. . . . But Job himself may for a time seem foul, especially . . . when greatness is the mark and accusation is the game."

But later on, when the evidence began to pile up against him, he changed about face. Instead of denying the charges, he admitted them and begged for the king's pardon. "I fly unto your Majesty with the wings of a dove, which once I thought would carry me a higher flight." He then confesses his "frailty," but expresses the hope that "your Majesty's heart which is an abyssus of goodness, as I am an abyssus of misery, will judge me, resting as clay in your Majesty's gracious hands, with the honour of your mercy."

And then, with the frankness of a Machiavelli, he offers to repay the king for his pardon. "Because he that hath *taken* bribes is apt to *give* bribes, I will . . . present your Majesty with a bribe. For if your Majesty give me peace and leisure, and God give me life, I will present your Majesty with a good history of England, and a better digest of your laws."

But, in spite of this plea, the king refused to interfere with the verdict of Parliament. Bacon was imprisoned in the Tower and fined forty thousand pounds. Some of the members demanded his expulsion from the kingdom. But Buckingham urged against this step. "The Lord Chancellor is so sick that he cannot live long."

After a few days, Bacon was released from the Tower. But he was deprived of all his public offices and banished from the city of London. He retired to the country, with plenty of time now to pursue his philosophy in the light of his disgrace. "The desire of power in excess," he reflected, "caused the angels to fall."

VI

The desire for excessive power, due to inadequate knowledge. This, in a few words, lies at the foundation of Bacon's philosophy. Let us not judge him too hastily. Though one of the wisest of men, he was a product of his time. The influence of Machiavelli was too strong in the Elizabethan Age. Bribery among high officials was the rule rather than the exception. The trouble with Bacon was his too great insistence upon worldly success. He underestimated the danger of his scramble for fortune at the expense of his friends. He was selfish, to be sure. But aren't we all? Unfortunately for him, his unenlightened self-love turned out to be self-hatred in the end.

Bacon disregarded this truth in his actions, but sensed it in his philosophy. He had tried to surround himself with all the trappings of glory. Yet at the same time he wrote: "Virtue is like a rich stone—best plain set." Having emptied the cup of luxury to the bitter dregs, he realized that what we need is not more luxury, but more light.

More light! This was the ultimate aim of his philosophical quest. Less blundering, through greater knowledge. Learn as much as you can, about as many subjects as you can, and live by your learning. Bacon lived in an age of general rather than specialized knowledge. *Bene vixit qui bene latuit*—the wider your interests, the better your life. "It is knowledge alone that doth clear the mind of all perturbations."

And so, if you dedicate your life to learning, you can reconcile yourself to life. A life free from "vain imaginations, ill-proportioned estimations, and the clouds of error that turn into the storms of perturbations." Raise your mind above the confusion of things. Therein lies your happiness, your contentment, your true delight.

But how can you best elevate your mind to the comprehension of what is your sovereign good? By learning to "rate things according to their real worth." Expurgate your intellect of its counterfeit values. Destroy the false images—Bacon calls them Idols—of the world.

Bacon divides these false images into four groups:

1. *Idols of the Tribe.* These include the "superstitions, dreams, omens . . . or the like"—fallacies that are common to all the

members of the human race. These fallacies lead us astray because we are prone to jump—or rather to fly—to conclusions without examining the facts. "The understanding must not be supplied with wings, but rather hung with weights to keep it from leaping and flying."

In other words, look and measure before you leap, and then you will be less likely to fall into the abyss.

2. *Idols of the Cave.* These are the errors due to our individual rather than to our universal defects. "For every one . . . has a cave or den of his own, which refracts and discolors the light of nature." Get out of the cavern of your little self. Step into the daylight and examine the surrounding vista. Do not succumb to your hindsight by relying too much upon the past, or surrender implicitly to your foresight by expecting too much of the future. Learn rather to "preserve the just medium," and guide your conduct by the best of what you have learned from yesterday, and by the most of what you can expect from tomorrow.

And thus you will "neither tear up what the ancients have correctly established, nor despise the just innovations of the moderns."

3. *Idols of the Market Place.* These errors arise "from the commerce and association of men with one another." Learn to use words that say what you mean, and mean what you say. We often use the wrong words either through ignorance, or through a guilty conscience, or through a deliberate attempt to deceive. Avoid counterfeit words as you would avoid counterfeit coins. They will only buy you retribution in the end.

4. *Idols of the Theater.* These are the errors that come from the wrong interpretation of the Drama of Life. Don't be fooled by the plots that you see on the stage. They represent "worlds of their own creation after an unreal and scenic fashion." Remember that "the stories invented for the stage are . . . more as we would wish them to be than true stories out of history."

And so you must allow experience—your own and that of the rest of the world—to light your candle, and then by means of the candle to show you the way.

For it is through knowledge alone that you can find your way to power—not the power to exploit the world, but the ability to govern yourself.

VII

In *The New Atlantis,* published two years before his death, Bacon describes a mythical island inhabited by people who are able to govern themselves. These inhabitants have reached a stage of superior happiness through superior intelligence. Here are no politicians, but only statesmen; no truckling for office through flatteries and bribes, but honest selection on the basis of fitness and character; no selfish exploitation by bankers and businessmen, but unselfish service by philosophers and scientists; no individual struggle of man against man, but a united effort of all men to control the forces of nature.

In Bacon's Utopia there is no strife for the simple reason that there is no greed. Nobody tries to surpass his neighbors in the acquisition of wealth. And thus all the goods are fairly distributed among all the people. For they have accepted the economic formula that "money is like muck, not good unless it be spread."

The business of these Utopians is of the most unusual sort. "We maintain a trade, not of gold, silver, or jewels, nor for silks, nor for spices, nor for any other commodity or matter; but only for God's first creature, which was light; to have light of the growth of all parts of the world." For this purpose, the Utopians maintain a class of businessmen called "Merchants of Light"—philosophers and scientists who travel throughout the world for the international exchange of new ideas and fair play.

And thus, through the leadership of these philosophical Utopians, the entire world will become converted to the gospel of co-operative good will.

This was the final dream of Francis Bacon after his fitful night-mare of glory and grief. For the first time he realized that "men are not animals erect, but immortal gods." He had become trans-formed, through his sad experience, from an arrogant minister of lust into a humble Merchant of Light.

And it was in this capacity that he ended his life. He died as the result of a scientific experiment. On a winter journey through the countryside, it occurred to him that it might be possible to preserve flesh with snow as well as with salt.

He descended from his carriage, purchased a fowl, killed it, and stuffed it with snow.

Immediately after the experiment, he suffered a chill. This de-veloped into pneumonia. A few days later he was dead. "My experiment," he wrote just before the end, "succeeded excellently well."

His funeral, unlike his life, was without pomp. He had learned his lesson. "I bequeath . . . my body," he had written in his will, "to be buried obscurely. . . . My name to the next ages and to foreign nations . . . my soul to God."

CHAPTER XV

John Locke's Bloodless Revolution

[1632–1704]

THERE ARE two kinds of men in politics—those who have ideals, and those who make deals. Locke belonged to the first category. And, as might have been expected, his government repaid him for his ideals with exile, persecution, and hate.

Yet he stuck to his guns until he succeeded in replacing the "divine right of royalty" with something much nearer to the heart's desire—the divine royalty of right.

Locke was one of the leading actors in the historic drama of transition from monarchy to democracy. He was the apostle of the Revolution of 1688—"the most moderate and successful," to quote Bertrand Russell, "of all revolutions."

So let us meet this quiet little fellow whose philosophy exploded the traditions that had misguided the world for several thousand years.

II

He was born (1632) in the midst of a thunderstorm. And he grew up in a hurricane of tyranny, dictatorship, and civil war. He was ten years old when the British people rebelled against their king, the detested Charles I. Locke's father, a country lawyer, joined the people's army under Oliver Cromwell. And Locke was seventeen when the king was defeated, arraigned for treason against his subjects, and beheaded.

It was an act unprecedented in history—the sheep destroying

the wolf. It was something to make people think. And it played a great part in the shaping of Locke's political thought.

Then came the dictatorship of Cromwell and the massacre of those who were opposed to his "benevolent" rule. The sheep, as Locke observed, were no better than the wolves.

The death of Cromwell (1658) was followed by a period of mental intoxication and spiritual insanity. "Let us eat and drink and be merry. For tomorrow the king may call upon us to die."

And so Merrie England, led by the dissolute Charles II, went off on a spree. The king sold out to Louis XIV of France, for an annual bribe of a hundred thousand pounds, the right to govern the foreign policies of Europe. He then abandoned himself to his horses, his women, and his dogs. When the Dutch sailed up the Thames (1667) and burned the English fleet almost under the very walls of the palace, the king "did sup with my lady Castle-maine"—the quotation is from Pepys' diary—"and there they were all mad, hunting a poor moth."

As for the king's subjects, they amused themselves with gambling and cheating, and hunting the Quakers for the crime of being too much in love with peace.

Such were the scenes that surrounded the education of John Locke.

III

Locke found his studies rather distasteful. The teachers, as a rule, were blissfully unaware of the turbulence of their day. They recited the poetry of the ancient Greeks and paid no attention to the politics of modern England. "My teachers brought very little light to my understanding."

And they prepared him for a career like their own. They appointed him instructor of Greek at Christ's Church.

But Locke was wiser than his teachers. He devoted his leisure to the study of medicine and government. And he interested himself especially in philosophy—not as an abstract theory, but as a practical way of life.

Life, he had learned, is a process of adjustment—the recovery from sorrow and the avoidance of pain. He had lost his entire family—his mother, his father, and his only brother. And he himself was stricken with the family disease—consumption.

But Locke paid little attention to his own disease. He was much more concerned with the sickness of his country. And in this concern he found a sympathetic helper—a former college friend, Lord Ashley, later to be known as the Earl of Shaftesbury. Like Locke himself, Ashley was disgusted with the frivolity of the people and the debauchery of the king. Together they threw themselves into an effort to bring sanity into an insane age.

Locke became Ashley's adviser, his children's tutor, and his family physician. Though he had never received a medical degree or training in surgery, he successfully removed a tumor from Ashley's breast. Locke was one of those rare possessors of universal knowledge—a master of the practical sciences as well as of the theoretical arts.

And now came a period when he had to exercise his skill in another field—the art of cheerful living under an adverse fate. Lord Ashley, in spite of his liberal ideas, had for several years enjoyed the favor of the king. Charles was too busy chasing his moths to trouble himself about his ministers. Though he paid little attention to Ashley's advice, he raised him to the rank of lord chancellor. And Locke's own star had risen along with that of his patron. But now there was a sudden turn for the worse. The king had become afraid of Ashley's influence with the liberal faction. He removed him from his office and threw him into the Tower. Locke escaped just in time to avoid a similar fate. He fled to France, but after a time the king relented and allowed him to return. Locke secured a teaching job at Oxford, but found himself almost immediately in hot water again.

The king had once more decided to distrust him. He hired a number of spies who attempted to goad the philosopher into arguments that would betray his "disloyalty." But Locke was too clever for them. "Not a word ever drops from his mouth," the spies reported, "that betrays any of his plottings within."

Yet the king hounded him out of Oxford and threatened him once more with the Tower. Again the philosopher managed to escape in the nick of time. He fled to Holland—"the refuge of liberal thought"—and, to the king's dismay, "vanished into thin air." Concealed in the house of a friendly Dutch doctor, he worked quietly on his system of philosophy—the foundation for a democratic world.

IV

The keynote of Locke's philosophy may be summarized in two words—contractual consent. All government, all human relationships, all life must be regarded as a business. The ruler, instead of imposing his will upon the people, must sell his services to them. And he must do it in accordance with a contract that is satisfactory to them as well as to himself. It was in the free commercial transactions of the middle classes, in their shrewd yet oftentimes honest efforts to buy and to sell goods on a basis of good will, that Locke recognized an entirely new field for the exercise of human reason. The philosophy of commerce, he said, must be applied to the business of government and to the ethics of our daily life. Honest words, serviceable goods, and fair play.

In order to live a rational life, said Locke, we must begin with an examination of reason. What is it, and how do we get it?

Locke's answer to this question resulted in the charting of a new course in philosophy. Reason, he said, is not inherent in the human mind. We are not, as is generally believed, born with an instinctive knowledge of good and bad, right and wrong, Heaven and Hell. We get all our knowledge later on, as a result of the experience that enters our mind through our senses. "There is nothing in the mind except what was first in the senses." At birth, the mind is a *tabula rasa*, a blank sheet; and the sense-experiences of sight, hearing, taste, smell, and touch are a textbook of knowledge written upon the mind from birth to death. This knowledge is organized into memory, memory into thought, and thought into reason.

Our human reason, therefore, is nothing but the reflection of the material world as it comes in to us through the gateway of our senses. Our mind is incapable of understanding anything but matter, for only matter can affect the sense.

Moreover, said Locke, different people see the world in a different way. For our senses, though externally alike, are differently attuned to the world. We can see an illustration of this fact in the indefinite meanings of our words. The same word can denote a number of things to a number of people. Take the word *hole,* for example. It can mean any of the following things: *a hollow place in a solid body, an excavation, a poor lodging, a figurative breach* (I made a hole in his argument), *a predicament* (he got himself into a hole), *a narrow channel, a small harbor,* and so on. Indeed, so far as our language is concerned—and it is only through our language that we can express our reason—there is nothing illogical in the Irishman's recipe for making a gun. "Take a hole," he said, "and pour metal around it."

Our language, therefore, can only inadequately express our thoughts. And this is due to the fact that our senses can only inadequately—and differently in the case of different people—perceive the world.

And what does all this lead to? The necessity of tolerance. Since at best we can see only probabilities instead of certainties, and since these probabilities appear differently to different people, we must never enforce our own beliefs upon others. The most logical attitude as between man and man is one of "mutual charity and forbearance." There is no reason why men cannot "maintain peace and the common offices of humanity and friendship in the diversity of opinions." Try to reason with your fellows, and then allow them to reason for themselves. "We shall do well not to treat others as obstinate and perverse because they will not renounce their own and receive our opinions . . . when it is more than probable that we are no less obstinate in not embracing some of theirs."

For none of us, in our state of human fallibility, has a right to set himself up as the sole measure of the truth. "Where is the man that has uncontestable evidence of the truth of all that he holds, or of the falsehood of all that he condemns; or can say that he has examined to the bottom all his own or other men's opinions?" Our intolerance is due not so much to the other fellow's perversity as to our own obstinacy. And this obstinacy is due to our imperfect knowledge. The more we know, the less we dispute. "There is reason to think that if men were better instructed themselves, they would be less imposing on others." Live and let live. Feel free to think your own thoughts, but beware of shackling the thoughts of other men.

And so Locke recommended a practical course for the exercise of human reason—the way of *co-operative toleration*. It is only through the mutual understanding *of*, and the mutual respect *for*, one another's views that we can hope to approximate the truth. Instead of reasoning one against the other, said Locke, let us learn to reason together.

In other words, let us return from the artificial to the natural state of man. That is, to a state of liberty for each and of mutual protection for all. Reason, which is our human understanding of the natural law, "instructs all mankind, who will but consult it, that being all equal and independent, no one ought to harm another in his life, health, liberty, or possessions."

Here we have, for the first time, the seed out of which grew our own *Declaration of Independence*—the natural right of every man to his life, liberty, and pursuit of happiness.

In order to maintain this right, continues Locke, men must unite into commonwealths and put themselves under government, so that the interests of one may not conflict with the welfare of all.

Good government, therefore, should not be a conflict between sovereign and subject, but a compact between man and man. The ultimate supreme power should not be vested in the scepter of the king; it should remain in the hands of the people. The community at large has the right to cancel the compact if the government has violated its conditions.

The rights of the individual, in other words, are to be *protected* rather than *restricted* by the state. The king has neither the divine authority nor the human right to set himself up as his brother's keeper. All men are equal in the eyes of God, and must be so regarded under the political laws of the government. "Political power I take to be the right of making and enforcing laws . . . for the public good." Kings, however, make laws and enforce them only for their own advantage. And so it is the height of folly, maintains Locke, for men to rely upon kings in order to protect themselves against one another. It is like asking the lions to protect the lambs. The only safety is for men to unite themselves into governments based upon *the consent of the majority.*

Such governments are to function *for* the people, and their expenses are to be borne *by* the people. But the taxes must be raised only with the consent *of* the people. In other words, there should be no taxation without representation.

Thus wrote the architect of American democracy a hundred years before the founding of the United States. All government, he said, is to be based upon the consent of the majority. It should allow freedom of speech, of thought, of election, and of religious worship. And, in order that it may be prevented from becoming too arbitrary, this democratic type of government should be regulated by a system of checks and balances. In other words, the government should be divided into three distinct branches—the legislative, the executive, and the judicial.

But what if the various branches of the government are opposed to one another? What if the executive, for example, fails to summon the legislative to exercise its function—as was the case when King Charles I (from 1628 to 1640) attempted to rule by himself without Parliament? In such an event, said Locke, the people have not only the right but even the duty to prevent such usurpation—if necessary, by force.

This prerogative of the people, however, must be exercised with the utmost care. "Force must be opposed to nothing but force." A democratic state must never be aggressive, but it must be ever on the alert for its defense.

This, in brief, is Locke's political philosophy as regards the government of individual nations. We must remember that this philosophy, so sound even today, was presented almost three hundred years ago to a world in which democracy was only a dream. But Locke's dream went even beyond the liberal government of individual states. It outlined the principles of international as well as of national government. The day of real progress, observed Locke, will arise when nations as well as men are united in a social contract of political interdependence. The trend of human freedom is from national to international democracy— from the cessation of duels among individuals to the abolition of wars among nations.

The purpose of all government—whether national or international—is to protect the life, liberty, and happiness of the citizens of the world. And thus, in the philosophy of John Locke, politics merges into ethics. The principle of justice depends not upon the sovereign's judgment but upon the people's need. Our reason —that is, the result of our experience based upon the evidence of our senses—shows us that "good and evil are nothing but pleasure and pain." But the determining factor as to what is pleasurable or painful for the individual or for society is not the law of the king but the voice of the people.

And the voice of the people is the will of God. Morality is not an imposition from without; it is an intuition from within. We have a faculty for justice—a fellow-feeling for one another's rights independently of any royal decree or dictatorial command. This universal faculty for mutual fair play—acquired, Locke insists, through our sensory experience of the world—is God's way of teaching us His will. It is the process of our divine education in the human world.

The principles that govern this educational process—that is to say, the laws of God—are as firmly based, and as decisively subject to demonstration, as the principles of mathematics. "The idea of a

Supreme Being, infinite in power, goodness, and wisdom, whose workmanship we are, and upon whom we depend, and the idea of ourselves as rational beings . . . would, I suppose, if duly considered and pursued, afford such foundations of our duty and rules of action as might place morality among the sciences capable of demonstration; wherein, I doubt not, but from self-evident propositions, by necessary consequences as incontestable as those in mathematics, the measures of right and wrong might be made out."

Locke would thus reduce ethics, like politics, to an exact science based upon the evidence of our senses. Virtue is action guided by prudence—that is, wisdom resulting from the evaluation of our experiences; and vice is action that fails to be guided by prudence. A sound analysis of our past failings is the best preparation for our future success.

And thus our ideas of success and failure, good and bad, right and wrong, are *empirical*—knowledge gained by experiment. And this experimental knowledge, observes Locke, has given us a number of "self-evident propositions." For example:

All men are born free and equal. Hence no man has a right to look down upon any other man.

It is our God-given duty to help rather than to harm one another.

Contracts, verbal as well as written, are sacred; they must never be terminated except by mutual consent, or by the failure of one of the parties to live up to the terms of the agreement.

Parents have a right to control their children, just as they have a duty to educate them. But the control of the parents ceases when the children have arrived at the (legal) age of reason.

The goods of the earth are common to all. Some of these goods may become the private property of anyone who has "mixed his labor" in their production of service—*provided*, however, "there is enough and as good left in common for others." In other words, let no man be too full until all men have satisfied their hunger.

This last pronouncement was, in Locke's day, a new note in ethics. And to many aggressive people even today it is an unwelcome thought. For it is a declaration, based upon "the intuitive law of divine justice," that the individual has a double duty to society: first, to appropriate nothing for which he has not labored; and second, to take only his rightful share so that others, too, may secure their share.

Good conduct, therefore, is that kind of behavior which leads toward happiness and away from pain. But the moral law requires that the conduct of the individual should lead to *the greatest happiness of the greatest number and the lessening of pain for all.*

V

Locke's own pain had now been lessened to a great extent. Charles II was dead—from natural causes. He had avoided assassination because, in spite of his occasional outbursts of cruelty, he had learned an important lesson. The people must have a voice in the government—through Parliament—if the king is to retain his head. Charles had received this lesson largely from the teachings of John Locke, the very man he had hounded into exile.

But now Charles was dead, and England was ruled by a new king who relied upon old ideas. King James II tried to set himself up against the will of the people, and the people decided that the king must go.

Not, however, by violence. John Locke had shown that it is possible to have a revolution without bloodshed. At first the king was stubborn against the people's demand for his abdication. But finally, rashness yielded to reason. He gave up his throne (1688) without the firing of a single shot.

The new king, William of Orange, was imported from Holland —the country which had sheltered Locke during his exile. The philosopher was now a free man. The next few years were the most prolific of his entire career. "My life really began at sixty." He sat on the Board of Trade, helped to found the Bank of England, organized the education of the masses, and wrote a number of books and pamphlets defending the rights of labor, the freedom of the press, and the democratic against the monarchistic way of life.

He remained a teacher to the end. He loved to be among "young and eager minds." He preferred the hopefulness of youth to the disillusion of old age. "Two groaning old people make but an uncomfortable concert." And his preference for looking forward to tomorrow's sun, rather than backward to yesterday's clouds, helped to preserve his physical as well as his mental strength up to the age of seventy-two.

Shortly before he died, a friend asked him how he felt. "John Locke," replied the philosopher, "is very well. The cottage in which he lives is becoming shaky, and the wind is beginning to blow in through the cracks. But Mr. Locke himself is quite well, thank you; and he is about to move into a better house, not built by human hands."

CHAPTER XVI

Spinoza's "Expulsion"
from the Human Race

[1632–1677]

SPINOZA was eight years old when he witnessed a scene that he never forgot for the rest of his life. It was at the Amsterdam synagogue. A man by the name of Uriel Acosta was lying alongside the threshold while the members of the congregation trampled over his body as they passed into the street.

"What has he done to deserve this punishment?" Spinoza asked his father.

"It's a long story, Baruch, but I shall tell it to you in a few words. Uriel Acosta disagreed with the laws of our religion. They drove him out of our society for his free thoughts. But Acosta felt lonely and asked to be taken back. And this is his punishment before he can become a member of our synagogue again."

"Tell me, Father, can you make a man a good Jew by trampling over him?"

"I'm afraid not, Baruch, any more than you can make a man a good Christian by burning him at the stake."

Little Spinoza went home in a thoughtful mood. The ghetto was all agog over the news of Acosta's punishment. Most of the people agreed with the synagogue authorities. The few who dared to dissent were afraid to raise their voice. They spoke in bated whispers. Baruch tried to say a kindly word for the victim, but one of his playmates hit him on the face.

The next day, the Acosta tragedy came to a head. Unable to stand the humiliation, the poor fellow shot himself to death.

A strange world, thought little Spinoza. He was wise beyond his years. The Spinozas had acquired their wisdom through their suffering. They had not only *studied* history, they had *lived* it. The Inquisition, the prison, the torture rack, the stake—all the instruments of man's inhumanity to man had been the common experience of almost every Jewish family in the Middle Ages. The Jews had been driven, like so many pieces of wreckage, from country to country. Some of them had drifted from Spain and Portugal to Africa, where they were murdered for the jewelry which they were reported to have concealed or swallowed. Others had sailed to Italy and to England, where they were told that they were not wanted. Still others took ship to Holland—one of the few countries where they received at least a measure of tolerance if not a heart-warming welcome.

The Spinozas were one of the Jewish families that had migrated from Portugal to Holland. Baruch had been familiar from his infancy with the saga of suffering and dispersion and courage and faith known as the history of the Jews. He had heard many stories about the cruelty of the Gentiles. But here, in the tragedy of Acosta, he was learning something new—the cruelty of his own people. The persecuted had turned into persecutors. The Jews, under the lash of their Christian tutors, had become apt pupils in the school of hate.

The world needed a new kind of teacher. Dimly the idea was dawning in the child's mind. When he grew up, *this* was the sort of thing he would like to do. He would try to teach people to drive the hatred out of their hearts.

II

Spinoza's education was not confined to his book learning. He learned a great deal from the book of life. And the pages of this book brought him into a number of unhappy experiences.

First of all, he discovered that there was great admiration but little love between Gentile beauty and Jewish philosophy. His

Latin teacher, the Dutch scholar Van den Ende, had a charming daughter. Spinoza was rash enough to propose to her. But she rejected him—she adored his Jewish mind, but despised his Jewish face—and she offered her hand to a Gentile suitor.

Spinoza swallowed his disappointment, and went on to other disillusioning blows. When his father died, his sister attempted to cheat him of his inheritance. This time he met the situation with a greater show of fight. He brought his sister into court and won the case against her.

And then he showed his true mettle. He tore up the judge's decision, and turned the money over to his sister. Let justice be served, but let kindness prevail.

His greatest test came when the elders of the synagogue tried to dissuade him from his unorthodox views about the Bible. They offered him five hundred dollars a year if he would consent to keep his thoughts to himself. He refused the offer; and on July 27, 1656, he was publicly excommunicated from the "homes and the hearts" of his people.

He was twenty-four at the time. It was a terrible experience to be condemned to utter loneliness for the rest of his life. A living ghost to whom no Jew must ever give food or shelter or even a word or a smile. This decree was proclaimed amidst the wailing of the congregation and the sounding of the ram's horn, while the candlelights were snuffed out, one by one. A symbol of the snuffing out of Spinoza's existence as a member of society. A man accursed among his fellow men. "Let him be accursed by day, and accursed by night; accursed in his lying down, and accursed in his rising up; accursed in his going out and in his coming in. May the Lord never pardon him; may the wrath of the Lord burn against him; may it load him with all the curses written in the Torah, and may it blot out his name from under the sky . . ."

As the final curse is proclaimed, the last light is extinguished. The congregation is in total darkness. Spinoza, by the decree of the Elders, has been blotted out of the world. "Let none hold converse with him by word of mouth, or communicate with him by writing. Let no one do him any service, or abide with him under the same roof, or come near him, or read any document dictated by him or written by his hand."

Spinoza stands in the darkness, listening to the condemnation of the rabbi, the blast of the shofar, and the wails of the people, and his mind reverts to the scene of his childhood. The trampling of Uriel Acosta. What a savage madness possesses the human heart!

Yet, in the midst of his suffering, he feels no rancor against his judges. "It is my business not to criticize, execrate, or condemn, but to understand." This will be his business from now on. Left relentlessly alone, he will try to understand the mind of God and the nature of man.

III

In the acceptance of his excommunication, Spinoza was a true child of his people. A race stubborn to follow its own way to Heaven. The Jews had suffered for their refusal to accept Christianity, and now Spinoza suffered for his refusal to accept Judaism. He could have recovered the warmth of fellowship through conversion to another faith. But he preferred to remain alone. He wanted to study the world through his own eyes. "Those who wish to . . . understand the things of nature as philosophers, and not to stare at them in astonishment like fools, are considered as heretical and impious by the mob." So be it. He would not exchange the flattery of one mob for that of another. He would spend the rest of his life with but a single companion— his own peace of mind.

But even this sort of life was for a time denied him. One night a zealous member of the synagogue attacked him with a dagger. Spinoza escaped with a minor cut in the neck. He decided to move to a quiet attic in one of the suburbs of Amsterdam, and to change his name from Baruch to its Latin equivalent, Benedict. He learned to polish lenses for a living; and he watched the battles of the spiders in his attic for his amusement.

He found a great deal in common between spiders and men.

Such amazing ingenuity in the weaving of their webs and the building of their homes, such utter stupidity in the wanton destruction of their handiwork!

In his spare time, he began to build the structure of his own philosophy. His hosts moved to Leyden, and Spinoza went along with them. They were peace-loving Mennonites—a Christian sect who tried to live and let others live. Occasionally Spinoza would smoke a pipe with them and explain his ideas in the simple language of their hearts. And they, in turn, would minister to his simple wants—a diet of bread and raisins and milk—and take care of him when he was sick.

For he was a victim of tuberculosis. He knew that his time was short, and so he worked feverishly to complete his books before he died.

In this he was not altogether successful. The last—and perhaps the best—of his four books, *A Treatise on Politics,* remained unfinished at his death. And even his other books—*A Treatise on Religion and the State, On the Improvement of the Mind,* and *Ethics*—contained but a "fragment of the truth." For even the greatest philosopher, he confessed, looks upon the world like a prisoner, through a chink in the wall of his body, which is his lifelong cell.

Yet this view, however narrow, is a *true* vision if we regard it "in the framework of eternity." This is the substance of Spinoza's philosophy. The battles of the spiders, the conflicts of men, the tortures on the rack, the excommunications from the synagogue, the misunderstandings and the hatreds and the plots between individuals and families and nations—these are but the darker threads in the eternal weaving of the pattern of life. These, as well as the brighter threads, are essential if the pattern is to be complete.

And what is the meaning of this pattern? *The unity of the world in a river of eternal life.* Imprisoned as we are, we catch only temporary glimpses of this divine life. Yet, to Spinoza, these illuminating glimpses are enough to demonstrate the fact that God and Man and the Universe are One.

This philosophy, known as *pantheism*—from the Greek *pan* (everything) + *theos* (God)—means that God is in every one of us, and every one of us is a part of God. The cruelty of an inquisitor, the suffering of a consumptive, the disappointment of an unrequited love, the ending of a life—all these are but the passing shadows over the face of God.

But the ultimate substance of God is light, eternal light.

And every human body is a part of God's substance, just as every human mind is a part of God's mind. Let us not, however, confuse our own puny intelligence with the infinite intelligence of God. The world is governed not in accordance with our individual desires but in accordance with God's comprehensive design. All things, to be sure, partake of the intelligence of God. But in this world there are different grades of intelligence. The mind of a tree, for example, has very little in common with the mind of a dog; the mind of a dog has very little in common with the mind of a man; and the mind of the average man has very little in common with the mind of a great poet. But even the mind of a Shakespeare, as compared to God, is like the mind of a tree as compared to Shakespeare.

Yet—and here comes the heartening phase of Spinoza's philosophy—your destiny is greater than you think. Your present life on earth is but a stage in your ultimate education. Every one of us—from the vagabond in the gutter to the king on his throne—is an equally important pupil in the classroom of eternal life. At any given moment we happen to be in different grades, depending upon our present capacity to learn. But all of us are scheduled in time to reach the senior class of the elect.

For the present, therefore, let us be friendly schoolmates in the Alma Mater of the Universe. Let us look up to those who are ahead, and help those who are behind. Instinctively, declares Spinoza, all of us are inspired with an "intellectual love of God" —that is, with an intelligent and fraternal affection toward our fellow men. This, indeed, is the basis of our education in the school of eternity. There is a bond of "infinite love" that exists between our better—that is, our divine—selves. And "he who clearly and distinctly understands his divine nature" will surrender himself to this infinite love which emanates from God and embraces all living things.

This "divine nature" of ours, if only we follow its guidance, will lead us to the ultimate objective in life—human happiness. "A man's happiness consists in this, that his power—his zest for living—is increased." And this increased power—for life, for work, for creative effort—can come about only through "the love of self." The self-love of Spinoza is not the narrow egotism of the aggressor, the schemer, the man of strife. It is rather the enlightened selfishness of the humanitarian, the conciliator, the lover of mankind.

For the entire human race is an organic unit of life. When you hurt another, you are hurting your own body, your own mind, your own soul—"the divine essence of your better self." Every act of aggression sows the seeds of further aggression; and so on and on, until someone is sane enough to shame hatred, through forgiveness, into love. It was no mere bravado that induced Spinoza to give his inheritance to his sister. "He who wishes to revenge injuries by reciprocal injuries will always be unhappy." For he will live—as the world is living today—in a perpetual atmosphere of suspicion and retaliation and war. Spinoza recognized only one kind of warfare as being always and everywhere just. A universal aggressiveness for peace. "The greatest victories," he declared, "are to be won not by force of arms, but by nobility of soul."

And who is there to say that our philosopher was wrong? After all, Spinoza's kind of war has never yet been tried. Spinoza distrusted the tried but untrue methods for settling quarrels. Force, he maintained, leads to resistance; and resistance, to further force. Hatred, rancor, malevolence, oppression, vindictiveness, jealousy, strife—these, said Spinoza, are the symptoms of a spiritual myopia. We are unable to see beyond the quarrels of today. How much bloodshed we could avoid if each of us learned to look at the world through the other fellow's eyes! Because of our unwillingness to do this, "many of our ideas are mutilated and confused."

We must cultivate the proper perspective. We must see others as we see ourselves—the related members of a living pageant marching over the highway of eternity. When this eternal movement brings happiness to others, it brings happiness to you. If you reach the summit of a mountain, it is only to describe the view to the rest and to hold out your hand that they, too, may reach the top. Do not rejoice in your strength unless you can share it with the weak.

This eagerness to share is what Spinoza calls "the strength of the wise man." The ignorant man, on the other hand, "is driven forward by lust alone."

The truly wise man, in other words, is the *social* man. He gives himself to others because he knows that all of us are children of eternity. He enjoys the only freedom worth while. Freedom from hatred. "The greatest injury you can do me is to plant hatred in my soul." Freedom from passion and fear. "A free man fears nothing, not even death." Freedom from tyranny and slavery. "A free man is master of himself, servant of none." Freedom from jealousy and spite. "When you and I are free, why should we despise each other?" Freedom from ignorance, misunderstanding, prejudice, and doubt. "Wisdom leads to forbearance, and forbearance to further wisdom."

Hence the completely free man—that is, the completely *wise* man—"will desire nothing for himself which he will not also desire for the rest of mankind." This, in brief, is Spinoza's formula for the attainment of "true peace of soul."

IV

Spinoza was one of the few men in history who enjoyed this perfect peace of soul. His body was wracked with coughing, his larder was often empty, his clothes were shabby—"a mediocre article should not be put into a costly wrapper"—but he went serenely ahead with his work. Once he was almost lynched. The situation had its humorous as well as its dramatic side. He had visited the headquarters of Prince Condé, who was invading Holland at the time. When he returned from the visit, he was met with stones and angry shouts: "Renegade!" "Atheist!" "Traitor!" It was with difficulty that he succeeded in convincing the mob of his innocence. He had gone to the enemy's camp for the simple purpose of a philosophical chat with Condé. To Spinoza, the physical battles of men were of less interest than their spiritual needs.

And his own material welfare was of less importance than his mental independence. On at least two occasions he turned down flattering offers for his advancement. At one time Louis XIV, the "Sun King" of France, asked him to dedicate his next book to His Resplendent Majesty in return for a generous pension. Spinoza politely refused the request. At another time the Regent of Germany offered him a professorship in philosophy at the University of Heidelberg. There was only one condition attached to the offer—Spinoza must refrain from criticizing the established religion of the state. Again Spinoza refused the job. "A free man is master of himself, servant of none." Spinoza was determined to remain alone with his poverty and his freedom and his thoughts.

And so he sat in his garret, and polished his lenses, and sent his thoughts adventuring into the mysteries of Heaven. And it was thus that death found him, on a quiet Sunday afternoon (February 20, 1677). He was only forty-four at the time. His host and his hostess were in church. The only one present was Dr. Meyer, his physician and friend. Spinoza died in Dr. Meyer's arms.

V

It was only after he was gone that the world recognized his greatness. Today, in front of the house where he lived, the philosopher sits carved in stone. His eyes gaze into infinity, as his hand inscribes an enduring thought. For his, in the words of the French historian, Renan, "was perhaps the truest vision ever had of God."

CHAPTER XVII

Rousseau—Father of the French Revolution

[1712–1778]

A RESTLESS LIFE of poverty, crime, hatred, beggary, ingratitude, pity, suspicion, folly, and wisdom—this, in brief, is the story of Rousseau. His philosophy is not a system of thought but a saga of emotion. "Through the whole course of his life," observes the English philosopher, David Hume, "Rousseau only *felt*." Very few people in history have been so sensitive to the buffetings of fate and the injustices of the world. "He is like a man," continues Hume, "who was stripped not only of his clothes, but of his skin, and turned out in this situation to combat with the rude and boisterous elements."

Let us follow the odyssey of this supersensitive philosopher against the aggressive hostility of his age.

II

Born (1712) of poor parents, he lost his mother in his infancy. His father, a watchmaker and dancing-master, brought him up on a diet of hard crusts, severe Calvinism, and dissolute morals. At twelve he left school. At sixteen he ran away from his native city of Geneva. Drifting from place to place in an effort to make a living, he finally found himself in a monastery at Turin. Here he sought out a priest and asked to be converted to Catholicism—in order, as he later confessed, to feed his body rather than to satisfy his soul. "I could not dissemble from myself," he said, "that the holy deed of my conversion was at bottom the act of a bandit." Some years later he reverted to Protestantism. And then he left the Church altogether, to live alone "with his conscience and his God."

But by that time he had accumulated a considerable fund of iniquities that he felt obliged to confess to the world. His *Confessions,* a masterpiece of autobiography, is also a monument of exaggeration. He loved to "bare his soul" to the plaudits of the world. But, stripped of all its extravagance, his story reveals him as a man "destitute of all the ordinary virtues and endowed with extraordinary genius."

When he left the monastery at Turin, he became a servant to a lady named Madame de Vercellis. The lady died a few months later, and Rousseau was found with a trinket he had stolen from her. He told the police that he had received the trinket from a maid with whom he was in love. The maid, convicted on his evidence, was punished while Rousseau went scot free. Later, in his *Confessions,* he excused himself for his testimony on the subtle ground that he had thought *of* the maid as a scapegoat because he had thought *about* her as a lover. In the twisted morality of Rousseau, love justifies all crimes—even against your beloved.

And now, having lost the affection of the imprisoned servant, he became a prisoner to the allurements of a rich lady, Madame de Warens. For nine years he cherished her as his "mother and mistress." But he was content to share her favors with another man. And when this man died, Rousseau was delighted to get "the rival's clothes as well as the lady's caresses" all to himself.

On his vacations from his amatory adventures, he went off vagabonding either alone or in the company of other reckless romantics like himself. Sometimes he robbed his companions; at other times they robbed him. During one of his escapades as a free-lance scoundrel, he met the dissolute French Ambassador to Venice. The ambassador hired Rousseau as his secretary. Rousseau's work was satisfactory; but he received his pay in compliments instead of cash. Rousseau brought his grievance to the French Government. Everybody admitted the justice of his complaint, but nobody did anything about it.

This callousness on the part of the French rulers marked a turning point in Rousseau's life. From now on, his drifting was at an end. He had a definite objective to live for, a concrete battle to fight. The overthrow of the existing government in France. The end of *all* government that functioned without the consent of the governed.

He settled down to a life of quiet domesticity. But not respectability. Disbelieving in the legalized convention of marriage, he entered into a "family partnership" without benefit of clergy. His "partner" was Thérèse le Vasseur, a servant at his hotel in Paris. He lived with her for a number of years. Though he strayed occasionally, he managed to have five children by her. But he didn't raise them himself. He took them to the foundling hospital right after their birth.

What he discovered in Thérèse to attract him, nobody knew. She was a slattern with an ugly face and an ignorant mind. He taught her, with great pains, to write her name; but he could never teach her to read. He couldn't even get her to memorize the names of the months, or to add up the simple expenses of the day.

But that was not all. In contrast to her mental apathy, she had an avaricious physical appetite. And a great passion for stableboys. "I like them," she said, "because they're my kind." Perhaps Rousseau put up with her because she was a "simple barbarian" —the ideal of his philosophical dream. He liked the primitive in human character—the inability to think evil because of the incapacity to think at all.

But whatever the reason for his putting up with Thérèse, she attended to his comforts and gave him an interval of comparative quiet for the development of his philosophical thought.

III

Rousseau was almost forty at the time of his adventure into philosophy. The Academy of Dijon had offered a prize for an essay on the subject, Have the Arts and Sciences Corrupted or Purified Society? Rousseau entered the contest and won the prize. Smarting under his insults at the hands of the educated *élite,* he had maintained the thesis that culture is an evil rather than a good. Many of the world's injustices, he declared, are due to the fact that we have allowed our minds to outstrip our hearts. The wider our knowledge of the world, the greater our thirst to possess it. And thus, the ambition of the educated classes leads to the subjugation of the ignorant masses.

Knowledge and virtue, asserted Rousseau, are incompatible. Every science is the result of an ignoble aim. Astronomy rises out of astrology—the desire to make the stars serve our personal ends. Eloquence is the offspring of politics—the ambition to lord it over others less aggressive than ourselves. Geometry is the outgrowth of our greed for the possession of land. And so on and on. Even the art of printing is an opiate administered by the rich to pacify the rebellion of the poor. "There is a saying among the philosophers themselves that ever since learned men have appeared, honest men have disappeared."

A thinking man, therefore, "is a depraved animal." So let us abandon our overemphasis on education, at least until our hearts have caught up with our minds.

Rousseau admired the "noble savage" of nature—untutored, unambitious, unspoiled—the unsophisticated creature who allows his emotions rather than his intellect to guide his life. "Let us, too, stop thinking and begin to feel."

Encouraged by the success of his essay against learning, Rousseau himself began to live the simple life. He sold his watch, declaring that he would no longer need to tell the time. He "abandoned" civilization and "went back" to Nature—theoretically rather than actually. And he declared the equality of all men in the eyes of Rousseau and God.

He developed his theory more elaborately in another essay— *Discourse on Inequality.* "Man is naturally good, and it is only his institutions that make him bad." The worst of these institutions, declared Rousseau, is the private ownership of property. "The first man who, having enclosed a piece of land, bethought himself of saying 'this is mine,' and found people simple enough to believe him, was the real founder of oppressive government."

The only remedy for this "evil"—Rousseau argued—is "to abandon civilization." For all men are good in their natural state. The savage needs nothing but food for his happiness. When he has had his fill, he is at peace with Nature and the friend of all his fellow savages.

Rousseau sent a copy of this essay to Voltaire. The reply hurt him to the quick. "I thank you for your new book against the human race," wrote Voltaire. "Never was such cleverness employed in an effort to make us stupid. One longs, in reading your book, to walk on all fours. But since I have lost the habit for more than sixty years, I'm afraid I shall find it impossible to resume it."

This was the beginning of a series of quarrels between the two sharpest tongues of their generation. Voltaire called Rousseau "a mischievous madman." And Rousseau dubbed Voltaire "a trumpet of impiety—a splendid mind and sordid soul who, professing to believe in God, believes only in the Devil." Now and then Rousseau made an overture of peace, only to be repelled by another display of Voltaire's devastating wit. Finally Rousseau gave up. "I hate you," he wrote to his rival, "since you have so willed it. And I hate you all the more for the love with which I regard your books. If there is nothing in you that I can honor but your talents, the fault is yours, not mine."

These bitter quarrels were but the minor bickerings of two men engaged upon a major task. Rousseau, like Voltaire, was anxious to overthrow the established evils of his day and to build a better world for a happier race. He outlined the features of this dream world in a number of books—a novel, a treatise on education, an essay on religion, and various tracts on history, politics, and ethics.

These books—especially *The New Héloise, Emile* (which included *A Savoyard Vicar's Confession of Faith*), and *The Social Contract*—were destined to serve as a springboard for the French Revolution. They created the fashion for more than a century of political action and philosophical thought. And the echoes are still heard in the visions of the present-day idealists who are trying to kindle a divine fire in our human clay.

Briefly summarized, the philosophy of Rousseau may be reduced to two major themes—the beneficence of God, and the equality of man.

God, said Rousseau, is the power for good. "How do I know this? Because I feel it in my heart." The reasons of the heart, declared Rousseau, are clearer than the reasons of the mind. "Ah, Madame," he wrote in one of his letters, "sometimes in the privacy of my study, with my hands pressed tight over my eyes and in the darkness of the night, I think that there is no God. But look yonder: the rising of the sun, as it scatters the mists that cover the earth, and lays bare the glittering scene of nature, disperses at the same moment every cloud from my soul. I find my faith again, and my God, and my belief in His goodness. I admire and adore Him, and I prostrate myself in His presence."

Rousseau deduces his belief not from the "gropings of philosophy" but from the "vision of the soul." And this same vision, he contends, enables us to do the will of God through the promptings of our conscience. You don't have to be educated to be good. "Thank Heaven, we are freed from the shackles of reason. We can be happy without being cultured. We need no longer waste our life in the study of morals. We have, at less cost, a more assured guide in this immense labyrinth of human opinion." This trustworthy guide is our instinct, the philosophy of the heart.

Let us but follow the guidance of the heart, said Rousseau, and all men will be united in a single religion. A religion of eternal punishment for none, of ultimate salvation for all. A creed of natural kindliness, universal tolerance, freedom from dogma, and friendly understanding between neighbors and strangers alike.

This "new religion of the heart" exploded like a bombshell among the conservative leaders of France. The rulers of the court as well as the dignitaries of the Church assailed him for his idea of an impartial God. For each of them preferred to believe that he and his sect alone had found the one true road to salvation. Rousseau became a hunted man for his desire to harmonize the world under a single faith.

But even more explosive than his religious faith was his political creed. Rousseau was opposed to every form of coercion—whether by an individual ruler, or by a small group of aristocrats, or by an organized mob. "Man is born free," and he must exercise this birthright at all times. Yet many governments display a tendency to shackle the weak to the interests of the strong. And thus freedom suffers from tyranny through the enslavement not only of our bodies but of our minds.

And what is the remedy? A social contract between the government and the people. An agreement, such as advocated by the English John Locke, that the people will respect the just laws of the government and that the government will protect the human rights of the people.

This ideal type of social contract, Rousseau believes, can best be realized in a democracy. But it must be a democracy in which *all* the people have an equal voice. A government that has no direct primary for the nomination of its candidates for office is not a democracy but an "elective aristocracy." In a true democracy, the will of the people must be represented not by a group of appointed delegates but by the direct votes of all the citizens. "If the people, being furnished with adequate information, made their individual decisions . . . the total decision of the majority would always be good."

A democracy of this pure nature, Rousseau concedes, is impossible except in a small state. For the voting machinery in a larger state is too unwieldy to enable all the people to elect all the officers or to enact all the laws. "Were there a nation of gods, their government would be purely democratic. So perfect a government is not for men."

But in spite of our human limitations, we can *approximate* such a government. First of all, we must abolish the "divine right" of kings. Next, we must recognize the human rights of the people. And finally, we must establish a social contract—a legal constitution which defines the rights and the duties of all parties to the agreement. This is the only sort of government in which there can be no masters and no slaves.

IV

The *Social Contract* became, in the words of Bertrand Russell, "the Bible of most of the leaders in the French Revolution." And it so infuriated the established rulers of France that they clamored for Rousseau's death. He escaped, however, and tried to find an asylum in Switzerland. But the Swiss Government refused to harbor him. His books were burned in public, and Rousseau was driven on.

For a while he found shelter at the court of the enlightened Frederick the Great. But the surrounding peasantry, the "noble savages" of Rousseau's romantic dream, tried to murder him because he had "poisoned their minds against religion" and was now reported "to be plotting to poison their bodies." He fled to England and to the hospitality of David Hume.

But his mind had given way as a result of his sufferings. He became the victim of a persecution mania. He even suspected that Hume was trying to kill him. In his more lucid moments he embraced his benefactor and exclaimed, "No, no, Hume is no traitor!" But his delusions finally overcame his reason, and he escaped from the "plottings" of his most faithful friend.

He was allowed to return to France. For, in the present state of his depression, he was no longer regarded as a danger to the state. The retainers of the king looked upon him as "already dead." But they forgot that his books were still very much alive.

V

He devoted the last years of his life to his *Confessions*—a book which, as we have already noted, contains perhaps as much fiction as truth. In the enfeebled sunset of his mind, the shadows of his sins appeared much longer than the substance. Finally his mind became completely dark. He lived on for a while, in poverty and neglect. And when he died, it was suspected that he had committed suicide.

Rousseau's philosophy had developed out of his suffering. "His bread," to paraphrase Goethe, "was seasoned with his tears." Unfortunately, however, we are inclined to forget the philosopher in the contemplation of the sinner. Rousseau's name to this day is anathema to many people. Dictators hold him responsible for the spread of socialism. Socialists are inclined to blame him for the upsurge of dictatorship. Religious fanatics denounce him as an atheist, and atheists excoriate him as a religious fanatic. But this has been the fate of many a thinker who has expressed new ideas that clash with old prejudices. Perhaps we can best strike a balance between the views of the extremists if we look upon him as a man who, blundering painfully through many wrongs, had finally stumbled upon the highway to religious freedom and social justice.

CHAPTER XVIII

Voltaire's Adventure in Laughter

[1694–1778]

HIS CONTEMPORARIES called Voltaire "the laughing philosopher." Referring to this title, Voltaire remarked: "I laugh to keep from hanging myself."

For, at that period, there was much in the world to make people sad. Injustice, poverty, oppression, dishonesty, greed, dissipation, intolerance, superstition, and war. The princes bought their splendor with the sufferings of the peasants. Diderot, one of the French prophets of a nobler day, has given us a vivid picture of the ghost of Louis XIV pointing out the beautiful palace of Versailles to the ghost of his grandfather, Henri IV. The old king looks at the palace and shakes his head:

"You are right, my son. It *is* beautiful. But I should like to look at the hovels of the peasants of Gonesse!"

"What would he have thought had he known that in the country around these imposing palaces the peasants slept on straw and hadn't even a roof over their heads or bread in their mouths?"

It was Voltaire's great sorrow to see both sides of the picture. And out of this sorrow came the whirlwind of his laughter. He appointed himself the unofficial jester of royal France. And jesters, as G. K. Chesterton has observed, are the most serious people in the world. They conceal their bitter indignation under a grinning mask.

II

The laughter of Voltaire swept the world clean of its ancient superstition about the divine right of kings. He completed with his cynicism the job that Rousseau had begun with his censure. Louis XVI, when he saw the works of Rousseau and Voltaire just before his execution, exclaimed: "Those two men have destroyed France!" What he meant was that they had destroyed the *despotism* of France.

And Voltaire, like Rousseau, paid a high price for his enlistment in the cause of human freedom. He suffered vituperation, exile, imprisonment, the suppression of his books, the loss of his health, and even occasional attacks against his life. But he accepted these hardships as occupational risks in his effort to fumigate the world. "He annihilated with his laughter"—to quote the Danish critic, Georg Brandes—"his own sufferings as well as many of the stupidities of his day."

So let us meet François Marie Arouet—this was Voltaire's real name—at the Duc de Sully's château. There is a dinner party held in his honor. He has just scored a tremendous success with his epic poem on the life of Henry of Navarre. He is still a little shaky on his feet—the result of a serious attack of smallpox. But his tongue is as nimble as ever.

This unbridled tongue of his has already cost him a term at the Bastille. But some of the very men who have imprisoned him are now among the dinner guests at the château. They listen with amusement, not unmingled with dismay, at the barbed sallies of his wit. "My trade," he tells them, "is to say what I think"—a dangerous business during the regency of Louis XV. One of the king's favorites, the Chevalier de Rohan, is trying to bait Voltaire. But Voltaire outwits him at every point. Finally the chevalier loses his temper. "Who is this young man," he asks rudely, "who dares to contradict us in so loud a tone?" "My Lord," replies Voltaire, "he is a man who drags no great name after him, but who honors the name he bears."

This insult is too much for the chevalier. He leaves the house, to the general chorus of "Good riddance!"

But this is only the beginning of the episode. A few days later, when Voltaire is again at the château, a footman tells him that there is somebody outside who wants to see him. As soon as Voltaire leaves the house, he is attacked by a gang of Rohan's hirelings. The chevalier himself looks on in amusement. "Don't spare him," he cries, "but be careful not to hit him in the head. Something good may come out of it yet."

Tattered and limping and half dead, Voltaire finally escapes into the house. He begs the Duc de Sully and his other "noble friends" to go with him to the police. But their only reply is laughter. Why help a mere poet who has been thrashed by a peer?

The next day Voltaire challenges the chevalier to a duel. But Rohan, taking fright, appeals to his cousin, the minister of police, to protect him. Voltaire is arrested and finds himself once more in the Bastille. And when he is released, he is ordered to go into exile in England.

And the French nobility witnessed the spectacle "with outbursts of laughter."

From now on, determined the young philosopher, he would fight them with their own weapons. "And I will show them whose laughter it is that can be the loudest and the best."

III

Voltaire was thirty-two at the time of his exile to England. He found no difficulty in learning the English language. But he retained his Parisian accent and his French attire. There is a story that one day he was attacked by a mob because they were annoyed at his foreign clothes. Mounting a bench, he held out his arms and said: "My brave friends, please bear with me. Am I not luckless enough already, not to have been born an Englishman?"

Whereupon they gave him nine rousing cheers and carried him home triumphantly upon their shoulders.

Voltaire loved England. "It is a country where men think freely and nobly, unhampered by any slavish fear." He read with delight the works of Pope, Addison, Congreve, and Swift. "Here are people who are permitted to say what they please." Having espoused the civilization of England, he embraced it with the exaggerated devotion of a lover on his honeymoon. He praised the philosophy of Bacon, but he forgot Bacon's dishonesty. He admired the English Quakers who were trying to convert the Christian nations to Christianity. But he overlooked the persecution of the Quakers at the hands of the government. He was delighted with the friendliness that the British showed toward their foreign visitors. But he was blind to the hostility with which they treated their own cousins in America.

Yet, on the whole, he was correct in his estimate of the British love for freedom. As compared to France, England was at that period a country of enlightened thought—with its elected parliament, its political tolerance, its intellectual honesty, and its legal protection of the weak against the encroachments of the strong. He met Swift, and found in him a fellow satirist after his own heart. He attended Newton's funeral, and was impressed by the honors paid to that great and modest scientist. "Not long ago," he wrote, "a distinguished company were discussing the . . . frivolous question, who was the greatest man—Caesar, Alexander, Tamerlane, or Cromwell? Someone answered that without doubt it was Isaac Newton. And rightly. For it is to him who masters our minds by the force of truth, and not to those who enslave them by violence, that we owe our deepest respect."

Voltaire recorded his admiration for the independence of England in a series of *Philosophical Letters*. They provided one of the sparks that kindled the fire for the independence of France.

He returned to his native country after an exile of three years. For a time he remained in hiding. But finally he wrote to the Regent, asking leave "to trail his chains in Paris." The leave was granted, on one condition—that he would promise not to attack "the established order of the world."

He made the promise, came back to Paris, and promptly forgot the agreement to hold his tongue.

IV

Though sickly at birth, and an invalid for the greater part of his life, Voltaire stormed through the world in a restless round of activities. From place to place, idea to idea, infatuation to infatuation. He had a weakness for other men's wives. But his attachments were intellectual rather than physical. In that period of moral laxity, it was not unusual for a woman to enjoy a husband and two lovers—the husband for her material comfort, the first lover for her mental improvement, and the second lover for her physical tastes.

Voltaire had begun his *affaires de coeur*—or, rather, his *affaires de tête*—at any early age. On his return from England he was a past master of the art. And his gallantry toward women, especially of the so-called "disreputable" class, brought him to many a disturbing situation.

One such event occurred only two years after his reinstatement in Paris. An actress whom he had greatly admired, Adrienne le Couvreur, had just died. The Church insisted upon her burial, "along with other outcasts," in unhallowed ground on the banks of the Seine. Voltaire criticized the action in a scathing poem. Once more he was threatened with arrest, but he managed to escape to a village in Normandy.

And then came another "black mark" against him. His *Philosophical Letters* were printed, without his consent, by a dishonest publisher. The book aroused a hurricane of abuse. The magistrates ordered it to be burned "in the Palace courtyard . . . by the common executioner, as being scandalous, contrary to religion, good morals, and the respect due to the ruling powers." The burning of the book was followed by another decree of exile for the author.

Voltaire took this new decree with his usual cynicism. He accepted the offer of the Marquise du Châtelet to take refuge with her at her château of Cirey. This castle was situated on the French border close to Lorraine, whither he could easily escape in the event of pursuit by the gendarmes. Here he lived with his hostess and mistress for fourteen years—one of the most scintillating periods in the intellectual history of France.

Madame du Châtelet was married to a professional soldier who was away with his regiment when Voltaire took possession of his castle and his wife. But the marquis offered no objection to the arrangement. His wife was too philosophical for the appetites of a military man. A student of Latin, a brilliant mathematician, and an essayist of unusual charm, she was a perfect companion for Voltaire.

But it was a companionship not without its storms. There were many flashes of lightning, followed by the thunder of invective, in the duels of their excitable minds. They were both competing for a prize offered by the Academy of Science on The Nature of Fire. And, to Voltaire's chagrin, the marquise carried off the prize.

Yet, in spite of their quarrels, they had the greatest admiration for each other. The marquise regarded Voltaire as "the finest ornament in France." And Voltaire referred to the marquise as "a great man whose only fault is being a woman."

And thus they insulted and adored each other, and worked together in a chemical laboratory which they had built at Cirey, and offered shelter to rebellious souls, and produced private plays for the most brilliant audiences of France, and gave sumptuous dinners spiced with conversations on poetry, science, philosophy, politics, music, and art.

And it was at Cirey that Voltaire began to pour out a veritable cascade of philosophical romances—each of them a jewel of wisdom in a setting of wit. His friends were amazed at the quantity— he wrote no less than ninety-nine volumes—as well as at the quality of his work. It is one of the world's mysteries how a man of his frail constitution could have accomplished so prodigious a task. He seemed to be carried along not by his physical strength but by his flaming spirit. "We must do our best," he said, "to feed the flame that God has entrusted to us."

He worked at a breathless pace—sometimes at the rate of fifteen thousand words a day. And he read them aloud at night to his friends.

Shall we join some of these audiences at Cirey and listen to Voltaire as he spices his bitter truths with the gaiety of his jests? Note the vivacious little figure, the haggard face, the whimsical upcurve at the corners of the mouth, the nervous hands, and the dancing eyes. He acts out every part as he reads. A born mimic, with the cynicism of a devil and the soul of a saint.

He is reading one of his latest stories—*L'Ingénu*. It is a whimsical satire upon human propensity to mistake ritual formalism for religious faith. A group of explorers have brought back an American Indian—a prototype of Rousseau's "noble savage"— to Paris. An abbé gives him the New Testament in an effort to convert him to Christianity. Having read it with great relish, the Indian decides to become a Christian. He asks for circumcision as well as for baptism. "For I do not find in your Bible a single person who was not circumcised." When it is explained to him, though not to his satisfaction, that baptism alone is now essential for a good Christian, he is ready for the next step. He confesses his sins to the abbé. But as soon as he is through, he drags his confessor into the penitent's chair. "Now," he declares, "you will confess *your* sins to *me*. For the Bible distinctly tells us, 'We must confess our sins to one another!' "

And so on and on. In a narrative that ripples under the sunlight of his eloquence, Voltaire points out the many contradictions between the teachings of the Bible and the practices of the various creeds.

Another evening, another story. *Zadig,* the tale of a Babylonian philosopher "who knew as much about the mystery of life as any man has ever known in any age—that is, little or nothing at all." Having loved a princess and a peasant, he found them both alike empty of affection and full of deceit. His picaresque adventures took Zadig to every corner of the earth, and to all sorts of women and men. On one occasion he rescued a woman from her husband's blows. Whereupon the woman turned upon Zadig and almost killed him. At another time he entered the service of the king; and after he had brought prosperity and peace to the country, the king tried to poison him because he suspected him of being in love with the queen. Escaping to India, he abolished the practice of suttee—the cremation of a wife together with her dead husband. The method by which he accomplished this reform was very simple. He induced the king to pass a law requiring the young widow to spend a couple of hours, just prior to her martyrdom, in the company of a handsome young man. The married women found the new custom very pleasant, but the married men drove Zadig out of their land.

As a result of his varied adventures, Zadig concluded that "the human species . . . is a parcel of insects devouring one another on a little atom of clay. This true image seemed to annihilate his misfortunes, by making him sensible of the nothingness of his own being. . . . His soul launched into infinity and, detached from the senses, contemplated the immutable order of the universe. . . ."

And now let us listen to a story—*Micromégas*—which ranges over vast regions of the universe. It is a fantasy which outswifts Swift—a *Gulliver's Travels* constructed upon a superhuman scale. Two inhabitants from other planets—a 500,000-foot giant from Sirius and a 1,000-foot "pigmy" from Saturn—come on a visit to the earth. As they stroll through the Mediterranean, a little puddle that barely wets the Sirian's heels, the two visitors converse with each other.

Sirian: How many senses do your people possess?

Saturnian: Unfortunately, only seventy-two—hardly enough to give us more than a glimpse into the mystery of life.

Sirian: And how long do you live?

Saturnian: Just a trifle of fifteen thousand years. We begin to die the moment we are born. Our existence is no more than a point, our duration a puff of wind, and our globe an atom of dust.

In the course of their stroll, they pick up a ship which the

Sirian balances upon his thumbnail. The humans aboard the ship appear to him no bigger than microbes. Bending over them like a cloud, he addresses them as superior creatures because of their infinitesimal size. "O ye intelligent atoms, in whom the Supreme Being has been pleased to manifest His omnipotence and omniscience, there can be no doubt that your joys on this earth are pure and exquisite. For, being unencumbered with matter and possessing little else than souls, you must spend your lives in the pleasures of reflection. . . . Nowhere else in the universe have I seen true happiness. But now at last I have found it on earth."

"We enjoy little happiness," replies one of the passengers, "but we do a great deal of mischief. . . . At this very moment there are a hundred thousand animals of our own species, covered with hats, slaying an equal number of their fellow animals, who are covered with turbans. And this has been going on from the beginning of time."

"Scoundrels!" exclaims the indignant Sirian. "I have a good mind to trample the entire nest of such ridiculous assassins under my feet."

"Don't give yourself the trouble," replies the passenger. "These soldiers are industrious enough to secure their own destruction. At the end of ten years, not one out of a hundred among them will survive. . . . Besides, the punishment should be inflicted not upon the soldiers, but rather upon the barbarians, who, sitting idly in their palaces, issue orders for the murder of a million men, and then solemnly thank Heaven for their success. . . ."

And thus they spent their evenings at Cirey, enjoying the bittersweet laughter of Voltaire, and absorbing the ideas that were to shatter the foundations of the Bourbon throne. And the satire of these romances, though they are rarely read today, has found an echo in much of the more thoughtful laughter of our own century. Such writers as Mark Twain, Anatole France, and Bernard Shaw have dipped their pens in the fountain of Voltaire's inexhaustible wit. The earth, as Voltaire observed, is perhaps a lunatic asylum for those who have gone mad in the other planets.

But, thanks to the possession of a sense of humor, we may be able someday to laugh ourselves back to sanity again.

V

Voltaire's happiness at Cirey was terminated by a tragedy. The Marquise du Châtelet had become somewhat tired of her soul mate, just as she had become tired of her husband. But, instead of dismissing them, she added another lover to her ménage. Like her husband, Voltaire accepted the situation. For he realized that he was "strong in learning, but frail in love."

And now, at forty-four, the marquise was about to become a mother. Voltaire had a premonition that she would not survive the ordeal. And he was right. She died a week after the birth of the child.

For a time, Voltaire wandered about the château "in the extremity of despair." When a friend asked him what the marquise had died of, he exclaimed: "Don't you know? It was he who killed her, the brute! He gave her a child!"

But finally he regained his zest for life. He had received from Frederick the Great an invitation to come and live with him at his palace. He accepted the invitation—to the relief of his own king, who was glad to be rid of the thorn in his side. "There will be one fool the more at the Prussian court," said Louis XV, "and one fool the less at my own."

But Frederick thought otherwise. A man of enlightened ideas— this was before his ambition had got the better of his discretion —he found a congenial companion in Voltaire. And Voltaire relished the friendship of the king, the lavish sums of money bestowed upon him—he believed in a full purse as well as a free mind—and the murmurs of admiration from the people whenever he passed by. "There goes Voltaire, the great Voltaire!"

But he had enemies in the palace. Nothing sours a courtier like a rival's success. Slanderous gossip began to pass around in the aristocratic circles of Potsdam. The king regarded himself as somewhat of a poet, and he often asked Voltaire to correct his manuscripts. On one such occasion it was reported to Frederick that Voltaire had remarked: "Here's some more of the dirty linen His Majesty sends me to launder." At about the same time, it was whispered to Voltaire that the king had said: "I shall need him for another year. The way to handle an orange is to squeeze out the juice and to fling away the rind."

Finally the trouble came to a head. The king accused the philosopher of a shady business transaction. The accusation was probably justified; Voltaire's financial dealings were not always aboveboard. But, taking umbrage at the "royal distrust," he replied in a pamphlet that irritated the king. The pamphlet was burned by the public hangman, Voltaire was sent to jail, and after his release he was ordered to move on.

He was now, at the age of sixty, a man practically without a country. "I can taste liberty no more in Germany than in France."

VI

He bought an estate on the shore of Lake Geneva, and began to sign his letters "Voltaire the Swiss." Here, at Ferney, he remained for twenty years "a dying man." His laughter had now become rather subdued. He no longer adhered strictly to his own motto, "Walk ever on the path of truth—with a sneer." He was still in search of the truth, but the sneer was gone. His main business now was to think right and to do good. And little by little he spent on others the money he had accumulated—somewhat too eagerly, perhaps—in his earlier days. He cleared the land around his estate, he built houses for workers, and he sold them at low cost and on easy terms. "I have left abundance," he said, "where there was want before. True, only by ruining myself. But a man could not ruin himself in a more decent cause." He set up workshops which he managed on a basis of the highest possible wages and the lowest possible profit. And he instilled in the workers a sense of dignity, friendliness, and tolerance toward all sorts of ideas and creeds. "In my hamlet . . . nobody notices that there is more than one religion."

The Voltaire of Ferney is generally regarded as the true Voltaire. A man with a hatred of sham and a hunger for God. Not the God of any particular sect, but the Creator and Caretaker of the Universal Garden known as the world. He dedicated himself as a priest of this rational faith. He expressed it in a flood of booklets published under various names. And the recurring themesong of these booklets was "Crush the infamy!" Destroy the madness of superstition and sectarianism, and enthrone religion in their place.

And what is the Bible of this religion? The great Book of Nature. This is the only book that can reveal the majesty of God. "The splendor of creation betokens the Creator. . . . Nobody can doubt that a painted landscape—a mere reproduction of the original . . . is the work of a skilled artist. If the copy springs from an intelligent mind, can the original be a matter of chance?"

The only true religion, therefore, is to worship God by doing your allotted work in His Cosmic Garden.

And this brings us to the most famous of Voltaire's works—his *Candide.*

Voltaire wrote this book as an answer to the easy optimism of Leibniz. "Everything," the German philosopher had written, "is for the best in the best of worlds." This assertion, said Voltaire, is not true. You can't sit back and feel that all's right with the world. There's too much wrong in it. But it's up to you to *make* it right.

And to prove this assertion—to expose the ugly spectacle of man's inhumanity to man—Voltaire assumed once more the jester's mask. *Candide* is a smiling parable of human folly. The hero of this story—a rich young nobleman—is a pupil of Pangloss (Leibniz), professor of metaphysicotheologicocosmonigology. "It can be easily demonstrated," declares Pangloss, "that everything is for the best." Thus, for example, the nose has been formed to bear spectacles . . . legs have been designed to fit into stockings . . . pigs have been made to supply us with pork . . . and fleas have been created to give us the pleasure of scratching. "And therefore," maintains Pangloss, "it is foolish to assert merely that all is well. The truth is, that all is for the best."

While Candide is listening to this lecture, his father's castle is attacked by a Bulgarian army. Candide is captured and compelled to become a soldier.

One fine day he decides, as a free man in this "best of possible worlds," to go for a walk outside the camp. He is caught and court-martialed. "You can have your choice of two punishments," he is told, "either to be whipped six and thirty times through all the regiment, or to receive two balls of lead in your brain." "But our human will is free," Candide protests. "I therefore choose neither the one punishment nor the other."

Compelled to make his choice, he decides, "by virtue of that gift of God called liberty, to run the gauntlet six and thirty times."

After a while he escapes, only to learn from Pangloss that his parents have been murdered and their castle burned to the ground. "This, too," observes Pangloss, "was necessary; for out of our private misfortune comes the public good."

In order to avoid further individual misfortune "as an aid to the general good," Candide flees to Lisbon. He arrives there just in time to be caught in an earthquake that destroys thirty thousand souls. "How happy the dead must feel that the others have suvived!" exclaims Pangloss.

From the earthquake Candide escapes to the Inquisition—"another example of justice in the best of all worlds." And from the Inquisition he goes to a Dutch colony where the black slaves "enjoy" a bitter life to make sugar for their white masters. He observes that one of the slaves has one arm and one leg. "How did this happen?" he asks. "When we work at the sugar plantation," explains the slave, "and we lose a finger, they punish us by cutting off a hand. And when we try to run away, they cut off a leg."

And thus Candide goes from misfortune to misfortune, and tries to fit his experiences into the picture of a good world, and becomes ever more and more perplexed. "Do you believe," he asks a fellow traveler on one of his voyages, "that men have always massacred one another as they do today, that they have always been liars, cheats, traitors, ingrates, brigands, idiots, thieves, scoundrels, gluttons, drunkards, misers, murderers, graspers, fanatics, hypocrites and fools?"

"Do you believe," inquires his fellow passenger, "that hawks have always eaten doves?"

"Without a doubt," replies Candide.

"Well, then, if hawks have always retained their character, why should you imagine that men have changed theirs?"

"But," argues Candide, "there is a tremendous difference. For men have free will. . . ."

And thus debating, they arrive at their destination. Candide settles down as a farmer on a small plot of land in Turkey. Pangloss is at his side. He still tries hard to prove his point to his pupil. "There is a chain of events in this best of all possible worlds," he declares. "For if you had not been kicked out of a castle . . . if you had not escaped from an earthquake . . . if you had not fallen into the hands of the Inquisition . . . and if you had not undergone all the other hardships . . . you would not now be here eating preserved citrons and pistachio nuts."

"All this may be very well," replies Candide. "But let us cultivate our garden."

This is the crux of Voltaire's philosophy. And the picture of Candide in his garden is the final picture of Voltaire himself. The best solution of your own troubles and the world's iniquities is to do your honest share of work. In spite of his infirmities, Voltaire was busy to the very end. "The further I advance along the path of life," he wrote, "the more do I find work a necessity." The writing of books, the clearing of fields, the planting of trees, and the cultivation of friends—"these have become the greatest of my pleasures."

Cultivate your garden, whether physical, mental, or moral. Attend to your own plot of land and don't cast greedy eyes upon your neighbor's plot. Eat your bread by the sweat of your labor, bend to your plowing, be patient for the harvest, and build houses for shelter and chapels for peace.

He lived to the age of eighty-four—"so busy that he had no time to be buried." And one of his repeated hopes was that someday philosophy might bring an end to malevolence and bloodshed. "I love wisdom," he said, "and I despise war."

CHAPTER XIX

Kant—the Hunchback Who Defied the King

[1724–1804]

HE LIVED in a turbulent age—the Seven Years' War, the French Revolution, and the Napoleonic madness. But he managed to weather the storm. "I am so small and insignificant, the winds pass over me without hurling me to the ground." Immanuel Kant had the body of a child—he was scarcely five feet tall—and "the most towering intellect" of the nineteenth century. Every afternoon he took a walk under the linden trees of Königsberg. "There goes our animated timepiece," said the neighbors as they set their watches at exactly three-thirty—the moment of his stepping into the street.

The neighbors knew that this twisted little bachelor was as precise as a clock in his personal habits. But few of them understood how accurately he was able to measure the stupendous clock of the universe.

One day he failed to appear for his regular stroll. "Something very strange must have happened." But this "strange" interruption to his daily routine was nothing more than a book. Rousseau's *Emile*. For several days "the little professor" interrupted his timetable and stayed indoors to read and reread this book. He was delighted to find a fellow adventurer out of the darkness of disbelief. They were both aiming at the selfsame goal, but in different ways. Rousseau had tried to discover God through his emotion; Kant, through his reason. And now, in his *Emile*, the philosopher of the heart was calling out to the philosopher of the mind. Rousseau was helping Kant to lay down the complete foundation of his new philosophy—to *feel* his way as well as to *think* his way to the mysterious language of life.

II

When Kant resumed his walks after the reading of *Emile,* his neighbors failed to recognize anything unusual about him. The same twisted shoulders, the same piercing little eyes and timid smile, the same gray cane tapping the pavement like the ticking of a clock. "But what a sharp contrast"—the quotation is from Heine—"between the outer life of this man and his destructive, world-convulsive thoughts! Had the citizens of Königsberg surmised the . . . significance of those thoughts, they would have felt a more profound awe in the presence of this man than in that of an executioner." For an executioner merely kills human beings. But Kant destroyed the orthodox worship of the kings and the traditional image of God.

When Kant read the book that revolutionized his own philosophy, he was just thirty-eight years old.

III

Kant's ancestors had come to Germany from Scotland. His parents were poor but deeply religious. His father, a maker of leather straps, used them frequently upon his eleven children. "Spare the belt, and spoil the brat." His mother, an overzealous Puritan, brought up her family to a strict observance of the rituals and the rigors of her faith. Kant's school life, like his home life, was saturated with Puritanical dogma. "I would gladly," said one of his teachers, "sacrifice a hundred scholars to save one soul."

As a reaction to his early training, Kant refused to attend church throughout his mature life. Yet he felt, at all times, a great and growing hunger to reach out from the human to the divine.

As a young man, he read Locke and Hume, and found that their intellectual fare was deficient in the meat of reality. Locke had declared that the mind at birth is a blank sheet and that all we know has come to us through our experience. If this were so, said Kant, how explain our human conscience, our instinct that right is superior to might? We follow this instinct even though our experience has shown that the powers of evil are often triumphant over the promptings of justice. Locke, believed Kant, had failed to grapple with the practical meaning of life.

And Hume, with equal impracticality, had maintained that the mind is not even a blank sheet. It is merely a vague name for a series of observations and thoughts. Hence, the mind does not exist save as an abstract mirror of matter; and matter does not exist save as an equally abstract mirage of the mind. And thus, according to our human reason, said Hume, the whole world is a dream, nothing more. Is this picture of the world a mere trick of philosophical juggling? Not at all, insisted Hume. It is the conclusion of the best and the most honest effort of our human thought.

If this is so—if the best that our reason can do is to plunge us into an empty abyss—is it not time to examine reason itself? So thought Kant before he read Rousseau's attempt to abolish reason altogether and to replace it with feeling. Here was a new and powerful flock of ideas that had come to disturb his mind. And it took Kant almost twenty years to reconcile these new ideas with his own speculations, and to weave them all into the most complete system of philosophy within modern times.

Externally he still remained the quiet little hunchback with the timid voice. A man of the lower strata of society who seemed to know his place. He was an obscure teacher, and two of his sisters were housemaids. Nothing about the Kants to startle the world. For fifteen years he tried to get a promotion to a professorship at the University of Königsberg, but without success. "He hasn't the personality for a professor." And his ideas about teaching were peculiar, to say the least. "I pay most attention," he said, "to the students of mediocre ability. The geniuses can help themselves, and the dunces are beyond all help."

An average teacher for average students. Even when he was finally appointed professor, nobody expected him to create a sensation. He was already past fifty—"a bashful lover of philosophy," as he remarked, "though my mistress has shown me few favors as yet." He was looked upon as one of those unimpressive college lecturers who used "sesquipedalian words"—words six feet long—"to convey useless thoughts." Referring to his lectures, one of his students remarked: "Sometimes he talks less and less about more and more, until he tells us nothing about everything. At other times he talks more and more about less and less, until he tells us everything about nothing." And another of his students observed: "He carries us over a sea without shores in a vessel without sails." As a teacher he was beyond the depth of his pupils —and quite beyond their concern.

Or the concern of anybody else.

But nobody knew that there was a volcano of ideas seething within that modest little head. And, at the age of fifty-seven, came the eruption of flame that illumined the world under a new light.

IV

The book that so startled the intellectual world was *The Critique of Pure Reason*. The title of this book means *a critical analysis of reason in its pure state of independence from the experience of our senses*. That is to say, an examination of perfect knowledge as distinct from our imperfect observation of the world.

Kant's books, like his titles, are extremely difficult to understand. For he uses a new terminology, and he frequently packs an entire chapter into a single phrase. When Kant sent the manuscript of his *Critique* to Herz, a friend who was an eminent scholar, Herz returned it without finishing the book. "If I go on with it, I am afraid I shall go mad."

But we can find, at the very beginning of the book, a trail of light that will guide us through the mazes of his complicated thought. Let us try to follow this trail.

Kant begins his philosophy with a challenge to Locke and to Hume. Our knowledge does not come entirely through the senses. And our mind is not merely a bundle of impressions. There is such a thing as *absolute* knowledge, a *definite entity* known to us as *mind*. This knowledge, this mind, is not dependent upon the experience of our sight, hearing, taste, touch, or smell. It is *a priori* —that is, *prior to our own experience.* "General truths . . . are clear and certain in themselves"—regardless of any appearances that our imperfect visions may observe. "How far we can advance independently of all experience, in *a priori* knowledge, is shown by the brilliant example of mathematics." No matter what we may see or think, it is an absolute certainty that two times two will always make four.

Locke is wrong, therefore, when he insists that there is no knowledge outside of experience. And Hume is wrong when he denies the existence of certainties in this world. The mind is not merely a *collector,* but a *director* of observations. It organizes the world, by means of mathematical and other *a priori* truths, into an intelligible unit. It enables us to transform chaos into order, random experiences into organized knowledge, individual perceptions into universal wisdom. And to grope from human wisdom to divine light.

Human wisdom, therefore, is *organization*—the ability to use eternal truths for the understanding and the ordering of our temporal affairs. An idiot observes the same world as a Shakespeare. But only Shakespeare can weave his observations into a pattern of beauty and sense.

Let us, therefore, depend less upon our senses and more upon our sense. Our senses give us a world of appearances, but our sense directs us to the reality behind the appearances—the *thing-in-itself.* "Kant's greatest contribution to philosophy," wrote

Schopenhauer, "was his distinction between the real world and the apparent world."

The apparent world, as seen through the senses, is like a jumble of bricks, iron, glass, wood, and stone scattered over the ground. But the real world of the sense is a complete building constructed out of these materials into a beautiful architectural unit.

And it is the function of the mind to discover how the mass of disorder has been organized, and to get some idea of this ultimate order, of the exact nature of the *thing-in-itself* that lies hidden behind the veil of our defective vision.

Yet we are doomed to remain partially blind. We shall never understand the exact nature of reality. "It remains completely unknown to us what the world may be by itself and apart from the receptivity of our senses. We know nothing but our manner of perceiving it." We know merely that the world exists.

How did it come into existence? Has it been created by a Supreme Artist, and is it guided by a Supreme Mind? To these questions, Kant replies, "there can be no answer dictated by reason."

But possibly there is an answer of another kind, dictated by emotion? The feeling of right, for example? Is there perhaps an absolute principle of morality, just as there is an absolute principle of mathematics? This is the idea that Kant developed in the next book of his philosophical structure—*The Critique of Practical Reason*. The moral principle, like the mathematical, is inborn; it is prior to, and independent of, our experience as derived from our senses. This moral principle is the basis of our religion, the demand of our conscience, the very center of our existence.

Good conduct is an absolute commandment from within. Mutual kindness is a *must*. We feel—and it is a feeling born with the birth of our body—that we are spiritually *bound* to one another. We know instinctively that we ought to do our duty. This sense of social duty—the principle of a world organized as a unit —not only prompts our hearts toward the right ends, but guides the stars in their appointed course.

"The starry heavens above, the moral law within"—these are the two aspects of the selfsame principle that can lead our reason and our emotion to a better understanding of the world. The mathematics of the heavenly bodies and the ethics of our earthly existence are the expression of a divine law. And this law, translated into human terms, means that we must live in accordance with the organized process of Nature. "Act as if the maxim of your own conduct were to become by your will the maxim of all the world's activity." In other words, avoid any action which, if adopted by all other people, would make social life impossible. Are you tempted to break your promise? Your conscience—which serves as the interpreter of the universal principle—informs you that a world of broken promises would become a jungle of snarling beasts. On the same principle, "the moral law within" condemns aggressiveness, cupidity, intolerance, extortion, treachery, malevolence, murder, theft.

And, for the same reason, the moral law sanctions the virtues which are opposed to these vices. Our conscience is an infallible guide to our actions. It not only demands honesty *when* it is the best policy. It declares that honesty *always is* the best policy. Honest behavior may mean your own temporary loss, but it also means humanity's permanent gain. The aim of morality is to do your duty by making others happy. For in this way you will make your own self worthy of happiness.

Our conscience, in short, prompts us to keep the world organized on the basis of unstinted labor from, and adequate compensation to, every member of society. Let every man be "an end in himself," instead of an instrument wielded by somebody else. *Thou shalt not exploit thy neighbor.* "There can be nothing more dreadful than that the actions of a man should be subject to the will of another man."

This *a priori* prompting of the conscience—the absolute command to duty—leads to three important conclusions: the freedom of the will, the immortality of the soul, and the existence of God.

1. *The freedom of the will.* It would be meaningless to have a sense of duty—a feeling that we ought to do the right thing—

unless we felt free to choose between the right and the wrong. We can prove our free will not by our theoretical reason, but by our practical emotion. Whenever we have a moral choice to make, we know—not through our acquired senses, but through our innate sense—that we can, if we will, choose the right way. This inborn knowledge of our ability to do our duty, of our creative power to fashion the imperfect world of our experience into the perfect world of our heart's desire, is the manifestation of a free will "as definite as the multiplication table." To every moral choice, as to every mathematical problem, there is but one true answer. We cannot reason, but we can feel, that this is so. We have an instinctive feeling for the right, an instinctive desire to find it, and an instinctive power to follow it. In other words, we are endowed with a free will.

2. *The immortality of the soul.* In like manner, we have an instinctive feeling that we are endowed with an immortal soul. We look upon the drama of a human life, and we find that it is quite different from a stage drama. On the stage there is a definite plot that provides a reward for every virtue and a punishment for every sin. But in life we see no such poetic justice. On the contrary, we see "truth forever on the scaffold," injustice ever on the throne.

And thus the drama of life, as we observe it, violates our instinct for a good play. It appears like the fragment of a single act, without symmetry or sense. And therefore we feel that this is not the entire story, and we try to act accordingly. Our moral sense tells us to do good in spite of our suffering and to avoid evil regardless of our reward. Why? Because we sense that our life on earth is only a part of the drama, and that the final story is symmetrical, satisfactory, and complete. Hence our determination to do our duty in the face of evil. This desire, observes Kant, would have no meaning unless we knew instinctively that our death is but the end of a chapter—to be continued with a further, fuller, and happier development of the plot in another life.

3. *The existence of God.* Our moral sense tells that there is a Mind which has created this human drama. We feel that we are justified in facing today's suffering for tomorrow's joy. The action of the drama in the next world will explain the suspense and the mystery of the present world. Our instinct—that is, our *a priori* knowledge—takes immortality for granted. And this "postulate of immortality . . . must lead to the supposition of the existence of a cause adequate to this effect. In other words, it must postulate the existence of God."

We cannot prove, but we can feel, the workmanship of God—the Dramatist of the Perfect Play. And our feeling is prior to, and independent of, our reason. Our moral sense is sounder than our material observation.

Kant was unable to discover God in his mind. But he found and enthroned Him in his heart. As Heine somewhat playfully observes, the Königsberg philosopher created God for the sake of his old servant, Lampe. "Hitherto," writes Heine, "Immanuel Kant has appeared as the grim and inexorable iconoclast. He has stormed heaven, put the whole garrison to the sword; the ruler of the world swims senseless in his blood; there is no more any mercy or fatherly goodness or future reward for present privations; the immortality of the soul is in its last agonies—death rattles and groans! And old Lampe stands by with his umbrella under his arm as a sorrowing spectator, and the sweat of anguish and tears runs down his cheeks. Then Immanuel Kant is moved to pity and shows himself not only a great philosopher but a good man. 'Old Lampe,' he observes, 'must have a God, or else the poor man cannot be happy; and people really ought to be happy in this world. Practical common sense *requires* it. Very well, then, let practical reason *guarantee* it.' "

As usual, Heine conceals an aspect of the truth behind a comic mask. It *was* the kindness of Immanuel Kant that led him to postulate the existence of God. Kindness not only to his servant but to all humanity. We know that God exists, he said, because there is so universal a need of Him. In this world of distorted justice, there would be no place for happiness or hope without a Providence that patterned the whole into a unit of sense. The feeling of the heart is a better guide than the logic of the head. For the heart, to paraphrase Pascal has reasons of its own which the head can never understand.

V

Kant finished his philosophy of the head and the heart at the age of sixty-nine. He hoped to settle down to a peaceful old age. But his hope was not to be realized. His denial of religion on the basis of reason aroused a storm of abuse. And his insistence upon the duties rather than the dogmas of Christianity whipped the storm into a hurricane. The Pharisees of the world called him a dog; and many of them called their dogs Immanuel Kant.

But Kant went on, in his quiet way, to point out the inadequacy of religion as practiced in his own country. "Christ," he declared, "has brought the Kingdom of God nearer to earth; but he has been misunderstood; and in place of God's kingdom the kingdom of the priest has been established among us." The word religion means a binding together of heart to heart. But, instead of being bound together by kindness, men are torn apart and divided into creeds. Religious worship, declared Kant, has degenerated into "a sort of heavenly court service by means of which a man may win by flattery the favor of the ruler of heaven."

These words, declared King Frederick William, sounded like treason not only against the ruler of Heaven but also against the rulers of the earth. He issued a decree to stop all such "subversive" teaching in Prussia. Kant had just written another essay on religion. The manuscript was about to be published in the *Berliner Monatsschrift*. The king ordered the magazine to suppress the article.

But the king reckoned without his rebellious little hunchback of seventy. Kant sent the article to a friend in Jena—a city which lay beyond the jurisdiction of Prussia—with a request that it be published there. When the article was finally issued, the king flew into a rage. "Our highest person," he wrote to the philosopher, "has been greatly displeased to observe how you misuse your philosophy to undermine . . . many of the most important and fundamental doctrines of the Holy Scriptures and of Christianity. We demand . . . that in future you will give no such cause for our anger. . . . If you continue to oppose this order, you may expect unpleasant consequences."

But Kant had already spoken his final word on religion. With tongue in cheek, he wrote to the king: "Your Majesty, I will add nothing further to what I have already said."

VI

Kant was an amazing personality. His mental development seemed to be contrary to the laws of Nature. Instead of turning from the liberalism of youth to the conservatism of old age, he reversed the process. He started as a resigned conservative and ended as a passionate liberal. At the outbreak of the French Revolution, most of the college professors in Europe declared their allegiance to the institution of monarchy. But Kant, in his youthful enthusiasm of almost seventy years, hailed the Revolution with tears in his eyes. "Now I can say like Simeon, 'Lord, let Thy servant depart in peace; for mine eyes have seen Thy salvation.' "

One of his latest books, written at seventy-one, was a plea for a world federation of free states, bound together by a treaty to outlaw war. In this book, *Eternal Peace,* Kant complains—note the modern ring of the complaint—that "our rulers have no money to spend on public education . . . because all their resources are already placed to the account of the next war." He advocates not only the reduction, but the abolition of all military forces. "Standing armies excite states to outrival one another in the number of their armed men." And this means intolerable hardship as well as unnecessary expense.

In order to avoid this hardship and expense, Kant insists, we must organize our states on a democratic basis—so that "war cannot be declared except by a vote of all the people."

For the function of government, like the function of religion, is to "respect every man as an absolute unit in himself," and to "bind all men into a world-wide unit of peace." This, declared Kant, is the goal toward which all humanity is striving under the Providence of God.

And why do we need this God as our Guide? Because only such a Guide can reconcile our aims and rectify the struggles of the world. Kant's great heart, a biographer has observed, felt the truth that his great mind was unable to see.

CHAPTER XX

An Adventure Toward the Light—
the Philosophy of Goethe

[1749–1832]

GOETHE was no academic philosopher. He lectured at no university, and he created no complicated system of thought. Yet his was one of the world's greatest contributions to philosophy. In his physical activity, as well as in his mental speculations, he stumbled always instinctively toward the light. Goethe's books, especially his dramatic poem on Faust, may be regarded as philosophy applied to life. It is for this reason, we believe, that he deserves a high place in the adventure of human thought.

II

He was a man with a magnetic personality. One day, as he entered a restaurant in Strasbourg, the diners dropped their knives and forks to stare at the magnificent stranger. "This man," whispered one of the guests, "has just descended from Olympus."

"Yes," replied his companion. "It must be Apollo, the god of light!"

He was the handsomest and the most gifted German of his day. And the most restless of lovers. He experienced the first of his many passions at fourteen, and the last at seventy-four. His life was a restless search for new emotions, new actions, new avenues of approach to the "secret heart of the universe." He was, in turn, a rebel and a conservative, a pagan and a Christian, a follower of Satan and a disciple of the saints. In his effort to touch life at every possible point, he even flirted for a time with the idea of killing himself. "This, perhaps, will be the greatest adventure of them all."

But he decided to live on. "What if death is really the end?" Take no chances. Accept the certainty of further hazards, rather than the possibility of eternal oblivion. He must live a full life. "And the fulfillment of life is the pursuit of an ever receding goal." It isn't what you are, but what you may become, that puts the zest into the banquet of life.

Goethe, like Faust, was anxious to taste all the savory dishes of life. In his universal hunger for living, he was unable for a time to settle upon a career. He thought of medicine, business, law, teaching, poetry, painting—and finally concentrated upon the last two possibilities. In order to express himself most adequately, he would become a writer or an artist. One day he walked along the banks of the Rhine. His mind was agitated with the beauty of the landscape: hazy mountains in the distance, a precipice at his feet—and in the depths of the gorge below, the river flowing under a grotto of maples and willows. If only he could paint this scene!

Or describe it in words that would take fire and come to life! He took a jackknife from his pocket. "Let me put my decision to the test. I will throw this knife into the river. If I see it drop into the water, I will become an artist. If it disappears into the shrubbery, I will devote myself to writing."

He received no clear answer from the experiment. He couldn't see the knife as it fell into the stream, but he heard the splash of the water. He took it as a sign that he was meant to be a combination of the artist and the poet. He would devote his life to the painting of man and nature through the medium of human speech.

And this, he tells us in his autobiography, is how he decided to become a painter-poet-philosopher at an early age.

III

He started as a romantic rebel. He became a leader of the storm-and-stress movement of intellectual revolt against the traditions and the conventions of the world. And he put all his fiery enthusiasm into a drama about the life of Götz von Berlichingen —a German counterpart of Robin Hood who defied the rich to help the poor. This, declared Goethe, is the meaning of life—to rebel against injustice, even though it may result in your imprisonment or death.

But, like Faust, Goethe was still groping. Götz, he realized, represented but a single aspect of life. Rebellion. What about some of the other aspects? Renunciation, for example? Goethe had just emerged from the tempest of an unhappy love affair. The young lady of his choice was engaged to another man. What to do in a case of this sort? Renounce your love and suffer? Or renounce it and die? He settled the problem by turning his own sad experience into a novel—*The Sorrows of Werther*. Like Goethe himself, Werther has loved and lost. But, unlike Goethe, Werther puts an end to his life. After all, he hasn't the poet's ability to transmute his sorrow into song.

The success of the novel was tremendous. But it was a bitter sort of success. It resulted in a wave of suicides. Overwhelmed by Goethe's eloquence, many of the young men and women of Germany accepted annihilation as the answer to frustrated hope.

But Goethe knew better. An insurmountable obstacle in your way is not a sentence to death. It is rather an invitation to seek for another—and perhaps superior—way. One does not have to be a genius like Goethe to come up fighting after a defeat. Even the ant, he observed, has learned to crawl *around* a rock if it is unable to climb *over* it. Goethe was greatly distressed over the adverse results of his novel. He had meant to depict Werther not as a hero to be followed but as a weakling to be pitied and scorned.

Renunciation, to Goethe, meant the rejection of the unattainable and the redirection of one's energies toward something that might be attained. Goethe himself, though generous to people who had failed, had nothing but disdain for failure. As he grew older, his rebelliousness subsided. He learned more and more to adapt himself to the world. He sought the acquaintance of the powerful and the rich. "You can do most good to others when you are well off yourself." He accepted the post of private secretary to Karl August, moved into a "garden house" near the palace at Weimar, and divided his time between his poetry and his prince.

He became fairly conventional in his public life. "It is always advantageous to be courteous at court." One day he was strolling with Beethoven when the prince and his retinue happened to pass by. The rebel composer threw out his chest and walked unbowed through the royal retinue. But the philosopher poet stepped aside, removed his hat, and made a profound bow. Afterwards, when Beethoven twitted his friend on his subservience, Goethe replied with a smile: "Render unto Caesar the things that are Caesar's."

And unto God the things that are God's. From his conventional retreat at Weimar, Goethe surveyed the infinite and tried to find his way to the secret of life. He continued, in his novels, his poems, his essays, and his dreams, to question the conventions of the day. Is this the best approach to God? Is our life, as lived in our perplexing world, headed in the right direction? To his readers, his works were masterpieces of literature; but to himself, they were merely desperate attempts to stumble upon the one true way. In his *Stella* and in his *Elective Affinities,* he examined the institution of marriage and found much to criticize in the rigid yoking of men and women into a frequently distasteful bond. (He himself, it is interesting to note, lived with a woman for many years without benefit of clergy.) In his *Egmont,* his *Wilhelm Meister,* in many of his other major and minor works, he asks himself the selfsame question: "Whither are we going? And why?" And always he tries to find a newer and better answer.

Yet the answer never satisfies him. Rebellion, renunciation, submission, aggressiveness, victory, defeat—not one of these ideas appeals to him as a solution to the eternal riddle. A world of meaningless customs, insane hatreds, useless pursuits, irrational hopes. All is vanity, without reason or rhyme. A bitter wine, and bread seasoned with tears, this life of ours. "We are dragged into the world, compelled to sin against our will and to suffer for our unwilling sins." We are lost in a jungle of chaos, and nobody knows the way out.

Yet Goethe tried again and again to find a way. And at last, in the words of Emerson, "he hazarded a step beyond chaos" and saw the sun. In a century of exploring expeditions, Goethe made perhaps the most important discovery of all. An approach to the meaning of life. He had made several minor discoveries—especially in the field of science. He wrote original essays on botany, physiology, and anthropology. And he developed a new, and scientifically sound, theory of colors. Every color, he said, is a mixture of darkness and light.

Like life itself—a mixture of darkness and light, suffering and serenity, evil and good. Pleasure can be appreciated only when contrasted with pain. There is no salvation without sin. Like Spinoza, whom he deeply admired, Goethe had come to the conclusion that we can best understand the fitful colors of our existence if we look upon them *sub specie aeternitatis*—under the perspective of eternity.

This was the final philosophy of Goethe. But, instead of elaborating it into a system of abstract thought, he built it into the concrete story of a human life. The story of Faust is Goethe's final answer to the question, What is the purpose of man's adventure into the world?

Man, declared Goethe, is a pawn in the eternal Chess Game between God and the Devil. The play of *Faust*—it took Goethe over fifty years to write it—begins with a Prologue in Heaven. God and the Devil make a wager about the soul of Man. God is the Creator and the Devil is the Destroyer of life. Yet the Destruction, argues Satan, is more important than the Creation. Non-existence is better than existence. "I am the necessary surgeon to the disease called life."

For no life, insists the Devil, is worth the while. No man is good enough to be brought into the world.

The Lord: But what about Faust?

The Devil: He, too, is like the rest.

To prove his contention, the Devil offers to tempt Faust. "Give him to me but for a while, and I will damn his soul forever."

The Lord agrees to the wager. For He feels certain that Faust is going to win.

> Throughout his groping journey in the night,
> Instinctively Man travels toward the light.

IV

Having concluded the wager, the Devil comes to the earth to tempt Faust. He finds the old philosopher disgusted with the world from which he is about to depart. "I started with the aspirations of youth only to end in the disillusions of old age."

But the Devil offers Faust a new life, new knowledge, new aspirations, new adventures, and new hopes. He will restore his youth to him and serve him on one condition. "I will be your slave in this world, if you will consent to be my slave in the next."

Faust: And how long are you to serve me in this world?

The Devil: That is for you to say.

Faust: Agreed. I shall live from pleasure to pleasure, in an ever ascending ecstasy, until I reach that moment to which I can say, "Linger on, thou art so fair!" From that moment, I am your eternal slave.

He seals his compact with a pen dipped in his blood; and the Devil becomes his servant until that fateful moment of earth's highest bliss. What or when that moment may be, neither Faust nor the Devil is as yet able to tell. With the help of the Devil's magic, Faust is transformed into a young man again. And then he starts off on his exciting adventures in search of the happy life.

The first half of the story is familiar to most readers. Faust, in the company of the Devil, tastes the sensual pleasures of the world—the drunken gaiety of Auerbach's cellar, the obscene sensuality of the witches' kitchen, and the wild debauchery of the Walpurgisnacht—and he finds them all unpalatable and stale. Not in these pleasures will he reach the moment of supreme bliss.

And then, still guided by the Devil, Faust experiences his beautiful and evil romance with Marguerite. After the seduction of his beloved, he abandons her to her sins and her sorrows and plunges once more into an orgy of material pleasure. All the riches and the revels of the earth are at his command. But here, too, he fails to find the moment that will satisfy his soul. As he pursues a nymph in one of his orgies, he sees a little red mouse running out of her mouth. Ugliness springing out of beauty. Not this the final meaning of life.

He returns to Marguerite in her prison, too late to undo the ruin he has brought about. He has disgraced Marguerite, poisoned her mother, and killed her brother in a duel. The child of his passion for Marguerite is drowned, and Marguerite is condemned to death for the murder.

Thus ends the First Part of *Faust*—the story of a man's hunger for the material prizes of life. What has been the result of this breathless pursuit? Nothing but a bitter taste. No joy conferred upon others, no lasting joy for one's self. No moment to which Faust—that is, Universal Man—could say, "Linger on, thou art so fair."

The Second Part of *Faust* is not so well known, yet far more important from a philosophical point of view. When Goethe wrote it, he was an old man. Like Faust, he had lived long and suffered much. "I have never uttered anything," he said, "which I have not experienced myself." The Second Part of *Faust* is the quintessence of almost eighty years of zestful living and profound thinking. In the first scene of the Second Part—Goethe was eighty-two when it was finished (1831)—we find our hero transported to a flowering hillside. He tosses about in a restless sleep. Above him hover the compassionate spirits of Nature. They try to comfort his troubled soul. The question is not whether he was a saint or a sinner. It is enough for them that he is unfortunate. And so they bring him the balm of forgetfulness in sleep. Why trouble him with remorse? Will it undo the evil he has done? What is the good of heaping future sorrow upon past sin? "Man stumbles in all his ways, but Nature forgives and forgets."

Faust awakes, like the spring out of the winter's sleep, renewed for another start in life. New flowers out of rotted seeds, new hopes out of old despairs. Nature is still waiting for the adventurous. Nobility may be had for the readiness to dare.

Faust looks into the sky and sees a rainbow painted on the clouds. The rainbow, he reflects, is like our human achievement—always obliterated, but always restored.

Life, death, and life again. But what of the brief span of existence on this earth? What is the tendency, what is the purpose of Faust's erring and stumbling through the mists of the world?

So far as Faust can see at the moment, there is no purpose at all. A blind groping and striking against one another in the dark. Better to end it all right now. He lifts a cup of poison to his lips, and is about to drink it down, but is checked by the sound of an Easter hymn. Memories of a religion long forgotten—a call to further life.

"A life of further uselessness, no doubt." But he may as well go on. Perhaps somewhere he may reach a road from which he can see the light.

So on to the new adventures of a new day! With the aid of the Devil, Faust becomes a councilor at the royal court. He wins riches, honors, wars—and finds them nothing but ashes in his mouth. The "glory" of victory brings death and devastation to victor and victim alike.

Another adventure in love—this time with the spirit of Helen of Troy. Faust—that is, Goethe—is trying to find the secret of the good life in a marriage between the classic beauty of ancient

Greece and the romantic restlessness of his own day. Together, Faust and Helen scale the highest peaks. Here, perhaps, they will come to the end of their quest. But again Faust is disillusioned. As he tries to follow Helen, she disappears into a cloud and leaves only her mantle behind. The beauty of ancient Greece is nothing but the splendor of a departed day. You can't find the way to the future by turning your footsteps back toward the past.

The next adventure of Faust is in the world of commerce. Activity, building, advancing, expanding—perhaps here he will find the supreme satisfaction of life. Disenchantment again. Not in the whirlwind of the market place can you hear the still small voice of God.

Next comes travel. But the escape from one place to another is no escape from the boredom of his mind. Whatever the surroundings, Faust is always Faust.

But one day, from a hillside, he gets a vision of the "one true way"—the way of escape from himself. In the distance, he sees the ebb and flow of the ocean over the flatlands of the shore. To reclaim the uninhabitable marshes, and to make them fit for human habitation—would not this, at last, be a career worthy of a man?

Faust gets busy with this project. He begins to drain the swamps and to build homes upon a free soil for a people who must daily reconquer their freedom against the winds and the tides of the sea. A succession of victories, followed by successive dangers with their challenge to renew the fight.

> It is the struggle, and not the goal,
> That brings salvation to the soul.

Faust has learned his last word of wisdom. To oversoar his own little self, a man must join with others in some united effort. And to deserve his life and liberty, he must win them anew from day to day.

Faust is thrilled at the thought of his contribution to this sort of life for millions of his fellow men. As a result of his labor, many generations will live in the heroic atmosphere between dangers already conquered and dangers still to be overcome. This restless and incessant striving, with joy in the strife, is the greatest happiness that a man can experience in the world. Faust has found the way at last.

And so he has reached the supreme moment to which he can say, "Linger on, thou art so fair."

This is the very moment which, according to the agreement, is to end his life and to enslave him to the Devil for all eternity. The Devil has won his wager, it seems. He comes to claim the victim's soul. But God's angels descend in a shower of roses and carry the soul up to Heaven. The victory is not the Devil's, but Faust's. For the moment of his greatest happiness is a moment of striving for others, rather than of fulfillment for himself. "He who has learned to strive forever," sing the angels, "he is worthy to be redeemed."

And Faust's job in Heaven will be to teach life—a life of wholesome fighting against destructiveness and hate—to the souls of little children who have died too young to join in the adventure of life. In Heaven, as on earth, the greatest happiness of the human soul lies in the eternal struggle for peace.

V

Throughout his own life, Goethe was consumed with a passion for peace. When his patron, Karl August, was waging a war against the French, he asked Goethe to write inflammatory songs for the German soldiers. But Goethe refused to do this. "How can I write hymns of hatred when I have no hate?"

He had an almost superhuman capacity for friendship—especially toward those, the poor and the hungry and the sick, who needed it most. And his friendship was not merely an abstract emotion but a practical fact. Out of an income of only a thousand dollars a year, he regularly supported two strangers who needed his help. And his home and his purse were always open to the so-called lower classes. "In God's eyes, perhaps these are the highest classes of all."

Like Faust, Goethe spent his last days in giving courage to those who daily had to renew their battle for life. His love for the underdog was similar to that of Walt Whitman. But, unlike the American poet who cried *vivas* to those who had failed, Goethe reserved his greatest admiration for those who kept on fighting even *after* their failure. "It is only by rising after every fall that we can hope to emerge out of the dark."

And his final utterance, as he lay on his deathbed, was a humble prayer to God: "Give me more light."

CHAPTER XXI

Schopenhauer's Struggle against Despair

[1788–1860]

ARTHUR SCHOPENHAUER was the philosopher of a world in ruins. He lived in an age very similar to our own. In order to recognize the similarity, let us briefly glance at the events of 1819. This was the year which saw the publication of Schopenhauer's epic of despair—*The World as Will and Idea.*

As Schopenhauer looked about him, he saw Europe turned into a shambles. The frightened human cattle were being driven from one slaughter to another. For humanity had lost its bearings. One by one, the blind leaders of the blind had destroyed their followers along with themselves. The will to power, as incarnated first in Robespierre, and then in Napoleon, had ended in ultimate defeat. Robespierre was dead, Napoleon was dying in disgrace, but the people were still smarting under the lash of a dictatorial will. This time it was Czar Alexander of Russia who held the whip. Under the guise of a "Holy Alliance" which was to establish the communal Brotherhood of Man, he had set out to enslave the entire world.

Change the names of the leading actors, and you have a similar world drama in our own generation. Substitute Trotsky for Robespierre, Hitler for Napoleon, and Stalin for Alexander, and you will understand the cynicism of a Schopenhauer in the nineteenth century just as you can understand the cynicism of a Hemingway in the twentieth.

II

Schopenhauer's philosophy stemmed directly out of the propensity of the aggressors to exert their will over their fellow men. The will to power, he declared, is the greatest evil in the world. For the world, it seemed to him, is governed not by a benevolent God but by a malevolent Devil. This Spirit of Evil has imposed upon us a universal plague—an overpowering will to live, and to kill others in order to preserve our own life.

Schopenhauer had good reason to hate unreasonable power. He had seen it not only in the devastation of Europe but in the frustration of his own desires. His father, a successful but quick-tempered merchant, had tried to force him into a business career which Schopenhauer hated. He preferred the adventures of the mind to the speculations of the market place.

But even after his father's death—by suicide, it was believed—Schopenhauer was unable to find peace. His mother, too, had a violent temper. Moreover, she was a brilliant novelist and insanely jealous of her son's literary ability. "Who ever heard of two geniuses in the same family?" she said. They quarreled and separated and came together again; and finally, in a fit of anger, the mother threw him down the stairs. Whereupon the son informed her that her ultimate fame would rest not upon her novels but upon his philosophy.

The temperamental mother and son never met again. A hatred of authority and a disdain for women became the centermost ideas of Schopenhauer's philosophical creed.

This hatred and disdain were intensified during his college years. He disliked the arrogance of his professors; and they, in turn, disliked the impudence of their pupil. He fell in love, only to be rejected as an "unromantic lout." For a time he tried to serve as host to his neighbors—his father had left him a comfortable income—but his neighbors accepted his toasts and rejected his thoughts.

And so he withdrew under his own skin—a bitter, suspicious, pessimistic porcupine of a man who stayed away from people and stung them with the needles of his sarcasm if they tried to get too close. He never married, and never made friends. "A man is your friend only for what he can get out of you. . . . A friend in need is not a friend indeed; he is merely a borrower."

Schopenhauer lived alone, kept his purse and his pipes under lock and key, and did his own shaving because he wouldn't trust his neck to another man's razor. When he went to sleep, he placed a loaded pistol at his bedside. He generally avoided conversation as "meaningless noise." His pet aversion, indeed, was noise of any kind. This was due no doubt to his hypersensitivity. But he attributed it to his intellectual superiority. "The amount of noise which anyone can bear undisturbed," he declared, "stands in inverse proportion to his mental capacity. . . . Noise is a torture to all intellectual people."

Yet there was one sound that he wanted desperately to hear all his life. The applause of the public. But this pleasure was denied him for many years. He remained almost to the end unrecognized and alone.

A man living in the silence of his own philosophy. He wrote book after book and sent them out to an unresponsive public. The only pay he ever got for any of his books was a free copy now and then. The great majority of his publications were sold as waste paper. "But what can you expect?" he said. "A book is a mirror of the reader's as well as of the author's mind. If an ass looks in, you can't expect an angel to look out."

For a while he tried to emerge from his ingrowing bitterness. He accepted a teaching job at the Berlin university. He prepared a series of brilliant lectures, and delivered them to empty seats. The public was as reluctant to hear as to read his cynical thoughts.

So he decided, like Timon of Athens, to let the people go hang on the trees of their own stupid planting. He moved into a two-room apartment in Frankfurt, where he remained for the last thirty years of his life. His only companion was a little poodle—"another cynic like myself." He had named the poodle *Atma*—

which is the Hindu word for *Universal Soul*. But the townspeople called it *Young Schopenhauer*.

For the most part, he stayed in his rooms. But he ate his dinners at the English Hotel. "Here come the two philosophers," the waiters would whisper to one another as Schopenhauer walked in with the poodle on the leash.

As he sat down to dinner, Schopenhauer always placed a gold coin upon the table. And he always replaced the coin in his pocket when he finished his meal. "Do you mind telling me, Herr Schopenhauer, why you do this?" a waiter once asked him.

"It's a bet I've made with myself," replied the philosopher. "I will drop the coin into the poor box the first day I hear the customers at this restaurant talk about anything except horses, women, or dogs."

His unconventional bluntness made him *persona non grata* not only to the general public, but to the intelligentsia as well. The universities refused to recognize him because his work possessed both clarity and wit. These two characteristics were frowned upon as almost criminal in the philosophical circles of the day. The metaphysical pedants rejected Schopenhauer because his thoughts were so daringly different from theirs. It was the age-old dislike of the unlike. The academicians resented his ability to "think on his feet"—to come quickly to the core of an idea that it took them years of dusty application to elaborate.

But Schopenhauer was cynical about their academic disdain of his unacademic thinking. In *The World as Will* he devastated his critics with an anecdote about the contemporary actor Unzelmann, who was in the habit of ad-libbing on the stage. The directors frowned upon this audacity on the actor's part, and finally they forbade him to improvise.

"Soon afterwards he had to appear upon the stage on horseback." Right after the entrance, the horse was guilty of an indiscretion not provided for in the script. "The audience began to titter; whereupon Unzelmann severely reproached the horse: 'Don't you know that we are forbidden to ad-lib?' "

Schopenhauer's entire philosophy, like Unzelmann's acting, was full of startling and, his critics not unjustly maintained, sometimes indelicate, unconventionalities. But it was an honest and realistic picture of the world—and "realism has its ugliness as well as its beauty." The world as will, observed through Schopenhauer's dark colored spectacles, appears as a somber and frightening but none the less fascinating drama. Nobody before Schopenhauer had dared to look so directly into the face of reality.

And what he saw was aggression, hopelessness, and pain.

III

The greatest misfortune in the world, said Schopenhauer, is man's aggressiveness—his will to live. It is a blind and useless will. For human life is a thing of no value. Man is essentially a creature of pain. We are the slaves of life. Overmastered by our desire to go on living, we are forever impelled to seek one object after another, and always at one another's expense.

Yet the moment we attain our objective, what follows? A terrible boredom, an empty void. And thus our existence becomes a meaningless series of pursuits and disillusions—a pendulum swinging continuously between the pain of desire and the emptiness of fulfillment. For all the satisfactions of life are of a negative quality. When we reach the goal, we have merely removed one hunger to become the immediate slaves of other hungers. Paradoxically enough, as Schopenhauer points out, it is only the *absence* of bliss that can make us *appreciate* bliss. We love best the things we haven't got. Happiness is but a dream. The only reality is pain.

This, then, is the sort of world we live in. The Platonic world of Ideas becomes, in the philosophy of Schopenhauer, a world of One Idea—an eternal will to persist in a life of frustrated hopes. We can look forward to nothing except the pursuit of empty dreams, the tedium that follows the attainment of these dreams, and the propulsion of the will to enter upon another and equally worthless pursuit.

Is there, then, no end to this? Cannot even death put a stop to this maddening race after meaningless shadows? Must we remain forever enslaved under this cosmic will to exist? Is there not somewhere a Buddhistic Nirvana, a Haven of Forgetfulness from the stormy nightmare of existence? Unfortunately, no. The craving for life is eternal. Even if he tries to escape by way of suicide, declares Schopenhauer, the individual can not put an end to the universal hunger for living. For each of us is a part of the cosmic unit of life. And though the part may die, the whole moves persistently onward. Death may be the enemy—or, rather, the friend —of the living individual. But the universal will to live is the implacable enemy of death.

The enemy of undisturbed rest, of final surcease from pain. And thus the universal will plays an eternal joke upon us. It impels us, before we die, to bring another generation into the evil of life. "The relation of the sexes is the invisible central point of all action and conduct. It is the cause of war and the end of peace. We see it at every moment sitting upon the throne as the hereditary lord of the world, and laughing at our futile efforts to bind it, or to imprison it, or at least to limit it and to keep it concealed."

It is the reproductive hunger of the species, maintains Schopenhauer, that keeps us continually chained to the wheel of life. Nature has deceived us into perpetuating the misery of our race. "She has endowed woman with a wealth of charm—for a few years at the expense of the rest of her life—so that during those years of her bloom she may capture the fancy of some man to such a degree that he is hurried away into undertaking the honorable care of her. . . . Then, just as the female ant, after fecundation, loses her wings . . . so, after giving birth to one or two children, a woman loses her beauty. Her mission has been accomplished."

The individual in love is thus a blind instrument of Nature. And when Nature has served her purpose to bring another group of draftees into the battle of life, she opens the eyes of the lover. And then comes the bitterness of disillusion. The man is no longer a demigod but a gorilla called *husband;* and the woman has changed from a winged angel into "an undersized, narrow-shouldered, broad-hipped and short-legged creature" called *wife.*

"Thus the individual discovers, too late, that he has been the dupe of Destiny." His lyric of love has become soured into a croak of disenchantment. "If Petrarch's passion had been gratified, his songs would have been silenced."

There is therefore no free will for the individual. He is only a leaf blown about by the winds of life, a river flowing downward over a channel predetermined by the nature of the land, a torch sputtering for a moment in a relay of fitful flames. "Everyone believes himself to be perfectly free, even in his individual actions. . . . But, through experience, he finds . . . that he is not free, but subjected to necessity; that in spite of all his resolutions and reflections he does not change his conduct, and that . . . he must carry out the very character which he himself condemns."

A character in a tragedy over which he has no control. And the plot of the tragedy is a horrible succession of wars. This was the picture of life in Schopenhauer's day, as it is the picture of life today. Every individual fights "for the matter, the place and the time" of every other individual. "The bulldog ant of Australia affords us the most extraordinary illustration of this truth. For if it is cut in two, a battle begins between the head and the tail. The head seizes the tail with its teeth, and the tail defends itself by stinging the head. And this battle lasts until they are both dead or are dragged away by other ants."

We find this hunger for killing in every species until we come to the human race. And it is then that the conflict assumes its most diabolical aspect. Humanity has developed almost to perfection the insanity of war as a manifestation of the will to live.

War is the ultimate evil in our life of pain. There is no suffering in the next world greater than the suffering of this world. "Where did Dante take the materials of his Hell but from our actual life here on earth?"

For our earth life is a farcical tragedy—a farce if we examine it in part, and a tragedy if we survey it as a whole.

Then what is the remedy? A wise and calm acceptance of our fate, declares Schopenhauer. Let us realize that "our life is a business which does not cover expenses." So let us stifle the craving for competition and cultivate an instinct for contemplation. "Not wealth but wisdom is the way." Let us concentrate not on what we *have*, but on what we *are*. And each of us is, or can be, one of two things—a slave of impetuous will, or a master of serene knowledge. We can train our intellect to disobey our will. "What the bridle and the bit are to an unmanageable horse, the intellect is to a willful man."

Cultivate your intellect. Not, however, by passive reading but by active thinking. "The inclination of most scholars"—and here Schopenhauer was aiming another blow at his academic critics—"is a kind of vacuum suction." The emptiness of their own mind draws into itself the thoughts of other people. "So it comes about that if anyone spends too much time in reading . . . he gradually loses the capacity for thinking."

Read few books, but the best. Use your own experience as your text, and your reading as a commentary.

For, after all, it is your own past that can serve as the best guide to your future. "In the end, everyone stands alone." He is happiest who finds his strength within himself.

Within himself, but not *for* himself. The man of pure intellect will be his own guide, but he will not be another man's dictator. In this way alone can he find pure independence—complete freedom from the inexorable will to perpetuate the evils of life. The wise man's life is an adventure from suffering to serenity. "The peace which is above understanding, the perfect calm of the spirit, the deep rest . . . is an entire, unfailing gospel. Only knowledge remains, the will has vanished."

IV

And "the highest form of this will-less knowledge is genius." Not the infinite capacity for taking pains—as some thinkers have defined genius—but "the power of leaving one's own interests, wishes and aims entirely out of sight . . . so as to remain a subject of pure knowledge, and to attain to a clear vision of the world."

This was the kind of genius which Schopenhauer believed he himself possessed. His philosophy was partly an interpretation of an era ravaged by the arrogance of a few headstrong individuals, and partly an explanation of his own detached attitude toward the world.

But, at bottom, Schopenhauer's character was anything but detached. He reacted to his environment not with serene contemplation but with surly criticism. And at times his criticism descended even to physical violence. He was the headstrong son of two headstrong parents. One day, in an argument with a servant, he pushed her out of the room. She fell in the scuffle and broke her arm. A lawsuit for damages resulted in a verdict against Schopenhauer. He was compelled to support her for the rest of her life.

And always Schopenhauer feared for his own life. Again and again he insisted that his enemies were trying to kill him—with tainted food, overdoses of medicine, and even poisoned snuff.

He regarded himself as a giant in a race of pygmies. His physical like his mental appetite was stupendous. Once, when a man across the table looked at him in astonishment, he said: "Yes, I do eat three times as much as you. But I also *think* three times as much."

He smoked, as he ate, like a superman. His pipe was a contraption that curved almost five feet from his mouth to the ground. As he inhaled the enormous puffs of smoke, he gazed at the busts of two congenial spirits—Buddha and Immanuel Kant—and at the eyes of the only living creature that adored him—his poodle Atma. "I feel most at home," he said, "among demigods and dogs. They alone are free from the failings of men."

He was keenly aware of other people's faults and keenly insensitive to his own. Though extremely nearsighted, he refused to wear glasses; and whenever he bumped into other pedestrians, he snarled at them for their carelessness. "You idiot, can't you learn how to walk?" Always, in his quarrels with other people, he insisted that it was they who were entirely to blame. He called himself "a tender spirit in an iron age." "And he belongs," observed one of his critics, "behind iron bars."

V

His pessimism was really the outcry of a wounded soul. He mocked the world because the world refused to notice him—until it was too late. He was old now, with his sight and his hearing almost gone, his gums toothless, and his appetite for food and fame no longer keen, when at last he got his recognition. Applause for a dying man. He acknowledged it with a wry smile. "Now that I have spent a long, lonely life of insignificance and disregard, they escort me to the end with trumpets and with drums."

And the rest of the world? Still blowing its trumpets and beating its drums for war, and more war. That diabolical will to win! 1860. Rumblings in Germany, France, Italy, Austria, the United States. *Homo homini lupus.* Not men but human beasts, ready to spring at one another's throats.

The urge to be born, the tempest of life, the peace of death. Perhaps it would be wise for the entire race to commit suicide. To kill in all men the desire to perpetuate the evil of life— through a sour and solemn adoption of universal celibacy.

Ah, but life—even Schopenhauer's life—has been a thrilling adventure! It is better to have loved and lost, lived and died, than never to have loved and lived at all. The laughter of children, the beauty of art, the joy of understanding, the rebirth of spring after winter's death—are not these pleasures worth all the pains of life, and more?

The joy of understanding—the rebirth of spring. What if there is some connection between the two—complete understanding in a new birth? Not *Nirvana,* Eternal *Nothingness,* but *Vita Aeterna, Eternal Life.* Perhaps the will to live is the real meaning of existence—and life *is* the final word?

"Herr Schopenhauer, you are ill!" It is his landlady speaking. He is sitting in his armchair, his head bent over his breast. She comes closer. The Old Pessimist is dead.

But now at last there is a smile on his face.

CHAPTER XXII

Auguste Comte's Journey
from Suicide to Sanity

[1798–1857]

A MAN, declared Comte, is not entirely a product of his environment. The seed is as important as the soil. The same earth
will produce fruit trees as well as brambles, flowers as well as
weeds.

His own life was a proof of this assertion. A contemporary of
Schopenhauer, Comte was subjected to the selfsame spectacle of a
world on the verge of disaster. But, instead of dismissing the world
with a growl of disdain, he tried to convert it into something
nearer to the heart's desire. Agreeing with Schopenhauer that the
idea of a benevolent Providence was inconsistent with the cruelties
of life, he tried to establish a new creed of Humanity—a religion
without God.

His philosophical religion was the outcome of a stormy life. An
unhappy marriage, a hopeless love affair with another man's wife,
an attack of insanity, the loss of his job, an attempted suicide,
and the final peace that comes from selfless devotion to others—
these were some of the ingredients that went into the formation of
his creed: "Fellow victims of a cruel fate, let us be gentle to one
another."

It was a creed of positive kindness in a shipwrecked and skeptical age.

II

He was a little fellow with a long name—Isidore Auguste Marie François Xavier Comte. Born at Montpellier in 1798, he grew up with a veneration for Benjamin Franklin, whom he called "the modern Socrates." He tried to model himself after this "wisest of Americans," who, at the age of twenty-five, had decided "to make all knowledge his province. . . . I, too, have dared to undertake this, though I am not yet twenty."

As a springboard for his mastery of universal knowledge, he became secretary to Saint-Simon, the famous Utopian who believed that all philosophy should be directed toward the social improvement of mankind. Though brought up as a Catholic, Comte fell under the influence of Voltaire's injunction, *Ecrasez l'infâme*—Crush the infamy [of religion]. But he also recognized the *virtues* of religion—especially the solicitude of many of the priests for the welfare of their parishioners. "Men are sometimes kinder than Nature apparently meant them to be."

If only they were left alone to do as their hearts dictated. "Why wait for a possible Paradise in Heaven? We can build a real Paradise here on earth."

But the builders of this Paradise were often among the most hunted of men. Look at the fate of Condorcet and Lavoisier. Education and science slaughtered by the Reign of Terror. The terrorism of the revolutionists was no wiser than the tyranny of the kings. The world was full of unthinking beasts whom the philosophers must somehow transform into thinking men.

But the demands of the world didn't allow a man much time to think. A quarrel with Saint-Simon set Comte adrift on the sea of the unemployed. A marriage to an uncongenial woman added further difficulties to a life already harassed by anxiety and want. A job at the Ecole Polytechnique dragged him into the distasteful politics of the academic world. And a final breach with the politics of the school left him once more unemployed.

He took up private tutoring for a precarious livelihood. Troubled from boyhood with a poor digestion, he finally suffered a complete physical and mental breakdown. He was taken to an asylum for a time. Here a man could think at last without too much disturbance. A madman among other madmen. Was this so different from the rest of the world?

He returned home after a while—though not completely cured. He suffered from dangerous lapses on several occasions. But, on the whole, his mind was clear and his heart at rest—until he met Clotilde de Vaux.

He was forty-six at the time. Two years earlier he had been separated from his wife. He was now giving lessons to private pupils. At one of the houses where he taught he was introduced to Clotilde, his pupil's sister. Her husband was serving a life sentence for embezzlement as a tax collector. Clotilde possessed that exquisite combination so rarely to be found in one person— beauty and intelligence and affection. Comte fell passionately in love with her. But it was a passion that came to a swift and tragic end. She died only a year after he met her.

A frustrated attempt to end his own life—and then, the calmness of resignation, and a new love. The human race. He witnessed, with more wisdom than hope, the Revolution of 1848. Humanity would not reach the millennium by a single blow, or by any succession of blows. The way of the sword was not the way to peace. What the world needed was progress through orderly education—not a series of explosive hatreds, but a gradually growing consciousness of Infinite Love.

III

And so Auguste Comte became the founder of a new religion— Christianity without Christ, a religion based upon the observations of science as opposed to the superstitions of theology and the abstractions of metaphysics. It was to be a world-wide faith growing out of philosophy, with positivistic knowledge at the root and humanistic morality in the flower.

Comte's philosophy therefore may be called either *Positivism* or *Humanism*—Positivism as an epitome of science, and Humanism as a system of ethics.

The essence of Positivism, said Comte, is concrete scientific knowledge. To plan for the future, we must understand the past. Hindsight is an essential preliminary to foresight. In order to clarify our vision of the past, Comte analyzed the various sciences and brought them into a logical unit. He arranged them according to their growing complexity and the general development of their subject matter—mathematics, astronomy, physics, chemistry, biology, anthropology, and sociology.

And thus, Comte observed, the historical structure of concrete knowledge began with mathematics as a base, developed consecutively into one after another of the more complex sciences, and culminated in sociology as the apex. Each new science rested upon the knowledge of the science before it; and sociology, as the latest of the sciences, is the result of all the accumulated knowledge of history.

And in each of the fields of knowledge, from mathematics to sociology, Comte defines a Law of Three Stages:

At first, the science was conceived *theologically*. Everything was worshiped as the person, or regarded as the instrument, of some divine creature. Thus the sun was a god, and the stars were the chariots of the gods.

Later on, the same science came to be considered *metaphysically*. The world became a "fiction of abstractions" instead of a series of fables and myths. For example, the stars were said to be spheres of music-making instruments because the sphere was valued as the perfect form and music as the perfect art.

Finally, the subject began to be observed *scientifically*. The phenomena of the world were subjected to experimental study and analyzed in accordance with the principles of cause and effect.

Thus the development of knowledge has carried us from the legends about the gods to the "Ideas" of Plato, and from the Ideas of Plato to the Laws of Nature. We have outgrown the fables of our childhood and the fallacies of our adolescence, and we are now ready to examine the facts. We have arrived at the age of scientific maturity.

And the most mature of the sciences—the culmination of positive knowledge to which all the other fields of knowledge are but stepping stones—is sociology, the science of human welfare. The most important study of mankind is man. "Let us come down to earth from the realm of dreams and speculations, and let us concentrate on human beings struggling from century to century toward a more abundant, more creative life."

In the philosophy of Auguste Comte, sociology is more than the culmination of the old sciences. It is the beginning of the new religion. The Tree of Knowledge as presented by Comte is quite different from that of the Old Testament. The eating of the fruit of *this* tree, maintains Comte, will not result in Paradise Lost. On the contrary, it will lead to Paradise Regained. A new Paradise of mutual good will, based upon a better understanding of the processes of Nature and the promptings of the human heart.

Sociology, in brief, is the bridge between science and religion. Comte regarded the betterment of human conduct as the final objective of all knowledge. His system of ethics may be defined as *Humanitarianism* rather than *Humanism*. Man, he said, is fundamentally a social creature. He has inherited this social instinct from the lower animals—refined and rationalized through the progressive learning of many centuries. Reason has been added to instinct, compassion is tempering our passion, and justice will ultimately overcome our tendency to strife.

In drawing this ideal picture of man, Comte was no visionary. He knew only too well that the history of the human race is a story of rivalries and hatreds and wars. He was realistic enough to foresee that the aggressions of a Napoleon would be repeated again and again, and every time on a larger scale. For the development of transportation was drawing the world more closely together into a unit. It would be very difficult in the future to keep a local conflict from spreading into a world war. Comte would have felt no surprise if someone with a prophetic vision had told him about the coming world wars of 1914 and 1939.

But, even in the light of today, Comte would have expressed the selfsame confidence in the ultimate triumph of Humanism. The human instinct, he insisted, *is* toward mutual co-operation, and the world *is* growing into a more compact and more friendly unit. Let us not be too distressed about "the struggles and the competitions" of mankind. They are but the growing pains of a socialized organism. A race of creatures with less intense emotions could not have developed into a closely knit society. It takes fire to fuse metals into a work of utility and art.

So let us be patient. And let us not be too sanguine about the immediate prospects of a millennium. Comte possessed the historic outlook on life. He saw human progress as a slow but certain growth. A single step in the right direction took not decades but centuries. Moreover, not every step was in the right direction. Men often stumbled in the march of time. But in spite of the fumblings and the falls, the march was definitely forward. Comte foresaw a United States of Europe similar to the United States of America. "The kings [and the dictators] may rage for war, but the people want to be left alone to the saner pursuits of peace."

Comte's religion, therefore, is a socialized effort to fulfill man's instinctive desire for mutual service. Humanism is friendliness organized on a world-wide scale, collective security based upon individual trust, the translation of the human instinct for pity into the divine gentleness of love.

In order to impress this religion upon his followers, Comte devised a system of rituals, sacraments, prayers, and priests. He prepared a calendar with a list of holidays commemorating not the victories of war but the achievements of progress.

Comte's Humanism was a heart-warming cult that spread rapidly over Europe. Humanistic churches were organized in several countries, especially in England. And the man who had abolished the deity lived to see himself almost deified by his followers. "There is no God," a cynic observed, "and Comte is His prophet."

And then his religion suffered the fate of many another creed. His worshipers concentrated on the external rituals and forgot the internal truths. "They adopted everything about the religion of humanity except the spirit of being humane."

Yet this criticism is not altogether true. Though the name of Comte is almost forgotten today—Bertrand Russell, for example, doesn't even mention him in his *History of Western Philosophy*— his teachings have colored nearly every phase of modern political and social and ethical progress. The United Nations, the socialization of medicine, the co-operative researches of science, the very name as well as the spirit of the new field of sociology, and the reawakening of the social consciousness in many of the Christian churches today—these are but a few of the many phases of modern life which show the widespread influence of the prophet-philosopher.

And even Bertrand Russell, who has rejected the name of Auguste Comte, has accepted his ethical teaching. Russell's doctrine of "enlightened selfishness" is nothing more than Comte's Humanism as applied to the life of the individual. For Humanism shows us that the kindness we bestow upon others is a means toward our own preservation. We are always repaid in our own coin. Not only that, but we see our own face reflected in the mirror held up to us by the world. Our every act, our every motive rebounds upon ourselves. The human instinct for mutual protection is a safeguard for the survival of the individual. We cut our own skin if we try to whip another. And if we try to deceive another, we lower ourselves in our own eyes.

And so—on this point nearly all modern ethics is derived from Comte—morality consists in helping others in order to help ourselves. *Vivre au grand jour*—Live so that all your actions can be seen under the light of day. The night prowler always runs the risk of stubbing his own toes. Comte's Humanism is a religion not of self-sacrifice but of self-realization—the advancement of each to the advantage of all.

IV

Comte spent the last years of his life in security, if not in comfort. His admirers, including Maximilien Littré and John Stuart Mill, raised a fund for his maintenance. They gave this to him not out of charity, but out of a sincere desire that he might be free to give his thoughts to the world.

And so he lived to become a strange phenomenon—a prophet honored in his own country and by his own generation. His disciples, like those of the Nazarene, expected miracles; they thought the Kingdom of Heaven would come to pass within a few years. But Comte smiled at their too optimistic hopes. "The Clock of Time, my friends, ticks off centuries for seconds. Don't expect too much too soon."

"But the world," exclaimed a disciple, "should be ready for Humanism right now!"

"I wonder." And then, remembering his early training as a Catholic, "Even Christianity has had to wait all these years."

"But Christianity has failed!"

"No, my friend. Christianity, like Humanism, has not as yet been tried."

CHAPTER XXIII

Thoreau's Adventure into the Simple Life

[1817–1862]

"THE MASS of men," observed Thoreau, "lead lives of quiet desperation." But he himself lived a life of quiet *inspiration*. And in so living, he enriched philosophy with one of its greatest spiritual adventures. He appointed himself "inspector of snowstorms and rainstorms," and surveyor of the highway that leads to God.

Thoreau was one of the few men who did not teach philosophy but lived it. "To be a philosopher," he said, "is not merely to have subtle thoughts, nor even to found a school, but so to love wisdom as to live, according to its dictates, a life of simplicity, independence, magnanimity and trust."

A life of simplicity. This, as he discovered, is the shortest way to Heaven. "Sometimes," he said, "as I drift idly on Walden Pond, I cease to live and begin to be." And in order to experience this supreme sort of being, he declared, you need to remember but a single rule: Find out not how *much* you need, but how *little* you need. When the entire country went mad with the California gold rush of 1849, he asked: "What's all the excitement about?" The sunlight reflected in a dewdrop was to him richer than any metal or precious stone. A snowfall he regarded as "the sweepings from heaven's floor." And a sparrow perching upon his shoulder gave him a greater thrill "than any epaulet" of military rank.

Who was this Yankee apostle of the noble mind and simple soul?

II

Henry David Thoreau was born (1817) on the outskirts of Concord, Massachusetts. And he remained all his life on the outskirts of the struggles and the ambitions of mankind. As a youngster, he helped his father to make pencils for a living. The family enjoyed their genteel poverty in the quiet surroundings of the New England village. Concord, the home of the Emersons, the Hawthornes, and the Alcotts, was more famous for the export of its thoughts than for the traffic of its goods.

And thus, Thoreau grew up in an atmosphere of plain living and high thinking. He was a voracious reader. He absorbed not only the works of the poets and the philosophers, but the even more important "books in running brooks, sermons in stones, and good in everything"—Nature's perennial commentary on the meaning of life. The mere sight of a soaring bird gave him "such simple joy . . . as might inspire the muse of Homer and Shakespeare."

At sixteen, he entered Harvard—the mecca of all the respectable young men in Concord. Here, as he said, they made him nibble at "all the branches of learning and none of the roots." Appointed to make a speech at commencement, he attacked "the commercial spirit" as "a blind and unmanly love of wealth."

After his graduation he taught public school for a while. But he lost his job because he refused to administer corporal punishment. Together with his brother John, he opened a private school. This venture, too, was unsuccessful. John died of a tetanus infection, and Henry was so shaken by the loss that he closed the school.

Once more he joined his family in the pencil-making business. His chief job, however, was "to discover God." And so he drifted from place to place—not aimlessly, but always "in the direction of heaven." He came to live in Emerson's household as handy man—"a wild, original character," to quote Hawthorne, "as ugly as sin; long-nosed, queer-mouthed . . . yet a keen and delicate observer of Nature . . . which shows him secrets that few others are allowed to witness." From Emerson's house he drifted to Staten Island, where he lived for a time with Emerson's brother William. Here he tutored William's young son, and devoted his spare time to writing, observing Nature, and visiting New York City, where he met "a million people but not a single man." And finally he returned to Concord and decided to divorce himself from the world for a while.

Not that he disliked human society. On the contrary, he was very fond of company. He enjoyed dancing and singing and sprightly conversation. And no one, observed his friend, Ellery Channing, laughed more heartily at a good joke.

But, much as he enjoyed his human contacts, he enjoyed even more his social companions of the forest. The fox and the wood-chuck, the martin and the squirrel, the trees and the clouds and the stars. He felt more closely related to the forest folk than to the townfolk.

And so he left his "acquaintances among the villagers," and went to visit his "friends and relations in Nature." He moved out of Concord and got himself a "house"—as he called it—at Walden Pond.

But the word house is an overstatement. His purpose in moving to Walden was to discover how small a shelter and how slender a purse a man needs for perfect happiness. His one-room hut, which he built at a cost of $28.12½ , was merely "a larger coat and hat—a sentry box . . . to walk into in rain or snow or cold." It measured ten feet by fifteen, and it contained two windows, a closet, a fireplace, and a door.

In a little garden outside the hut he planted the vegetables, on which he lived for the most part. All the other food he bought in the first year of his Walden adventure came to exactly $8.74.

This was the shelter, and this the money, that Thoreau needed for his journey into the infinite. He lived at Walden for two years —the most thrilling two years, perhaps, experienced by any man in the nineteenth century. For the Walden experiment proved to

Thoreau, and to many of his disciples, including such men as Gandhi and Tolstoy, that a man is happiest when he can act most completely under his own power. "Don't lean on other people if you can help it," he wrote. "As for myself, I mean to build my own house, bake my own bread, and wash my own clothes, in heaven as well as on earth."

Yet, even at Walden, Thoreau was no hermit. He enjoyed a constant stream of visitors who were anxious to meet "the New England disciple of Jesus." They found him rich beyond their wildest dreams—a man utterly content with the little he had. It took him only six weeks out of the year to earn his living expenses. All the rest of the time he spent in becoming better acquainted with life.

It was a life full of wonder and unexpected delight. The friendly little animals that stopped at his doorstep for a bite of food and an afternoon chat. The shimmer of the water at Walden in the shadow and the sunlight. The patterns made by the gliding fishes under the surface. The honking of the wild geese at midnight. The battle of the ants—a bloody Waterloo of the insect world—that made him wonder what these little warriors were fighting for, what all our human warriors are fighting for. As he sat in his boat and played a hymn on his flute to the setting sun, he felt that all Nature was one perpetual song, the music of everlasting creation. The voice of God was calling, reassuring you that you, too, are part of the song, an intimate part of the pattern, under the direct guidance of Heaven—if only you have the eyes to see, the ears to hear, the heart to understand.

All this, and much more, he put into his famous prose poem entitled *Walden*. A more appropriate name, perhaps, would be *Return to Paradise*.

III

In addition to *Walden,* Thoreau wrote thirty-nine other books —reflections on life in general, and observations on living things.

Of these books, only two were published during his lifetime. But they were enough to summarize his philosophical creed. As a matter of fact, this creed can be summarized in a single phrase: *contentment through simplicity.* "The more you simplify your life," he said, "the happier you can be."

This is the dominant note in all his writing. Cast away the complexities and the prejudices of society, and be yourself. He went to live at Walden, he said, in order to meet himself face to face.

And when you have done this, when you have made your own acquaintance, you will find that in the vast scheme of Nature you are only a trivial incident. "I come from the funeral of mankind," he said, "to attend to natural phenomena. The so much grander significance of any fact—of sun and moon and stars—of the evening and the morning and all the phenomena between them— when not referred to man and his needs but viewed absolutely."

Man is not, as we so arrogantly like to believe, the be-all and the end-all of creation. And the earth is not the center of the universe. In the eternal scheme of things, a king has no greater dignity than a cat. Yet the king would be much happier if he could understand that both he and the cat are humble but joyous playfellows in the exciting game of life.

Thoreau was keenly aware of this fellowship between the so-called lower animals and himself. In one of his most vivid passages he describes a race that he had with a fox. It was not a hunt, but merely a contest in speed and cunning between two friends. "Suddenly, looking down the river, I saw a fox some sixty rods off, making across the hills on my left. . . . I tossed my head aloft and bounded away. . . . It seemed Diana and all the satyrs cheered me on. . . . I gained rapidly on the fox; but he showed a remarkable presence of mind, for, instead of keeping up the steep and unwooded face of the hill, he kept along the slope in the direction of the forest, though he lost ground by it. . . . The course on his part was a series of most graceful curves. . . . When he doubled I wheeled and cut him off, bounding with fresh vigor. . . . Having finally got near enough

for a fair view, just as he was slipping into the wood, I grace-
fully yielded him the palm. . . ."

Thoreau felt most at home with his woodland companions.
For he found a common denominator in their mutual appetite
for the savor of life. Clifton Fadiman has observed that Thoreau
could get more fun out of ten minutes with a chickadee than
many a man could get out of a whole night with Cleopatra. This
statement, while grossly exaggerated for effect, contains nevertheless more than a germ of truth. Though he had no great zest
for physical love—he never married—Thoreau had an infinite
passion for a warm and understanding contact with all created
things. He found an equal dignity in all life.

An equal dignity, but not an equal simplicity. He best enjoyed
the animals because they had no hypercritical nonsense about
them. He wouldn't refer to a man as a dog because it would be
an insult to the dog. But on the other hand, "to have said that
one of his human neighbors was as interesting to him as a wood-
chuck"—we are quoting the editor of Thoreau's *Journal*—"would
have been to pay that neighbor a rather handsome compliment.
None of the brute animals, so-called . . . ever vexed his ears
with pomposity." To a visitor who ventured to pity him on his
solitude, he replied: "You have no idea how much there is going
on at Walden Pond." To another of his visitors he said: "A musk-
rat is a different sort of a man, that is all."

Thoreau's attachment to Nature was due to his philosophical—
we may even call it *religious*—conviction that every individual
little self is but a different expression of the all-embracing Universal Self. In one of his essays he asked, "Who hears the fishes
when they cry?" For even they, he declared, are not overlooked in
the ultimate scheme of things. Even the cry of the fishes is an important note in the Song of Eternal Life.

Regarded as an individual, therefore, the highest man is but a
trivial incident. But regarded as a part of the Whole, even the lowest creature is a necessary thread in a pattern of joy. Nothing is
isolated. Everything comes "straight down from the Maker of the
world." Even the snowflakes that fall upon your coat sleeve. "We

think that the one flake mechanically coheres, and that the other flake simply flows together and falls. But in truth they are the product of *enthusiasm,* the children of an ecstasy, finished with the artist's utmost skill." Every one of us is the handiwork of the "Universal Mind, which thinks while we are asleep."

This is the lesson that Thoreau learned in his solitary meditations at Walden Pond. "The great world exists for the enjoyment of the smallest living thing."

IV

But this is only half the story. Thoreau also learned how to apply this lesson to our everyday life. In order to be joyously alive, he said, disencumber yourself from the luxuries of the world. Get closer to the heart of Nature, to your own heart. Stop your breathless competition against your neighbors. Try to become better acquainted with them, and with yourself.

And, when you have done this, you will find that too many of us are losing our health in our scramble for riches. We have become "the tools of our tools." We are building machines to make speedier journeys. But our machines carry us faster than our thoughts. "We do not ride on our vehicles; they ride upon us." We raise towering buildings and monuments of stone. But "one piece of good sense would be more memorable than a monument as high as the moon." We have settled on earth and forgotten Heaven.

Our greatest curse, declared Thoreau, is our hunger for success. We try to bite off considerably more from the apple of life than we are able to chew. We fail to realize that "a man is rich in proportion to the number of things which he can afford to let alone." Our life is frittered away by counting the details we think we need. "I say, let your affairs be as two or three, and not a hundred or a thousand; instead of a million, count half a dozen, and keep your accounts on your thumb-nail. . . . Simplicity, simplicity, simplicity!"

Stop in your feverish hustle and listen to the workman at your side. Not the man you have hired, but "the Workman whose work we are."

And to do this, you need not withdraw from society. (Thoreau himself, we must remember, spent only two years at Walden.) Stay where you are. Accept the limitations of your time and place. "However mean your life is, meet it and live it; do not shun it and call it hard names. It is not as bad as you are." Thoreau was far from advising people to go off and live in a cave. Since "caves . . . are not plenty enough to accommodate all at the present day, it were certainly better to accept the advantages which the invention and industry of mankind offer." Adapt yourself to your environment but don't become a slave to it.

Above all, don't become a slave to your desire for wealth. "Superfluous wealth can buy superfluities only. Money is not required to buy one necessary of the soul." He despised the insatiable human passion for money. "The ways by which you may get money almost without exception lead downward." In the balancing of your ledger for happiness, try not to increase your income but to decrease your outgo. It takes little cash to buy the real values of life. "The man is the richest whose pleasures are the cheapest." The wisest men, Thoreau points out, have lived the simplest lives. The ancient philosophers, as well as many of the modern reformers, have belonged to a class "than which none has been poorer in outward riches, none so rich in inward." The most impoverished of all men are "those who have fettered themselves with chains of silver or gold."

V

Thoreau's own life remained utterly unfettered. Throughout his Walden experience he had "no lock nor bolt, not even a nail" over his latch or windows. He had nothing to fear because he had nothing to lose. His house, like his heart, was free to all comers. "I never fastened my door night or day, though I was to be absent several days. . . . The tired rambler could rest and warm himself by my fire, the literary amuse himself with a few books on my table, or the curious, by opening my closet door, see what was left of my dinner, and what prospect I had of a supper."

He was, however, molested on one occasion. And that was by the government, for his failure to pay his tax. It was a matter of principle with him. He refused to support a state which sanctioned slavery, and which bought and sold "men, women, and children like cattle." He was arrested and spent a night in jail. The next day his sister paid the tax and he was released.

When he left Walden, he carried the same spirit of gentle rebellion wherever he went. Though he believed that every organization, even the organized Church, may lead to oppression, he lived his entire life by the Biblical formula "What shall it profit a man, if he shall gain the whole world, and lose his own soul?"

He went back to making pencils for a living. He also accepted a job as the township's surveyor. But he found plenty of leisure for a frequent visit to his "forest relations"—at Walden, on the Merrimack River, and in other sparsely inhabited sections of New England.

Every return to Nature was to Thoreau a journey home. And also an adventure of discovery—an exploration of himself. Try this adventure, he advises his readers in the concluding chapter of *Walden*. "Be a Columbus to whole new continents and worlds within you, opening new channels, not of trade, but of thought." Sell your clothes, he declared, and keep your thoughts. "If I were confined to a corner of a garret all my days, like a spider, the world would be just as large to me while I had my thoughts about me." Wealth or poverty, fame or oblivion, good or bad fortune—these are but minor matters. "The setting sun is reflected from the windows of the almshouse as brightly as from the rich man's abode; the snow melts before its door as early in the spring. I do not see but a quiet mind may live as contentedly there, and have as cheering thoughts, as in a palace."

Therefore, observes Thoreau, you must "love your life, poor as it is. The faultfinder will find faults even in Paradise." Wherever you are, at whatever level you may have been placed, you are assigned to "walk even with the Builder of the Universe." Be assured that God is always at your side.

VI

Thoreau walked side by side with God to the end. At forty-five he fell a prey to tuberculosis. But he never lost his zest for life. He greeted everybody with a cheerful "Good morning" even after a night of sleepless pain. He insisted on eating his breakfast at the family table. "It would not be social," he said, "to take my meals alone." Once, when a friend talked to him about a future life, he said: "One world at a time." On another occasion, when an orthodox member of the household asked him whether he had made his peace with God, he replied: "I am not aware that God and I have ever quarreled."

As the last day approached, he looked forward to his new adventure. "There is more day to dawn. The sun is but a morning star."

CHAPTER XXIV

Nietzsche—Superman or Madman?

[1844–1900]

NIETZSCHE's philosophy is the product of an unbalanced mind. It fascinates and frightens the reader like the spectacle of a forest fire—gorgeous but destructive. "A man," he wrote, "must be built for my philosophy; otherwise the chances are that it will kill him." About three quarters of a century after this philosophy was written, it came near to killing the entire human race. And the danger is not yet over.

Nietzsche's mad adventure in philosophy was partly the result of his misadventure in love. His oversensitive mind gave way when the woman he wanted to marry rejected him. His resentment against one woman turned into hatred against all women. And his opposition to the rights of women became fermented into a poison against all human rights.

Nietzsche was a supremely gentle soul who, like many other people, admired everything that he was not. But, in his case, the admiration went too far. Devoid of the necessary qualities in the struggle for success, he exaggerated these qualities in the people who got to the top. A physical weakling himself, he turned brute strength into a religion. Though he grew faint at the sight of blood, he preached the gospel of bloodshed and war. Suffering from headache and eyestrain all his life, he came to see the world through a distorted spiritual as well as physical light. He was a great poet gone mad. He quarreled with God for the weaknesses of men. "Annihilate the millions of the bungled and botched," he declared, "to create one Superman"—the sort of pitiless and powerful Superman Nietzsche would have liked to be.

For, to his bitter sorrow, he himself was one of the bungled and the botched.

II

Nietzsche was born (1844) in Prussia—a comparatively small country which, like himself, was insanely anxious to become great. He lost his father, who was a minister, at an early age. His mother brought him up on a spiritual diet of fanatical orthodoxy. And he himself remained a fanatical orthodox up to the age of eighteen.

And then the pendulum swung to the other extreme. Nietzsche turned heterodox, but he retained his fanaticism. He became violently antagonistic to Christ, and conceived the irrational idea that he was destined to be Antichrist. Just as John the Baptist was the forerunner of Jesus, he believed that Machiavelli was the forerunner of Nietzsche. In his half-insane mind, he came to look upon himself as the prophet of a new religion—a religion without a God, based upon a scripture of hatred instead of love.

In addition to Machiavelli, Nietzsche adopted Schopenhauer as his philosophical mentor. At nineteen he read Schopenhauer's *World as Will and Idea*. The book threw him into an ecstasy of self-glorification. "It seemed as if Schopenhauer were addressing me personally. . . . In this book I saw . . . my own nature depicted with frightful grandeur."

At twenty-three he was drafted into the Army. The military life was too strenuous for him, and he was soon dismissed. From that time on, the soldier became an object of worship to him. "I felt for the first time that the highest Will to Life does not find expression in a miserable struggle for existence, but in a Will to War, a Will to Power, a Will to Overpower."

His will to power, however, was stifled in a sedentary life. He got a position as professor of classical philology at the University of Basle. Here he became addicted to the ancient Spartan doctrine that the power to destroy is the greatest aim in life.

He was obsessed by the idea of grandeur. Yet in spite of his glowing words about himself, he found no grandeur in his own soul. He found it, however, in another man of colossal egocentricity. Richard Wagner. In the blatant music of Wagner he saw a spirit akin to his own. The Freudians would probably ascribe this instinct to Nietzsche's inferiority complex—his desire to picture himself as a Superman because he failed to reach the stature of a man.

He became, for a time, a satellite of Wagner. But he left him in anger when Wagner, in his *Parsifal,* "succumbed"—as Nietzsche put it—"to the decadence of Christianity." This sort of "piety and pity" was too much for Nietzsche's "Spartan soul."

III

And then came his unsuccessful love affair and a complete breakdown in physical and mental health. He recovered only in part, to become more fanatical than ever before. He traveled to Italy in search of his health, and from Italy to the Alps, and from the Alps to the nebulous fantasies of the world "beyond good and evil." He used, as the mouthpiece for his new philosophy, the ancient Persian prophet, Zarathustra.

Thus Spake Zarathustra is one of the most fantastic dreams ever recorded by an insane mind—"a soul," as Nietzsche declared, "that overflowed all its margins." In his delusions of grandeur, Nietzsche exclaimed: "This work stands alone. Let us not mention other books in the same breath; nothing has ever been produced out of such a superabundance of strength."

The book is undoubtedly strong. But it is supercharged with emotion instead of being filled with thought. It turns the cold calculations of Machiavelli into a passionate creed. And it has swept unstable minds, like Hitler and Mussolini, into an orgy of self-aggrandizement at the expense of the world. "Live dangerously!" cries Nietzsche. "Live in a state of war!" He who wants to be a creator must first be a destroyer; he must break all the old values into pieces. The old gods are dead—they have laughed themselves to death. And there is no longer any God in the world. There is only Superman. "The Superman is a bridge, and not a goal; a destroyer, and not a builder . . ." For him there is only one satisfactory kind of morality—the morality of the *classes* as opposed to the morality of the *masses*.

Indeed, the masses must live only for the exploitation of the classes. The multitude of men must perish in order that the one Superman may survive. To Nietzsche this was merely a poetical hyperbole. But to a man like Hitler it became a gospel fact. Nietzsche was daydreaming when he saw himself as a savage warrior magnified to superhuman proportions. Hitler transformed this daydream into a nightmare of reality.

For Nietzsche's philosophy, like Machiavelli's, is a guidebook for dictators—the monomaniacs who see themselves through a magnifying mirror. They place themselves on a pedestal above the rest of the world. They regard themselves as Nietzsche's Superman —the blond beast who leaps over the heights and terrorizes the "inferior cattle" in the valleys and on the slopes.

In the effervescence of his imagination, Nietzsche was probably unaware of the mischief he was doing. He seems to have been more anxious to startle than to teach. Thus, in answer to the idealists who believe that we have had too much war, he declares that we have had too much peace. "There have not been wars enough to strengthen our souls." To be supremely good, declares Nietzsche paradoxically, a man must be supremely evil. "Doth my preaching break all your truths? Let them break! Thus spake Zarathustra."

And these words of Zarathustra are repeated, in somewhat different form, throughout the later books of Nietzsche. Unable, because of his sensitive eyesight, to face the sun, he shut himself up in an attic and drew down the blinds. And in this dingy atmosphere, he brewed the potion of his witches' dream. The entire purpose of this dream was "to destroy the old morality," the wave of the past, and "to establish the new immorality," the wave of the future. Ambition, ruthlessness, hate—these are the strength of the master. Compassion, generosity, love—these are the weakness of the slave.

In his lucid moments, Nietzsche was able to raise the curtains of his soul. And then he saw love under a different light. "The chastest utterance I ever heard is the quotation from the French: *Dans le véritable amour c'est l'âme qui enveloppe le corps*—In true love it is the soul that embraces the body." But such moments of truer insight were all too rare with Nietzsche. The bulk of his work is dedicated to the proposition that might is the only right. The Superman does not try to rationalize his desire for power. His only justification is, "This is my will." The master, declares Nietzsche, need not be ashamed of his selfish determination to rule. On the contrary, he should be proud of it. And by a subtle contortion of his logic, Nietzsche proposes a transvaluation of all values. He turns light into darkness, and wrong into right. "What is justice for the master is justice for the slave." And so, when the slave complains of his wrongs, he is merely railing against the supreme justice of the world—the right of the master to rule.

Hence the "evil virtues" of the strong must become the acceptable burdens of the weak. "All morality must be compelled to bow before the gradations of rank." The ambition of the Superman must become the morality of the world.

And the Superman must steel himself against becoming too soft. He must ever aim to "become better and more evil"—to revert to the "cruelty" that "constituted the great joy and delight of ancient man." This cruel happiness of the Superman—"the career of Napoleon, for example"—is "the greatest blessing that can come to the worthless herd of mankind."

For "not mankind but Superman is the goal." The world, as Nietzsche sees it, is a huge laboratory in which tons of rubbish are wasted to produce an ounce of gold. Don't protect the average, or help the mediocre, or pity the underdog. They are the expendables in Nature's experiment for the best. They are the soil that must be fertilized with muck in order that "the seed of man may grow into the flower of Superman."

Away, then, with the "softness" of Christianity—the "enervating" doctrine that all men have equal rights. The masses of men have only an equal duty—to refrain from rebellion and to leave their masters "free, in their wild-beast innocence, from every social restraint."

This aristocratic, "wild-beast innocence" of the Superman, as Nietzsche apprehensively confessed, is endangered by the spread of democracy. He called it the Judaeo-Christian "mania for counting noses" and treating all men alike. "We must destroy this Christian democratic notion before it is too late." And the pity of it is that men like Hitler and Mussolini took him at his word. Nietzsche's Superman is a distorted little paranoiac who would turn all human values upside down.

It is such paranoiacs who, inspired by Nietzsche's diseased imagination, have tried and are still trying to overrun the world. Note his words about the "ideal" ruling state—a perfect picture of Nazism, Fascism, or Communism. "A State of blond beasts of prey, a race of [would-be] conquerors and masters, with military organization . . . unscrupulously placing their fearful paws upon the population . . ." The "Superman ruler" of such a state has no need of the consent of the masses, no contractual understanding between his people and himself. "What has he to do with contracts who is master by nature, who is able to command with violence in demeanor and deed?"

The most likely soil for this violent "Super-State," believed Nietzsche, "is Russia." Its people have for generations been trained to a "stubborn and resigned fatalism" which readily submits to the cruelty of the masters—the blond beasts of Europe.

These blond beasts, he prophesied, would try to "rescue" the world from the "democrats, the Christians and the cows" otherwise known as "the herd."

And the aim of all this? "To overthrow the old society and to build the new." This new society, said Nietzsche, "must be constructed like a pyramid. It must stand upon a solid foundation of willing mediocrity at the bottom, with a commanding apex at the top." For the only important thing is "the Ego whole and holy, and selfishness blessed."

IV

Such was the evil dream of the philosopher who had lost his mind. His poetry is a Niagara of eloquence, his imagery is superb, and his observations on human foibles are often as keen as a razor's edge. But for all his brilliance, it is a sickening experience to read him today. Especially in the light of the world tragedies we have experienced—partly as a result of his sadistic credo—in the last fifty years. In this framework, the philosophy of Nietzsche glitters like the sunlight reflected in a pool of blood. We have paid too high a price in our effort to fashion the blond-beast Superman of Nietzsche's design.

For Nietzsche's Superman is a madman. Like Nietzsche himself. The older he grew, the more unbalanced his mind became. He looked upon himself as greater than Wagner, greater than Napoleon, greater than Christ. He regarded his books as the "supreme literary achievement of all time." To the critics who remained cold he cried, "My time is not yet. Only the day after tomorrow belongs to me."

His self-glorification was equaled only by his self-mortification. As time went on, he became more and more derisive about humanity, more and more bitter about himself. Indeed, his laughter was but the outcome of his bitterness. "Perhaps I know best why man is the only animal that laughs," he wrote in one of his lucid intervals. "Man alone suffers so excruciatingly that he was compelled to invent laughter."

And so he went on laughing and railing and rhapsodizing as his body was racked with pain. His sight grew gradually worse until at last he was almost blind. And in his madness he began to cry out that he was a pagan god nailed to the cross of human stupidity.

One day, in the winter of 1889, his madness became unmanageable. They took him to an asylum—"the right man," as Max Nordau remarked, "in the right place."

After a while they released him in the custody of his mother. But he was a complete wreck now. He was no longer able to write, or even to think. He merely babbled incoherent phrases. Now and then a brief quotation from his own work would come stumbling across his clouded mind. "Say thy word," he whispered on one of these occasions, "and break in pieces."

And at last, in 1900, death gathered up the broken pieces and swept them out of the world.

But the evil had been done. The mischief-makers of the world had found a powerful advocate. And mankind is still suffering from the chain reaction of his destructive thoughts. For the madman with a pen can be even more dangerous than the madman with a gun.

CHAPTER XXV

Christ in Calcutta—
the Vedanta Philosophy of Vivekananda

[1863–1902]

IN 1893 there was a Hindu invasion of the United States. It was not, however, a material but a spiritual invasion. And this is how it came about.

Vivekananda, a Hindu philosopher, had decided to come to America in order to convert the Christians to Christianity. He was a disciple of Ramakrishna—a strange, Christlike prophet who had founded a new religion to embrace all the other religions of the world. A Fellowship of Faiths. And Vivekananda had taken it upon himself to serve as a missionary of this new religion to the "civilized savages" of the West.

He collected funds for his mission, and sailed for the United States. In Chicago, he had been told, there was to be a World's Fair and a Parliament of Religions. Somehow he would try to bring his message to this parliament and put an end, as he hoped, to all future religious strife.

But he was more devout than practical. He arrived in Chicago in July 1893, only to learn that the Parliament of Religions would not open until September. He registered at a first-class hotel where the sharpers began to snipe at him as an easy prey. Within a few days he was robbed and cheated of most of his money. He had just enough left for a trip to Boston.

On the train he met a charming lady who, attracted by his brilliant conversation and picturesque attire, invited him to her Boston home and introduced him to her Beacon Hill friends, including J. H. Wright, professor of Greek at Harvard. Professor Wright took him under his wing. "Here is a man," he wrote to the chairman of the Fair, "who is more learned than all our learned professors put together." He sent Vivekananda back to Chicago, with sufficient funds and letters of recommendation to the influential members of the religious Parliament.

But again Vivekananda lost his funds—a philosopher and his money are soon parted—and, what was even worse, he lost his instructions. When he arrived at the railroad station, he didn't have the price of a hotel room. He spent the night in a dry-goods box in the train shed.

At daybreak he started out to look for the Parliament of Religions. Several times he lost his way. But he arrived just in time for the opening of the first session.

And then the miracle happened.

He stood up, tired, hungry, and with no notes or any prepared speech. Restlessness in the audience. Confusion in his own heart. He began in a low, hesitant voice:

"My sisters and brothers of America . . ."

Encouraged by the deafening applause that greeted his friendly salutation, he went on: "I profess a philosophy, and I belong to a faith, whose sacred language, the Sanskrit, has no word for *exclusion*. The divinities we worship are all human beings, all living things throughout the world."

Again the house shook with applause. A new note had been heard in America. From that moment, he held his audience spellbound—like a messenger from another world.

Who was this man, and what was his message?

II

Born in Calcutta (1863), he grew up as the turbulent son of a wealthy lawyer. His favorite sport, his father said, was to "tear the family peace into shreds." It was often necessary to "duck the boy's head under water in order to cool his fiery temper." He had a special fondness for "holy pilgrims," upon whom he lavished a large share of his spending money.

In his high school, and later at the University of Calcutta, he was a leader in study, sport, and mischief. But, said his teachers, he had "a heart of gold." He was always ready to help the underdog, and to castigate those who "bit and barked at the top of the pack."

One day, as he was singing in the choir of a Brahma temple, he was startled to hear his name called in a loud voice. Turning around, he saw a gaunt stranger dressed in a loincloth. He recognized the man. St. Ramakrishna, whom he had met on one or two occasions.

"My son, my son! Why have you not come to me? I have been waiting in anguish. . . ."

Vivekananda left the temple and followed him.

The relationship that began between the master and his favorite disciple reads like a story out of the New Testament. Ramakrishna, like Christ, was said to have been the child of an immaculate conception. Every now and then, declared the Hindu sages, God comes down to earth, through a virgin mother, in order to renew the spirit of man. And Ramakrishna, according to this doctrine, was the latest of the divine incarnations.

Brought up in a small village, Ramakrishna had no formal schooling. Yet, at the age of ten, he confounded the scholars with his ability to interpret the Hindu scriptures. At seventeen, he became an assistant to his brother, who was a priest in the temple of Kali—"the Goddess-Mother of the Universe." To his brother's urging that he get a practical education, Ramakrishna replied: "What shall I do with mere breadwinning knowledge? I am not concerned with filling my stomach; I want to illumine my heart."

At his brother's death, he went into the wilderness "to meet divinity face to face." People called him mad. "The people are right," he said. "I am mad with the desire to bring sanity into the world."

In his effort to find the way to "sanity in an insane world," he made a study of a number of religions. And, one by one, he em-

braced Christianity, Buddhism, Mohammedanism, and Hinduism; and he found that each of these religions is but a different
path to God. "Suppose a man has several sons. The older boys
address him distinctly as *Papa* or *Baba,* but the little ones can
only call him *Pa* or *Ba.* Do you think the father will be angry with
those who address him indistinctly? He knows that they, too, are
calling to him in their sincere but fumbling way. All children are
alike to their father; and all worshipers are alike to God. All of
them are addressing the same Person. Though His names are
many, His Love is One."

All men, of all religions, are the children of one God. Ramakrishna illustrated this point in a beautiful parable. One day a
man was walking through the forest in a fog. Suddenly he beheld
a horrible shape looming out of the darkness and advancing upon
him as if ready to attack. In a fit of terror he discharged his gun
at the oncoming creature and killed it.

And then, when it was too late, he realized that the aggressive animal was his own brother coming to visit him after an
absence of many years. The fog had made a beloved brother seem
like a ferocious beast.

So it is, said Ramakrishna, with our entire life in this world of
illusion. We are living in a fog of misleading observations and distorted images that lead us into all sorts of deceptive ideas, stupid
hatreds, and tragic deeds. And we cannot truly be happy until
we can see through these deceptions and behold the truth—the
equality of all races, all men, in the eyes of God. This, in brief,
was the philosophy of Ramakrishna—the Hindu peasant who became one of the world's wisest men.

Like Jesus, Ramakrishna gathered a group of disciples around
him, and instructed them to spread his gospel through all the
provinces of India. All religions are equally true; they are but
different chapters in the Story of God. "A truly religious man
should realize that other religions also are paths leading to the
truth. We must always maintain an attitude of respect toward
other faiths."

Ramakrishna was a man of extreme simplicity and supreme

love. And his sensitivity was such that the contact of money made him physically sick. He was a devoted fighter against material greed, a soldier in the battle of peace.

And he died on the battlefield. As a result of his incessant labor, he was stricken with "clergyman's sore throat." This disease finally developed into cancer. His disciples took him to Calcutta, where the physicians ordered him to maintain the strictest silence. "But I must speak on; for I am the voice of the Lord."

He was unable to take any food now. His throat was almost closed even against liquids. But he called his disciples to him and delivered his final message to them in a whisper just before he died. "Go to the children of God, and teach them to be kind to one another."

III

One night shortly after their leader's death, Vivekananda was walking in a garden with another disciple. Suddenly, Vivekananda tells us, they beheld a Shining Figure before them. The face was that of Ramakrishna. "Both of us saw him at the same time, so it could not have been a mere illusion."

Ramakrishna was still alive, still in their midst!

Firm in this belief, the disciples traveled by bullock cart to the sacred village of Antpur. Here they gathered one starry night around a fire in the open fields. Vivekananda told them the story of Ramakrishna, and of another dedicated messenger of God— Jesus of Nazareth. "Let us teach the world to unite under these two prophets. Let us plant once more the seeds of peace and of good will among men."

And suddenly, as the young disciples listened to Vivekananda, one of them thought of something. "Do you know what night this is?"

"No," replied a companion. "Is it anything special?"

"It has just occurred to me that this is Christmas Eve."

IV

The consecration of the Hindu disciples on the birthday of Christ was a mere coincidence. But to Vivekananda it meant something more—the merging of two great philosophic systems, the religion of the East and the science of the West, into a worldwide unity of love.

This was the vision that had brought him to America. The son of the rich man had become a wandering teacher of mercy. Wherever he traveled in the United States, he found an enthusiastic response. At first the crowds came out of curiosity. His appearance was sensational. He put on a "good show." He stepped upon the platform, wrote a journalist of that time, "attired in Oriental garb, consisting of a scarlet robe of soft cloth, which reached below the knees, bound round the waist with a crimson girdle. On his head was a turban of white silk which set off to advantage the finely poised head, and the swarthy complexion of his smoothly shaved face." The ladies especially came in throngs to admire this "handsome interpreter of the New Thought."

But many of those who came merely to be amused went away convinced. This man with the radiant personality, golden voice, eloquent speech, and sincere devotion to God had really something new to say. "My goal is simply to fill all America with the spirit of the eternal, universal religion of tolerant understanding. Are you a Christian, a Buddhist, a Hindu, a Mohammedan, a Jew? I do not ask you to abandon your religion and to adopt mine. On the contrary, I urge you to remain true to your own faith. But I beg of you to respect all men of other faiths. Keep all the paths to heaven free from bigotry, bloodshed and hate."

Vivekananda was not a Christian. But he had the deepest reverence for Christianity. He accepted the doctrine of salvation, but he interpreted it into a philosophy of individual effort as well as of vicarious atonement. It is not enough to say that Jesus sacrificed Himself for your sake. To save your soul you need more than His sacrifice. You need your own labor. "Every soul must pay the price of its salvation."

And the price we pay covers a period of many hundreds, perhaps many thousands, of years. The salvation of each soul is a long evolutionary process that goes on from life to life. Vivekananda believed in the transmigration of souls. And he adapted this belief to the Darwinian theory of evolution. This is a new and interesting point in Western philosophy. The life of the individual, like all life in general, goes through a process of evolution from the lower to the higher forms. But the individual development is *spiritual* instead of *material*. "The same soul gradually purifies itself by successive reincarnations."

This doctrine, declared Vivekananda, is the only one that can explain the omnipotence and the benevolence of God. "If we had only one life, how could we account for the failures and the frustrations of the world?" Every life, however lowly, seems to hold some divine promise. Yet every death means a promise unfulfilled. The greatest men of genius have declared that their realizations have fallen far short of their conceptions. Death often comes in the midst of preparation to do something great.

What is true of genius is true, in a lesser degree, of us all. Every one of us feels that the world has "let him down"—that he hasn't had his "real chance" in life, that what he has been *allowed* to do is but the merest fraction of what he has been *able* to do. "Shall we now think that this frustration of our soul is the entire story of our life?" Is it not more reasonable to conclude that the present life of an individual is but a single episode in the evolution of his soul?

And these episodes tell a consecutive story, from migration to migration, until the development of the individual soul is rounded into a unit of fulfillment. How, asked Vivekananda, could it be otherwise? "If we had only one birth and one death, how could we regard God as all-powerful and all-wise and all-just?" Would such a God create us with unequal endowments and unequal rewards in a world which offered us but a single chance? Would He send us to an eternity of punishment for one short life of sin?

It takes more than a single lifetime, said Vivekananda, to untangle the complicated distinctions between right and wrong.

Indeed, our main business in the world is to learn these distinctions gradually, a little in each successive life—just as a child learns his lessons in each successive grade. Every transmigration is a certificate of admission into a new and more advanced course of study.

And the final graduation, the salvation of the soul—that is, the merging of the individual person with the divine personality of God—comes for each of us when we have learned the great lesson of infinite love. This is the aim of all knowledge, the merging of all paths, the secret of all religions, the fulfillment of all hopes. This fulfillment comes through suffering. Even God suffers along with His human children. "In creating the world," writes one of Vivekananda's followers, Dr. S. L. Sarkar, "God has sacrificed Himself." But there is joy in self-sacrifice, happiness in suffering endured for another's sake. This is the meaning of creation—the creation of the world, of a work of art, or of a more merciful way of life. "All creation connotes sacrifice. And the more rigorous the sacrifice, the happier the result. Thus, self-sacrifice must be the road which every human life is called upon to travel."

For the way to God is long, and our footsteps are stumbling and weak. But we are headed in the right direction—every single one of us. Through all our stumbling along the road of our many human transmigrations, we have the divine instinct to reach the one true goal. Through the lessening of one another's pain. "So patience, my brothers, patience. In the end, we shall all come face to face with God."

V

Vivekananda had brought to America the patience of the East. And he brought back to India the impatience of the West. Impatience with unnecessary suffering, poverty, disease. Ramakrishna had been content with the health of the spirit. His own physical welfare, the physical welfare of the people, had meant very little to him. All India, in his day, was like a gigantic poorhouse. But Vivekananda changed all that. He merged the social service of Christianity with the spiritual meditation of Hinduism. He founded schools for the children, hospitals for the sick, and food centers for the famine-stricken masses. He spent the last years of his life shuttling back and forth between India and America, bringing the best features of each for the improvement of the other, and building a bridge of better understanding between the East and the West.

Again and again his health broke down. At one time he wrote: "The way is long, the time is short, evening is approaching . . . I feel my task is done." But, like Ramakrishna, he forced himself to go on against his doctor's advice. He was determined to carry his burden until he could at least see the firm foundations for "the Universal Religion of the World." The merging of all creeds into a single service for all mankind. However tired, however sick, he couldn't say *no* to a request for help.

At last, "like a spent torch he fell to the earth." Just before the end, he received a visit from a young French poet, Jules-Bois. He was lying ill in one of his Monasteries of Service. "From a small skiff on the Ganges, as we approached the Monastery," writes the poet, "Calcutta receded into the distance. Finally the Temple came into sight, all white in the midst of a grove of palm trees, the trident of its pagoda rising high above the pleasant terraces . . .

"Vivekananda's first words, when I beheld him, were: 'I am free, my friend, free again. I have given away everything. In the poorest country of the world, I am the poorest man. And the happiest.' "

It was on July 4, 1902, that he ended his earthly journey. A mere stage of the journey, he would have insisted. "I shall come into the world again and again. For there is more work to be done, more suffering to be endured, more mercy to bestow upon a suffering world."

CHAPTER XXVI

Havelock Ellis and the Dance of Life

[1859–1939]

H E INHERITED his daring from his seagoing ancestors. One of them, Sir Henry, was famous as the hero of the Indian Mutiny. His father, Edward Peppen (nicknamed Pepper) Ellis, was a ship captain who defied the rebellion of his sailors and the storms of the Seven Seas. And thus Havelock was well equipped for his exploration into new ideas against the tempests of bigotry and hate.

His entire life was an adventure against prejudice. He was a sailor of the spirit who tried to bring humanity into a haven of peace. He realized, from his own experience, that the pioneer of thought faces danger on every hand, and that "a clear-sighted eye, a many-sided sympathy, a fine daring, an endless patience, are for ever necessary" for the noble life.

He showed the superior qualities of his character at an early age. One day, when he was eight years old, he came home from school with a hole in the back of his neck. In reply to his mother's questions, he told her that the hole had been made by a slate pencil held in the hands of a schoolmate with a perverted sense of humor.

"I hope you paid him back in his own coin!" cried the indignant Mrs. Ellis.

"No, Mother," he replied. "For then I should have been as nasty as he was."

This was to be his attitude throughout his life. "You can never cure evil with evil. . . . Of all our human emotions, the most futile is hatred."

At school he was regarded as a "sissy." But the other boys didn't understand the toughness of his moral fiber—nor his childhood prayer that God would give him "the power to translate the soul into words."

At sixteen (in 1875), he was threatened with tuberculosis. The doctors advised his parents to take him out of school. His father's ship, the *Surrey,* was about to sail for Australia. A sea voyage, said the doctor, might be a good thing for the young man.

"Would you like to come along as captain's clerk?"

"Indeed I would!"

II

A long voyage from his native England, a storm that nearly washed him overboard, sun-bathing on the deck, considerable reading, and the maturing of a mind poised in the vastitude between the sea and the sky—just exactly what Ellis needed for the strengthening of his body and his soul. In Australia he taught school for a time—in two hamlets separated by several miles of mountains. His working week was divided equally between the two schools, three days in each. And twice every week he traveled over the mountains on foot.

It was here in the wilderness, "where man in the bush with God may meet," that Ellis determined upon his life's work. He would bend every effort to the discovery of the *real* world—to learn whether there was any meaning behind its external mechanism. "What is the world that science reveals to us as the reality of the world we see? A world dark as the grave, silent as a stone, and shaking like jelly. Is that the ultimate fact of this glorious world? Why, you might as well say that the ultimate fact of one of Beethoven's quartettes is the scraping of the tails of horses on the intestines of cats."

Yet, for the present, Ellis was still unsure of himself. His thoughts had not as yet become crystallized in his own mind. Thus far he had found no reason to substantiate his hope that the world he lived in was friendly rather than hostile. And so he wrote at this time: "I could only wander restlessly, an ignorant and home-less child." Like Housman's Shropshire lad, he was "a stranger and afraid in a world he never made."

His soul had become a battleground between the scientist who denied God and the mystic who tried to find Him. For the mind of Ellis, at this period, was a mixture of disbelief and trust. He was a student at the University of Sydney. The intellectual trend of the day, still stunned from the impact of Darwin's revolutionary theory, had lost its bearings. Many of the intelligentsia had be-come so concerned with the individual threads of the universe that they had forgotten the cosmic pattern. Ellis had found him-self—or, rather, had lost himself—in this intricate labyrinth of doubt and despair.

Fortunately, however, he came across a book that showed him the way out of his perplexity. This book—James Hinton's *Life in Nature*—enabled him to harmonize the materialistic and the mystical elements that struggled within his mind. It taught him the important fact that, in their final analysis, *materialism and mysticism are one.*

Havelock Ellis had lost his religion through science; but now, through a better understanding of science, he found his religion again. "Thanks to *Life in Nature,*" he wrote to one of his cousins, "I have now finally left all doubt behind."

In his diary, Ellis referred to his new experience as a religious conversion. But it had nothing in common with the popular idea of "conversion"—the sudden turning of a sinner into a saint. It was rather a return to sanity. Writing about this experience many years later, he said: "The book showed me that the mechanism of the world is not the mechanism of a factory, but something vital, with all the glow and beauty of life. . . . The two opposing psychic tendencies [of my mind] were fused in delicious harmony. . . . I saw that the spiritual world has, and must have, its only real basis on the world of science; and that the scientific world is only a symbol for the measurement of the world of the spirit." This blending of the material and the mystical aspects of the world, said Ellis, changed his entire mental attitude. "It was no longer an attitude of hostility and dread, but of confidence and love."

Yet this "conversion" resulted in no acceptance of any specific faith. "There was not a single clause in my religious creed because I held no creed. I had found that dogmas were not . . . true, not . . . false—but the mere empty shadows of intimate personal experience. I had become indifferent to shadows, for I held the substance. . . . Henceforth I could face life with confidence and joy, for my heart was at one with the world."

And what, in this new vision, was the meaning of the world? "I see the World as Beauty. To see the World as Beauty is the End of Living."

When Ellis had arrived at this mature philosophy of life, he was just nineteen years old.

III

Ellis returned to England (1879) at the age of twenty. His life was dedicated to the establishment of beauty and the abolition of ugliness. One of the most glaringly ugly things he saw in the world was the suffering that resulted from the misconception and the abuses of the intimate relationships between the sexes. He realized that this was a dangerous field for the investigation of a young student. But Ellis was not the sort to run away from danger. He had already observed that his attitude toward many vital questions was unorthodox. "In coming to all these conclusions, I have not . . . been actuated by the spirit of opposition or the wish to have out of the way opinions . . . On the contrary, in many cases these [out-of-the-way opinions] have made me miserable. . . ." But the facts must be investigated, and the results made known to the world.

In order to prepare himself for a scientific investigation of the sexual functions, he decided to study medicine. But he rarely practiced it after he got his diploma. "A doctor's life," he wrote, "satisfies one's great desires—to know and to serve. . . . *But the work for me lies in the things I have to say some day.* I cannot help making even doctoring subservient to that."

The one branch of medicine that particularly interested him was obstetrics. He made his deliveries mostly among the poor. "Through my contacts with these people, I learn how they live and think." And also how they react to the problems of birth and population as applied to their material welfare. His very first case was that of a woman stretched on the floor in a drunken stupor amidst a brood of howling children. Destitution and desire, passion and poverty, joy in the gift of life, despair in the inability to provide for a living. "It is in the lying-in hospitals of the poor that we find the basis of our social science."

This, at least, was the experience of Havelock Ellis. But his overwork resulted in a physical breakdown. So much misery, so little power to help. Sleepless nights, followed by an attack of scarlet fever from which he recovered but which killed his mother when she contracted it from him.

The inclemency of Nature, the inhumanity of man. After his recovery from his illness, Ellis wrote a book—*The New Spirit*—in which he represented "all learning" as "but an art to live well." Intended as an effort to "harmonize Heaven and Earth," it was regarded in many quarters as an "invitation to Hell"—an "unpleasant compilation of cool impudence and effrontery"—an "immodest exhibition of the fleshly element in sex." The publishers of the book were only too glad to strike the "obnoxious item" from their list.

But this was only the beginning of the tempest of vituperation that was to pursue him through the rest of his life. He found some protection against the storm in the love of Edith Lees, a woman with less than five feet of physical stature and a towering courage to defy the stupidities of the world. They were married in 1891—with a vow of mutual frankness toward, and economic independence from, each other.

Shortly after their marriage, Ellis began his monumental *Studies in the Psychology of Sex*. The purpose of these—as of all his other studies—was to demonstrate that "our feet cling to the earth," but that "there are two wings by which we may raise ourselves above the earth: simplicity, and purity." Yet the publication of the very first volume in the *Studies* created a scandal, and Ellis was brought into court as the author of a "lewd, wicked, bawdy, criminal and obscene book." The publisher of the book, accused as a co-culprit with the author, was compelled to pay a fine of a hundred pounds. As for Ellis himself, he wasn't even allowed the opportunity to defend the scientific character of the work. The book was banned in England, and Ellis was pointed out everywhere as a "nasty" man.

But he did not retaliate. "For then I should have been as nasty as they were." And so he quietly accepted "the loss of friends, the pecuniary damages, the proclamation to the world at large . . . that the author of a scientific work is to be classed with the purveyors of literary garbage."

But, chastened by his battle with the vulgar tastes of the police —"the meddlesome members of that sad class against which the gods themselves are powerless"—he decided to have his *Studies* published in the United States. "I insist on doing my own work in my own way . . . I do not intend that any consideration shall induce me to . . . distort my vision of life." He was willing to dispense with position or wealth. But he was determined to retain the one possession he prized above all—the serenity of his soul.

IV

"Life is a perpetual risk and danger . . . a perpetual challenge to high adventure. But it is only in art that the solution of life's problems can be found. It is art alone which . . . justifies the pains and griefs of life . . . redeeming the pain of life by beauty." This was the sustaining principle of Ellis's philosophy. His scientific study of sex—its ecstasies and tragedies, its transgressions and prohibitions, its fervors and failures, and its tremendous power for good or evil—all this was but a prelude to his profounder study of the entire spectacle of life.

Life as a Spectacle of Beauty. "The mother who seeks to soothe her crying child preaches him no sermon. She holds up some bright object and it fixes his attention." It was the purpose of Ellis to explain "the beautiful vision" of the suffering and the fortitude of existence. "All the pain and the madness, even the ugliness and the commonplace of the world," would in his philosophy become "converted into shining jewels."

This was the vision of Ellis—to reveal a new aspect of the world as an Adventure in Beauty. And he set down this vision in a book entitled, appropriately enough, *The Dance of Life.*

The movement of life, declared Ellis, is a continuous pattern of rhythmical harmonies. No single event, no individual life is an isolated fragment of existence. Every sunset in one place is a sunrise in another place. "There is never a moment when the new dawn is not breaking over the earth."

This unending circle in the dance of light is equally true of the dance of life. "In the moral world we are ourselves the light-bearers, and the cosmic process is in us made flesh. For a brief space it is granted to us, if we will, to enlighten the darkness that surrounds our path. As in the ancient torch-race . . . the symbol of all life . . . we press forward, torch in hand, along the course. Soon from behind comes the runner who will outpace us. All our skill lies in giving into his hand the living torch, bright and un-flickering, as we ourselves disappear in the darkness."

In the torch-race of life, which is part of the rhythmical dance of the universe, we experience pain as well as pleasure. Havelock Ellis—as his biographer, Houston Peterson, observes—"knew only too well that the great dancer may have blood in her slippers," and that "the dance of life involves the dance of death." But that is how one learns to dance, and how one learns to live—to rise, to fall, and to rise again.

And let us not, in the bitterness of our pain, forget the joyous-ness of the spectacle to which we contribute our own little dance. Let us not mistake a twist in the thread for the pattern of the whole. "To allow our vision of Nature to be disturbed by our vision of Man is to allow the infinitely small to outweigh the infinitely great." We are but the tiny configurations in the design of the Eternal Dance.

To understand this dance, and to adapt our own little steps to its universal cadence—this, in the philosophy of Ellis, constitutes the essential Art of Living. The happy life, the serene life, is the ability to face the mastery of our art, in spite of the pain and the blood, with greater piety and courage.

Ellis found his own serenity of soul in the contemplation of Nature—the regularity of its rhythmic motion, the continuous process of its resurrection, the uninterrupted pulsation of its life. Spring, summer, autumn, winter—and then spring again. Together with Einstein, he felt that "in every true searcher of Nature there is a kind of religious reverence." In the midst of the chaos of World War I, he found his solace in the religious conviction that in nature there is no death, but only a rhythmic transition from life to life. He saw the living face of beauty behind the dead mask of ugliness. "A thrill of joy," he wrote (in 1915), "passed through me as we drove along the beautiful road and my eyes chanced to fall on the poppies in the field. . . . A friend said sadly . . . that for her the war had taken all their beauty from the daffodils. I do not feel that, but rather the reverse. Behind the insanity of Man the beauty of Nature seems to become more poignant and her serene orderliness more deeply peaceful. So when men tell me how they have lived in the trenches ankle-deep in human blood, I think how Nature has shed these great drops of her pure and more immortal blood over the green and yellow earth. . . .

"If we keep our eyes fixed on Nature, whose most exquisitely fantastic flowers . . . we ourselves remain, how little it matters! . . . Nature continues the process of her resurrections, whatever may happen to the animalcule Man."

The process of resurrection—the eternal Dance of Life! The joyous beat of the feet of children, the rhythmical swaying of the flowers in the breeze, the cosmic swing of the philosopher's thoughts, the continual resurgence of our human hopes. "To dance is at once both to worship and to pray"; for "the dance brings us so very near to God." Practically every religion, as Ellis points out, began with the ritual of a dance.

Ellis defines religion—or mysticism—as the "relationship of the Self to the Not-Self, of the individual to a Whole . . . in harmony or devotion or love." This definition, as he observes, is very similar to the definition of science—"the organisation of an intellectual relationship to the world . . . adequate to give us some degree of power over that world." And thus, both religion and science—the one through the heart, the other through the mind —enable us to find our individual place in the essential harmony of the universe. "It is only by the possession of an acquired or inborn temperament attuned to the temperament of Nature that a Faraday or an Edison"—or, Ellis might have added, an Isaiah or a St. Paul—"can achieve his results." It is the men of little knowledge and the men of little faith who find science and religion antagonistic to each other. But the greatest scientists and the greatest religious leaders have a wholesome respect for one another as the co-explorers of the mysterious way that leads to God. The seekers are the blood brothers of the seers.

And the Godward journey of the seekers and the seers, and of all the rest of us, pulsates with the rhythm of the dance, with the music of the moving stars and the beatings of the human heart.

But each of us must find the way for himself—often with great sacrifice and pain. "There is no other way of salvation. The Promised Land always lies on the other side of a Wilderness."

And so each of us may learn to become, in his own way, a courageous dancer over the painful road of life toward the divine; an expert in the art of harmonious living; a collaborator in the philosophy of beauty through the medium of love; "an artist whose work is his own life" woven into the pattern of universal life. A life of knowledge through suffering, of beauty through the sense of duty, of spiritual gain through material pain. "It is no doubt important to resist pain, but it is also important that it should be there to resist."

Be ready, therefore, to suffer as an actor in the pageantry of life, to mitigate the sufferings of others, and to help make the spectacle a more glorious vision for all of us to behold.

Above all, try to preserve your sense of humor. Learn to laugh at your own suffering. "Enjoy the spectacle while you will, whether comedy or tragedy, enter into the spirit of its manifold richness and beauty, yet take it not too seriously, even when you leave it and the curtains are drawn that conceal it forever from your eyes, grown weary at last."

This, in brief, is Ellis's formula for "the transcendent Adventure of Existence." Never despair at the ending of a life, of all life upon this little dancing platform known as the earth. It is but a tiny figure in the divine choreography of the universe. And out of the ashes of the old universe a new universe might well arise. For all life is continuous. Nothing ever ends. "Sunset is the promise of dawn."

V

Ellis advanced his philosophy not as a professional but as an amateur. "The world's greatest thinkers," he observed, "have often been amateurs. For high thinking is often the outcome of fine independent living; and for that, a professional chair offers no special opportunities."

Ellis never occupied a professional chair. He preferred to think and to live without any academic restraints. His philosophy was merely the story of life, the intellectual history of his own life, in the framework of the universe.

He lived serenely, bravely, unostentatiously. He didn't care for the splendors of society or the plaudits of the crowd. He spent much of his time answering letters upon all sorts of subjects from all sorts of people. But he had no secretary—he couldn't afford one. He delivered no lectures, and went to no parties. He didn't even have a dress suit.

After the death of his wife (in 1916), he lived alone. Yet he was no recluse. His greatest pleasure was a conversation with a friend; and his favorite topic, the happiness of contemplating the world's beauty without the burden of possessing its trinkets. See him striding with some genial companion along a country lane, in animated discussion about the miracle of a growing flower or a singing bird. Tall, ruddy, hatless, blue-eyed, white-bearded— a man, in the words of Edward Carpenter, with "a sort of grand air of Nature about him"—with the brooding of a prophet and the laughter of Pan.

And thus he went on brooding and laughing to the end, and pitying men, and prodding them to abandon their stupidities and to look up to the sublime. And accepting calmly the clamor of their jeers or their silent neglect. "The writer who brings a new revelation must be prepared to face the execration of the herd." But this need not disturb him in the least. "When the mob yell: 'Crucify him! Crucify him!' the artist, in whatever medium, hears a voice from Heaven: 'This is my beloved son!' "

CHAPTER XXVII

William James, Who Brought Philosophy into Business

[1842–1910]

IN 1898, William James was lecturing at the University of California. One morning he saw a coyote that had just been shot dead. He wrote about the incident in a letter to his children.

This letter is a summary of his own philosophy as an intrepid adventure against the sufferings of life. "The heroic little animal," wrote James, "lay on the ground [near the hotel], with his big furry ears, and his clean white teeth, and his jolly cheerful little body, but his brave little life was gone. It made me think how brave all these living things are. Here little coyote was, without any clothes or house or books or anything, with nothing but his own naked self to pay his way with, and risking his life so cheerfully—and losing it—just to see if he could pick up a meal near the hotel. He was doing his coyote-business like a hero, and you must do your boy-business, and I my man-business bravely too, or else we won't be worth as much as that little coyote."

"You must do your boy-business, and I my man-business, bravely." The philosophy of William James was a courageous performance of his duties in spite of physical pain. He was an invalid for the greater part of his life. For several years he thought of committing suicide. A man is not psychologically complete, he observed, unless he has at one time or another contemplated self-destruction. The complete man has stood "on the perilous edge," and has dared to turn back and *face* the Universe.

William James is a practical philosopher who teaches us how

to "hold ourselves erect and keep our hearts unshaken" in the perilous game of life.

II

Born at the Astor Hotel, in New York, James grew up in a city-life atmosphere—with its rough-and-tumble education for living in the midst of crowds. No rooted flower growing up in the country, but rather a restless bee flying inquisitively from place to place. As a child, he was full of mischief and rough games. To Henry, his younger brother who was rather on the quiet side, William said, "As for myself, I like to play with boys who curse and swear!"

He picked up his schooling—mere sips of the nectar of wisdom —in various countries of Europe. For his father, Henry James the elder, was fond of traveling. London, Paris, Bordeaux, Geneva, Bonn—a kaleidoscope of people, languages, experiences, customs, and thoughts. William James acquired a linguistic facility and a cosmopolitan outlook on life.

He was especially interested in the art galleries of Europe. For a time he thought of becoming an artist himself. He studied painting under William Morris Hunt, who was friendly enough to advise him that this was not his field.

So he laid down his brush and began to prepare himself for a scientific career. He entered the Lawrence Scientific School in Cambridge, Massachusetts—an eager, sociable, sickly young fellow of nineteen who looked forward to only a few years of activity in a world of pain. "One year study in chemistry, then spend one term at home . . . then a medical education, then five or six years with Agassiz (the great Harvard naturalist), then probably death . . ."

His college course, like his earlier education, was full of interruptions. He was in the Harvard Medical School when the Civil War broke out. Enlistment in the Army was out of the question for a man of his precarious health. But he joined Agassiz in a scientific expedition to Brazil, and almost died in Rio. When he returned to the United States, he suffered another breakdown and went to Europe in search of health. Added to his physical illness —a weak heart from childhood—was a mental depression which (as we have already noted) drove him almost to the verge of suicide. Unable to recover his health, he came back to Cambridge, where he managed to complete his medical course (in 1869).

But he never practiced medicine. He had neither the inclination nor the strength to take up the rugged life of a doctor. He just settled down to the "last years of an invalid's life." He spent only a few hours a day in reading—the doctors forbade any excessive strain to his ailing eyesight. And he was allowed to make only a few social calls—a terrible hardship to a man of his friendly disposition.

This was the unhappiest period of his life. He gives us a vivid picture of his mental depression at the time: "I went one evening into a dressing-room in the twilight . . . when suddenly there fell upon me . . . a horrible fear of my own existence. . . . There arose in my mind the image of an epileptic patient whom I had seen in the asylum, a black-haired youth with greenish skin, entirely idiotic, who used to sit all day on one of the benches . . . against the wall, with his knees drawn up against his chin, and the coarse gray undershirt, which was his only garment, drawn over them and inclosing his entire figure. . . . This image and my fear entered into a species of combination with each other. *That shape am I,* I felt, potentially. . . .

"I became a mass of quivering fear. . . . For months I was unable to go out into the dark alone. . . . The fear was so invasive and powerful that if I had not clung to scripture-texts like 'The eternal God is my refuge,' etc., 'Come unto me, all ye that labor and are heavy laden,' etc., I think I should have grown really insane."

The thing that finally saved him was Renouvier's essay on free will. The exercise of free will, Renouvier had declared, is "the [act of] sustaining a thought *because I choose to* when I might have other free thoughts." James found his reason for further living in this exercise of his free will—his willingness to believe that his salvation lay within himself. "My life shall [be built upon] doing and suffering and creating" in spite of suffering.

James had stopped drifting and was ready to swim. "I must *do* my man-business, bravely." Active daring, and not passive moping; courageous fighting, and not cowardly defeat. So, in spite of his physical illness, James threw himself fearlessly into the current of life.

III

He married and began to teach physiology at Harvard. From physiology he moved to psychology, and from psychology to philosophy.

But from the moment of his own salvation, he remained an active worker for the salvation of mankind. Philosophy, as he pointed out to his students again and again, is not a final answer to the One Great Problem of the Universe. It is rather a practical guide to the solution of the many problems that arise in our daily activities. He was not interested in founding a school or in winning disciples. His favorite quotation was from the prophet Ezekiel: "Son of man, stand upon thy feet, and I will speak unto thee."

And he spoke to the world in a colloquial style that everybody could understand. There was little of the professor about him. Slender, animated, and short, he looked like "a little boy with a beard." He was very popular with the students, who looked upon him as "a genuine guy." His sense of humor was greater than his scholastic dignity. One of his students at Radcliffe was the unconventional Gertrude Stein. On the day of the final examination she handed in a paper with no answers, but with the following explanatory statement:

"Dear Professor James: I really don't feel like taking my examination."

In due time, Professor James returned the paper with a note:

"Dear Miss Stein: I really don't feel like *correcting* your examination."

He gave Miss Stein a *B* for the course.

When asked to explain his unorthodox action, he said: "Miss Stein's mind is better than her style. Had she written out her answers, I would probably have given her a *D*."

William James, as an admiring student remarked, was a strange phenomenon at Harvard—"a professor who talked like a man." A "genuine guy" who taught "genuine stuff." He took philosophy out of the classroom and turned it into an adventure in living. Every one of us, he maintained, is a philosopher. Whether we know it or not, we are always called upon to make decisions about the things that concern us. And this necessity to make decisions—this instinctive groping toward wiser ideas and better actions—is what makes philosophers of us all.

In view of this fact, James developed a philosophy that would be helpful in the solution of our everyday perplexities. He called this philosophy *Pragmatism*—a name which is derived from the Greek word *pragma,* an act, and which means *a philosophy based upon practical action.* It is the philosophy of business. Not business in the narrow sense of exchanging goods in the market place, but in the far wider sense of honest understanding and fair dealing in all our human transactions.

The idea of Pragmatism is very simple. It submits our entire conduct to a single, concrete test: *Does it pay?* What is the *cash value* of anything we may desire to do?

But don't misunderstand this idea. By "cash value" James did not mean the return in dollars and cents. He meant rather the payment in terms of a healthier body, a stronger mind, a more courageous soul.

As we have already seen, it was out of his own need that James devised his practical philosophy. In the days of his depression, he had referred to himself as "a suffering vegetable, if there be such a thing." His philosophy of action was a means of self-defense—a challenge to his own soul to pull him out of his "vegetative" state.

At first, however, he approached his philosophy with a cautious mind. Practical American that he was, he wanted to prove its validity before he accepted it for himself.

And so he applied it to the various activities of his life, *and found that it worked*. His philosophy gave him a stronger incentive for living, a wiser tolerance toward others, a clearer outlook upon the universe, wider horizons, deeper satisfactions, greater peace. He was then ready to declare his philosophy to the world. "If it has been helpful to me, the chances are it will be helpful to you, too."

Suppose, then, we test this philosophy in the light of our own experience. How can Pragmatism help us in our work, our attitude toward our family, our belief (or disbelief) in God? Finally, what answer can this philosophy give us to the most vital of all questions: Is life worth living?

First, let us consider Pragmatism in relation to our work. James cautions us not to overemphasize the importance of "that bitch goddess, success." Don't aim at success, he tells us, to the exclusion of everything else. Whether you are a worker or an employer, the thing that pays best is friendly co-operation rather than competitive aggressiveness. "The bigger we grow, the hollower, the more brutal we become. . . . So I am against all big successes and big results, and in favor of underdogs always."

Don't hunger after too much money for yourself at the expense of your neighbors. It doesn't pay. "Of what good is profit to me if it means loss to my fellow men?" Whatever your occupation, you are laboring not only for yourself but for society. And you will find your greatest happiness in a society of mutual helpfulness and honesty and trust. In such a society—which it is your business to help create—your activity will receive the highest wages in the world. The currency of a contented mind.

The Pragmatism of the office and the shop is closely allied to the Pragmatism of the home. Said James: "My philosophy has taught me to be quieter with my home lot." He was a sociable soul, but he found his deepest contentment in the family circle. There is *cash value* in a harmonious family—the accumulated capital of unstinted love. "Human life," writes Lewis Mumford, echoing the philosophy of William James, "is a constant march upward." And another Pragmatist, Dean Inge, reminds us: "The road of ascent is by personal affection."

We have little to fear, declared James, so long as we can keep our affections—so long as we maintain a home to play *in,* and a family to play *with.* This is the meaning of Pragmatism as applied to our family life. The family satisfies our universal hunger for "the dear togetherness." In mutual service, every member of the ideal family arrives at its fullest spiritual growth. He finds that *it pays* to make our home cheerful with the brightness of love.

In his pragmatic idea of family relationships, James widened the home to the boundaries of the world. The world is our home, and all its inhabitants are the members of our family. The most profitable activity in the world is the friendly exchange of affection and good will among men.

And this brings us to the idea of Pragmatism as applied to religion. The perfect religion would be that which could unite all men into a family worship of one God.

At present we belong to different religions because we have different conceptions of God. No man, in our imperfect state of knowledge, can have a monopoly of *the* truth. Each of us is a spectator looking upon the universe from a different point of view. And no one has the right to assume that his is the only point of view which is infallible. "Neither the whole of truth nor the whole of goodness is revealed to any single observer, though each observer gains a partial superiority of insight from the peculiar position in which he stands."

Hence, instead of fighting about our different points of view, we ought to combine them into a comprehensive vision of the co-partnership of man under the guidance of God. But in our everyday life, each man's faith, each man's church, each man's God is for him true if it enables him to cope with his legitimate daily problems.

Just what God is, we shall perhaps never know. Our idea as to the nature of God, said James, is like the idea of an animal as to the nature of man. But let us not be dismayed on that account. In a letter to his daughter about a dog who was his housemate he wrote: "He doesn't understand who or what I am. But he feels I am his friend. His tail keeps wagging all the time, and he makes on me the impression of an angel hid in a cloud. He longs to do good."

You and I, too, are like angels hid in a cloud. We are the house pets of God. However obscure the mists that surround you, be confident of one thing: If you believe in God, this belief in itself will make God a reality in your life. The *pragmatic value* of your religion, therefore, is the spiritual *cash value* of your reliance upon a friendly moral power greater than your own.

It is a "good investment" to believe in God. It puts a definite purpose into our life. For it provides us with a powerful guide toward our nobler aspirations.

But if we expect God to be on *our* side, we must be on *God's* side. And thus we come to the most important aspect of James's pragmatic philosophy.

Is life worth living? "It depends upon the *liver,*" writes James with one of his habitual flashes of humor.

But then he goes on to give an inspiring answer to this question. Our life is decidedly worth while, he declares, if we plan to live *with God's help and as God's helpers.* James is neither a pessimist nor an optimist. He is a meliorist—a philosopher who doesn't blink his eyes at the evils of the world but who believes that we can, if we will, make the world better.

For the world we live in is not yet finished. There is much important work to be done before it is complete. And God is dependent upon us to be His faithful employees in this work—just as we are dependent upon Him to be our friendly Employer.

Do a good job, therefore, as a co-worker with God. Help to eliminate the imperfections in the unfinished structure of the world, and try to make it a more secure and more beautiful place to live in.

Your life, then, is an adventure in sweeping away the old structures and building the new. "It is a real adventure, with

real danger. . . . Yet we may win through if each several agent
does his own level best. . . . Will you join the procession? Will
you trust yourself and trust other agents enough to face the risk?"

The philosophy of Pragmatism, in short, is a call to your individual effort in the progressive construction of a better world. In
trying to make the world better, you can make your own life
happier.

This, observes James, is not an absolute promise; but it *is* a
definite possibility. The important thing, after all, is not the glory
of the conqueror but the courage of the fighter. Especially when
the fight is against odds. *And there is always the chance of victory.*
William James brings out this point in a stirring epitaph translated from the Greek:

> *A shipwrecked sailor, buried on this coast,*
> *Bids you set sail.*
> *Full many a gallant bark, when we were lost,*
> *Outrode the gale.*

So don't sit back because others have failed. Trim your sail to
the wind, and keep adventuring on!

IV

James kept "adventuring on" throughout his life. He lived
always in the current of practical affairs. He threw himself into
many activities to improve the political, social, and economic
conditions of the world. He worked not only for abstract causes
but for individual men. His own courage against ill-health was
a spark that fired others into an equal courage. All of us, he
declared, have a reserve energy which many of us never use. Take
advantage of this reserve power and you will be amazed to discover your capability for solving your own problems. *Stand upon
your own feet.* And face whatever dangers may confront you.
"Take life strivingly." Fight against your own afflictions and the
abominations of the world.

True to his own philosophy, James fought against the persecution of Dreyfus, the injustices of the sweatshop, the encroachments of imperialism, and the insanities of war.

He hated war, yet he realized that our human instinct for fighting is perhaps ineradicable. He therefore advocated the channeling of this instinct into a "war against nature." Let every young man, he said, enlist for two years in a fighting army—not for killing but for building. Let us clear the forests, drain the marshes, irrigate the wastelands, span the rivers, and conquer the floods. And let us devote our energies and our funds, so tragically wasted in killing, to the more humane adventure of healing. Let us unite in building a friendlier, happier, and healthier human race.

His own health, always precarious, finally gave out. In 1907 he resigned from Harvard. To the outside world he still presented the lithe, erect little figure of the smiling philosopher. But his friends knew that he was nearing the end. A final trip to Europe, and he came back just in time to die.

He left the notes for a book that he didn't live to write. The tentative title of the book was *The Psychology of Jingoism.*

To the very end a fighting crusader for peace!

CHAPTER XXVIII

Kropotkin's Progress from Riches to Rags

[1842–1921]

LET US glance at the pictures of two boys in the nineteenth century.

First Picture: A little Russian prince with curly hair and up-tilted nose is presented to Czar Nicholas of Russia (1849). The immense ballroom of the palace is filled with guests who are paying their respects to the emperor as he looks down upon them from an elevated platform. One of the chamberlains, in a gold-embroidered uniform, has just raised the little prince from the floor and placed him at the emperor's feet.

"So you are Peter Kropotkin?" asks the emperor in a patronizing voice.

"Yes, Your Majesty," the child manages to blurt out.

"And how would you like to live in the palace?"

"V-very much, Your Majesty."

"All right, then, I shall make you my page." He beckons to Peter to come close to him. "When you are a good boy, I shall treat you like this," and he passes his big hand over Peter's face downward. "But when you are naughty, I shall treat you like that," and he passes his hand upward, rubbing the child's nose none too gently with his fingers.

The tears come into Peter's eyes as he makes a mental note to himself: It will go hard with me if ever I disobey the czar.

Second Picture: A French peasant boy is about to be executed for his participation in the uprising of the Commune (1871). As the soldiers get ready to shoot, the boy asks the officer's permission to hand his silver watch to his mother, who lives close by. The officer, yielding to an impulse of pity, allows the boy to go, probably in the hope that he will never return. But fifteen minutes later, the boy is back. Taking his place amidst the corpses of the executed men, he tells the officer: "I am ready." Twelve bullets put an end to his young life.

Splendor and tyranny on the one hand, misery and courage on the other. Such were the contrasts that influenced the philosophy of Kropotkin and molded the adventure of his life. He started as a prince, spent much of his time in prison, and ended his days in poverty. And, in the course of this strange adventure, he gave a new code of ethics to the world.

II

One of Kropotkin's earliest memories was that of a celebration in honor of his father, who had just received a medal for the rescue of a child from a burning house.

"But weren't you afraid to rush into the flames?" asked Peter.

"It wasn't I who did it, Peter. It was my footman, Frol."

"Then why was the medal given to *you?*"

"Because it was *my servant* who displayed the courage."

A funny world, thought Peter. When the servant does something noble, it's the master who gets the praise.

And when the master does something stupid, Peter observed, it's the servant who gets the blame. His father owned twelve hundred serfs; and though not a bad man by the standards of the time, he treated them unmercifully when anything went wrong. One day, he struck Frol for an apparent shortage in the supply of hay. "But Your Highness," Frol kept insisting, "you must have made a mistake."

The prince repeated his calculations, and this time it appeared that there was more hay in the barn than there ought to be.

"You son of Ham," he shouted. "You've been stinting on the rations for the horses!" And he sent Frol to the police station with a note that he be given "a hundred lashes with the birch rod" for his "insubordination."

The flogging of the serfs, writes Peter Kropotkin, "was a regular part of the duties of the police and of the fire brigade."

And when the serfs were freed (1861) by a decree of the czar, their condition became even more intolerable. For they had to recompense their former masters at a price that was far beyond their capacity to pay. And thus they now became enslaved to the soil. Compelled to sell most of their produce in order to meet their redemption taxes, many of them starved to death. And some of the survivors who fell behind in their payments were sent off to Siberia to *freeze* to death.

It was in this political atmosphere that Kropotkin grew to early manhood. "I have at last," he wrote in a letter to his brother Alexander, "found a purpose in life—to help the downtrodden and ill-treated stepchildren of the world." He had just finished his education at a military school. He was offered an assignment of his own choice—the artillery, the Cossacks, the cavalry, the emperor's body guard—he could enter whatever branch of service he preferred. But, to the astonishment of his superiors, he selected the "graveyard" of every young officer's hopes. "I want to be sent to the garrison in Siberia."

For here, he thought, he would find a field for the practical application of his idea—to mitigate the sufferings and to advance the happiness of his fellow men.

And so, amidst the derision of his classmates, he put on the drab Siberian uniform—gray trousers, black blouse, and doeskin cap—and went off to battle against the rigors of the wilderness and the cruelty of man.

III

He spent five years in Siberia—"a time of genuine education," as he put it, "in life and human character." Here he found democracy and despotism living side by side. The municipal government of the townships consisted of citizens who were "elected by all the population, as freely as they might have been elected in the United States." But over and above the municipal government towered the military government, responsible only to the czar.

And many of the military governors exercised their power with the utmost brutality. They flogged civilians and soldiers to death under the least provocation. Once, after the beating of a woman —which, even in Siberia, was considered illegal—Kropotkin took it upon himself to make an investigation with a view to sending a report to the czar. He found his investigation no easy task. The peasants remembered an old Russian saying: "God and the czar are very far, while your chief is your next-door neighbor." Even the woman who had been flogged was afraid at first to sign a written statement. Finally, however, Kropotkin succeeded in getting sufficient evidence to have the governor dismissed.

But this was not the end of the story. Several months later, Kropotkin learned that the governor had been "kicked upstairs" —to a higher post at a bigger salary. "Finally," writes Kropotkin, "the governor returned to St. Petersburg a rich man. And he contributed to the reactionary press a number of articles full, as one might expect, of high patriotic spirit."

Disgusted with this sort of despotism, Kropotkin joined a group of nihilists who tried to bring about a "better world." The word *nihilist,* as Kropotkin points out, has been greatly misunderstood. It is not to be confused with *terrorist.* Kropotkin himself was one of the gentlest of men. And many of the early nihilists had much in common with the early Quakers. They were soldiers without a sword—reformers who worked for the peaceful regeneration of the human heart, men like Kropotkin and Turgenev who refused to bow to superstitions, prejudices, and customs which their own reason could not justify.

Kropotkin was determined to seek out the truth that had been thrust aside by the conventional lies of society. He was a philosopher undazzled by the splendor of the life into which he had been born. And he sensed the secret of the true life, the good life, in "the principle of Man's communion with Nature." Part of his job in Siberia was to explore the wilderness, to sail down the Siberian rivers in order to find new outlets from the interior to the sea, and to break new paths over the mountains in order to link the trade of Siberia, through Manchuria, with the rest of the Asiatic world. His official job in the Army was that of exploring geographer. He was a nineteenth-century Marco Polo with the mind of a philosopher and the soul of a poet. And as a result of his adventures through the heart of Nature—often at the risk of his life—he arrived at an instinctive idea which at first he was able to grasp only in a vague and general way: "The poetry of Nature is in harmony with the aspirations of Man."

But before he could define the idea with greater clarity, he needed more study, more experience, more adventures into the miseries of the world and the mysteries of life.

IV

After five years in Siberia, he resigned from the Army and returned to St. Petersburg. He refused an offer to become the Secretary of the Russian Geographic Society. He felt that he had more important work to do. "What right had I to the joys of discovering new horizons for geology and geography? What was the use of writing new books for the people when they needed more bread? Whatsoever money I should spend for the pleasure of my studies must needs be taken from the mouths of those who grew the wheat for others and had not bread enough for their own children." Kropotkin felt he had no right to the "luxury" of further explorations. "The peasant needs me to live with him, to help him along to a freer and easier life."

So he gave up his lucrative position and his princely rank—he was disinherited when he became a "rebel"—and joined the underprivileged masses of mankind. *V'narod*—To the masses— this became the motto of Kropotkin and of many other young nobles who had given up their worldly possessions for the people's sake.

In order to have greater freedom for his action, he went to live for a time in Switzerland. He became interested in a movement designed to bring about "an international brotherhood of workers, a transformation of the weapons of war into the tools of peace, and a federation of all men into a United States of Mankind."

But this complete transfiguration of society was too hazy a dream in the nineteenth century. Kropotkin settled down to a more concrete job—the education of the masses through lectures, pamphlets, and magazines. The support for all this work had to come out of the poverty of the people themselves. As may well be imagined, Kropotkin was often obliged to go without food. But he always managed to bring out his articles on time. "No matter what happens, the education of the masses must go on."

And so, too, must his own education go on. He became a profound student of philosophy. He read the works of the great thinkers, and he subjected their theories to the test of life as he saw it in the raw. And as a result of his testing, he became more and more convinced that there was an indestructible bond between the pattern of Nature and the happiness of man.

But what was the secret of this bond? Just how did it operate? As yet, Kropotkin didn't quite know the answer to this question.

In the meantime, there was further concrete work to be done. And danger to be courted in the doing of this work. His nihilism had developed into *anarchism*—another word which, Kropotkin insisted, has been grossly misunderstood. The anarchism or no-government theory of Proudhon, as interpreted by Kropotkin, was based upon the assumption that all men are naturally good and that it is only the interference of government, or coercion, which makes them bad. And therefore it is our business, maintained Kropotkin, to bring about the abolition of government—not through the violence of revolution, but through the peaceful method of evolution. Through the gradual enlightenment of the governors and the governed alike.

Educate mankind to the truth that the peace of a friendly co-operation is better than the war of a hostile competition. After a number of years as a voluntary exile—in Switzerland and in France—Kropotkin returned to St. Petersburg. For he was still interested in his scientific as well as in his sociological work. He began to write a book about his geographical discoveries. And once again the leading scientists of his country offered him a post of the highest distinction. They nominated him for the presidency of the Geographic Society.

As he was returning home after the nomination, unable to decide as to whether or not to accept the honor, the government decided for him. A gendarme stopped his cab. "Prince Kropotkin, you are under arrest!"

V

After a perfunctory examination, he was taken to the prison of St. Peter and St. Paul—an inferno of torture named, ironically, after two of the Apostles of joy. "As they drove me across the [Neva] river, I admired the beautiful scenery. . . . The sun was going down. Thick gray clouds were hanging in the west . . . while light clouds floated over my head, showing here and there patches of blue sky. Then the carriage turned to the left and en-tered a dark passage, the gate of the prison. . . . I had to take off all my clothes, even a silk undergarment, and to put on the prison-uniform—a green flannel dressing-gown, immense woolen stockings of an incredible thickness, and boat-shaped yellow slip-pers so big that I could hardly keep them on my feet when I tried to walk. . . . Then I was taken to a musty cell, a heavy oak-door was shut behind me, a key turned in the lock, and I was alone in the night."

They left him in almost complete silence for two years. The guards were ordered not to speak to him when they brought him his meals. But he did hear, from a cell right under his feet, the growing sounds of insanity. One of the prisoners was slowly being driven mad.

His own health broke down in the dampness of his cell. They admitted him to the prison hospital and allowed him to take an occasional walk in the courtyard. And one day, as a load of firewood was being delivered to the prison through the open gate, Kropotkin made his escape.

They searched for him in every likely place—but in vain, and for a very good reason. He was enjoying a hearty dinner—in elegant clothes provided by his friends and with his long beard shaved off—in the most *unlikely* of all places for an escaped prisoner. The Donon—St. Petersburg's most fashionable restaurant. "No one," his friends had told him, "will look for you at Donon." And they were right.

The next day he escaped, by way of Sweden, to England. "Prince Kropotkin," reported the gendarmes, "has disappeared."

"Nevertheless," declared the czar, "he *must* be found!" And he sent spies into every European city to recapture or to kill the "dangerous" fugitive.

But for several years Kropotkin managed to elude them and continued, under the assumed name of Levashoff, to help the "downtrodden and oppressed."

VI

"Enlighten the people so that their salvation must come from themselves." This idea had become his guiding principle. "I saw a new form of society . . . germinating in the civilized nations . . . a society of equals, who will not be compelled to sell their hands and brains . . . in a haphazard way, but who will be able to apply their knowledge and capacities to production, in an organism so constructed as to combine all the efforts for procuring the greatest sum possible of well-being for all, *while full, free scope will be left for every individual initiative.* . . . No need of government will be felt, because . . . the causes of conflict being reduced in number, those conflicts which may still arise can be submitted to arbitration."

Arbitration by, and in the interests of, all the parties concerned. And thus, Kropotkin's anarchism, or no-government, was really *self-government*—a government of the people, by the people, and for the people. Kropotkin was no violent revolutionist. He was merely a kindly lover of all mankind.

And it was this universal love that finally enabled Kropotkin to crystallize his own philosophy. *Mutual Aid.*

He got the idea of mutual aid, strangely enough, from Darwin's theory of the struggle for existence. Helpfulness, as opposed to ruthlessness. For, as Kropotkin has pointed out and as many scientists have failed to observe, *mutual aid* is as important a law of Nature as *mutual strife*. The *struggle* for existence applies only to the members of *different* species. Among the members of the *same* species, there is a spirit of *co-operation* for existence. Darwin himself, Kropotkin reminds us, has declared that *the survival of the fittest* means *the survival of those who are best able to work together for their mutual protection.*

This is the foundation upon which Kropotkin built his ethical philosophy. "The aspirations of mankind are at one with the laws of Nature." The progressive evolution of the human species is based not upon the aggressiveness of the individual, but upon the interdependence of society.

Kropotkin first expressed this idea in his *Mutual Aid: a Factor in Evolution*. He developed the idea further in his *Ethics*—a book which, unfortunately, he was unable to finish before he died. The main features of his theory, however, are adequately outlined in the two books. Our human code of ethics, declared Kropotkin, is based upon the principle of mutual protection—an inheritance we have received from the lower animals. For there is a "natural law of morality" that governs the evolution of man.

And thus Kropotkin tries to reduce ethics to a science. The Golden Rule—to treat others as we want them to treat us—is not only the commandment of God, but the law of Nature for the preservation of the human race.

And this law, Kropotkin points out, applies not only to human beings but to the lower animals as well. There is mutuality among beasts and birds as well as among men. This instinct is universal. Nature has given it to us for the preservation of our species. Those who exercise the feeling of mutuality survive; those who fail to exercise it die out.

To prove his point, Kropotkin cites numerous instances of mutual aid among lower animals as well as among savage tribes. Here are just a few examples:

"Captain Stansbury, on a trip to Utah, noticed how a blind pelican was fed by other pelicans—on fish brought a distance of thirty miles."

"Monkeys have been observed to pick thorns and brambles from one another's fur," to protect the weaker members of their "society" against the cold weather and their common enemies, and to share their food after a foraging expedition "organized for the benefit of all."

Even among the predatory animals, there is one general rule: *they never kill a member of their own group.*

Herds of deer or of goats, when engaged in grazing, select a number of sentries to signal the approach of a beast of prey. And, in the event of an attack, the males and the females encircle their young and protect them, if necessary, with their lives.

"Among the birds, too, we note the same instinct of mutual protection." Kropotkin cites the story told by Eckermann, the German zoologist, about a fledgling bird which fell out of the nest after Eckermann had shot its mother. The fledgling was at once picked up by a bird of another species and returned to its nest. Similar examples of a social instinct among birds, observes Kropotkin, have been reported by a number of other zoologists.

"Mutual aid, therefore, is the predominant fact of Nature. . . . It represents the best weapon in the great struggle for life. . . . Therefore, taken as a whole, Nature is by no means an illustration of the triumph of physical force. . . . It seems, on the contrary, that species decidedly weak, such as the ant, the bee, the pigeon, the duck, the marmot, the deer and the gazelle, having no protective armor, no strong beak or fang for self-defense . . . nevertheless succeed best in the struggle for life." It is their "instinct for sociality," maintains Kropotkin, that enables them to displace their much more powerful competitors and enemies.

In union there is strength—even among the lower animals. And in this "constant, everpresent identification of the unit with the whole lies the origin of all ethics."

And thus Kropotkin bases his ethics upon the theory of evolution. When man emerged from the lower animals, he guided his conduct by the example of the gregarious creatures he saw around him. He adapted himself to the supreme law of survival—*social interdependence*. He learned, little by little, that the individual could best serve himself by serving others. He discovered that the strongest shield for the protection of the individual is not his *aggressiveness against,* but his *affection for,* other individuals. This instinct for mutual affection—Kropotkin calls it "the feeling of sociality"—is our human inheritance from our pre-human ancestors. And it is "the origin of all ethical conceptions and all the subsequent evolution of morality."

This sense of morality, developed to the highest degree, has come to be known as *Justice,* or *Equity.* The word *equity,* which is allied to *equality,* means *fairness among equals.* Whether or not we admit it, declares Kropotkin, we feel instinctively that all men are equal. Religion teaches this fact, and science proves it. Injustice, iniquity, inequality—that is, individual aggressiveness at the expense of others—leads to contention and hatred and death. But justice, equity, equality—that is, social co-operation for the common good—leads to harmony and compassion and life.

When two men quarrel, therefore, there is a disturbance in their equality as prescribed by the natural law of survival. There is an effort, on the part of one and perhaps of both, to assume an unequal advantage over the other. And then justice must step in to "re-establish the disturbed equality."

This, explained Kropotkin, is the principal lesson of evolution. *The keynote for human survival is interdependence.* The world is not merely a battlefield in which the weak are exterminated by the strong, the sluggish by the swift, the simple by the cunning, and the timid by the bold. It is also a school for progress, a classroom for socialization, a platform for teaching the principles of life through the practice of intelligence, companionship, beneficence, sympathy, and love. The process of evolution instructs us not only how to *live,* but how to *live together.* Kropotkin saw the story of the human race as "the evolution of the inherent tendency of man to organize his life on the basis of mutual service—from the clan to the tribe, from the tribe to the nation, from the nation to the united nations of the world." For man is gradually learning to understand not only the identical direction of all human aims, but the natural identity of all human life.

VII

This was the ideal to which Kropotkin had consecrated his own life—"to harmonize the aspirations of man with the laws of Nature." But to the despots of Europe he was a man to be hounded as a dangerous rebel. And finally their spies caught up with him in France. Another arrest, and another prison term. "One who casts his lot with the advance guard must be prepared to spend a good part of his life in prison."

And then, freedom for Kropotkin and, as he vainly hoped, for all the Russians. The Communist Revolution. He returned to his native city after an exile of forty years—only to discover that his people had replaced one form of despotism with another form of despotism. He observed that the dictatorial government of Russia was "morally unstable . . . a mere head without a heart." The rulers had proclaimed the equality of all men, and reduced them to the equal helplessness of slaves. The dictator was only another czar under a different name. New slogans, new promises, a new aristocracy of the slums, but the same old injustice, the same oppression, the same individual lust for power at the expense of the social good.

Saddened by the events, Kropotkin retired to a village not far

from Moscow. Here he remained to the end of his life (1921)—
working on his *Ethics,* copying it by himself, for he couldn't
afford a secretary, subsisting on the poorest fare, and delivering
his final testament to the world: "Without equity there is no
justice, and without justice there is no peace."

CHAPTER XXIX

Croce—a Philosopher in an Earthquake

[1866–1952]

IN 1883 a wealthy Neapolitan landowner, Signore Croce, was enjoying his vacation with his family on the island of Ischia. They were caught in an earthquake which killed the signore and his wife and their only daughter. Their two sons, however, were rescued after they had remained buried in the debris for over twelve hours.

One of the two boys who so narrowly escaped death was the seventeen-year-old Benedetto. The catastrophe had broken his bones and left his health shattered for many years. But it strengthened his mind. The long convalescence gave him time to think about the physical and spiritual earthquakes that so dramatically interrupt the ordinary business of life.

II

Benedetto Croce's own life was destined to be filled with spiritual earthquakes and political storms. He was born (1866) in the midst of a revolutionary upheaval. It was the restless age of Mazzini, Garibaldi, and Cavour. Naples had overthrown the monarchy, Italy had liberated itself from the grip of Austria, the state had cast off the excessive power of the Church, and the people everywhere were looking forward to a united Italy, a united world. While the Croces were not immediately involved in the upheaval, their patriotic cousins, the Spaventas, were up to the hilt in the fight. And it was in the house of one of the Spaventas that Benedetto came to live when his parents were killed in the earthquake.

At this time Benedetto was described as a "studious and pugnacious" lad. He was not, however, so keen for a physical brawl as for a mental duel. He had given up his belief in an omnipotent God; and his readiness to assert his disbelief kept him out of tune with the world. "These were the saddest and darkest years, the only ones in which often, as I laid my head on the pillow, I keenly desired never to wake again."

He entered the University of Rome, but withdrew (in 1886) without a degree. For a time, indeed, he withdrew from the entire world—studying, brooding, waiting for something to turn up.

And something did turn up. A visit to the Spaventas from one of Croce's old professors, Labriola. In the course of the conversation, Labriola told his hosts about a book he was preparing on Karl Marx. "I asked him for the manuscript," writes Croce, "and I read it. My mind was fired. . . . The flame of this new enthusiasm burned away my abstract moralism, and I came to believe that the course of history has the right to drag along and to crush individuals . . . in the service of humanity redeemed by labor."

But "that political enthusiasm, that faith, did not last." Croce became revolted at the idea of "killing a man in order to set him free." Violent revolution was too much like an earthquake. It temporarily readjusted the surface of the earth, but it left too much suffering in its wake. The philosophy of Karl Marx was an elaborate system of destruction. What Croce wanted was a system that would promise to save, instead of threatening to destroy, the human race.

And so he decided to elaborate a philosophy of his own. It was toward the turn of the century—time for a complete survey of human thought, aspiration, and hope.

This survey, Croce believed, must be made by a man who was in the swim of things. No ivory-tower philosopher, protected against the tempests of life, would understand the shipwrecks and the heartbreaks and the courage of mankind. Croce was anxious to throw himself into the midst of the storm, to study the struggles of humanity from personal observation and at close range.

He began with the publication of a new magazine—*La Critica*. From the very outset, he made it the arsenal for a battle of ideas against the warriors of the world. "We intend to fight for a definite order of life," he wrote in the first issue, "a general reawakening of the philosophic spirit . . . unhappily interrupted after the Italian Revolution of 1860."

His associate in this venture toward sanity in an insane world was another young philosopher, Giovanni Gentile—an intellectual firebrand who, as Croce was to learn later on, was endowed with more heat than light.

For the present, however, Croce and Gentile lashed out against the shams and the oppressions of the world. Croce selected as his principal target the arrogant militancy of such writers as Gabriele D'Annunzio and other superpatriots who were inciting their countrymen to new and destructive wars.

Then came the tragedy of World War I—when Italy, along with many other countries, was plunged into a whirlpool of blood. But after the war, there was an interval of sobering reflection. A man of peace—the sedate and moderate Giolitti—was called to the helm of the Italian Government. He selected Croce (in 1920) as his minister of education; and the philosopher hoped at last to bring about a practical regeneration in human thought.

But his hope was short-lived. It was only two years later that Mussolini seized the government. And the man whom the dictator named as the new minister of education was none other than Croce's former co-editor, Giovanni Gentile.

Croce had parted company with Gentile even before the war of 1914. Foreseeing the coming crisis and the danger of Italy's involvement in the struggle, he had raised his voice in a passionate plea for peace. But Gentile had joined the military party. At last he, too, had become infected with the insanity against which he had fought in his earlier days. He looked upon the war as a "holy crusade." And later on, when the madness of militarism gave rise to the lawlessness of Fascism, Gentile joined the Fascists as the architects of a "new order of life." Croce found himself drifting farther and farther away from the man who had once served as his fellow crusader for peace.

The final breach came when Gentile supplanted him as minister of education under the terrorism of Mussolini. It was not his personal jealousy, but the public need, that motivated Croce's bitterness at this time. "It is sad enough to misgovern the old without the added evil of misguiding the young."

In his attack against Fascism, Croce braved not only the anger of Gentile but the enmity of Mussolini himself. Yet the dictator left him severely alone. Croce was too popular a man to be put out of the way. As a lame excuse for his failure to "liquidate" the philosopher, Mussolini pretended that he knew nothing about him. "I have never read a page of Croce." Whereupon Croce retorted that Mussolini had often quoted him. "But, of course, Mussolini may be telling the truth. For his speeches are not his own; they are written for him by others."

Even though Mussolini left the philosopher alone, some of the other Fascist leaders made it their business to torment him. They broke into his library and destroyed his books and his manuscripts. They kept him a virtual prisoner in his home, the Palazzo Filomarino in Naples. And anybody who dared to visit him was branded as an enemy of the state.

III

But "truth, crushed to earth, will rise again." Croce continued with his self-appointed task to liberalize the thinking of the world. His name was banned from public mention, but his ideas managed somehow to seep into the public mind. Quietly, fearlessly, persistently, "the perfect employe of himself" kept pouring out book after book on history, literature, philosophy, science, and art. Blueprints for the rebuilding of society after an earthquake. He who had lain at the point of death under the ruins of Ischia had nothing to fear from the catastrophes of Nature or the passions of men. When he passed through the streets of Naples, people whispered to one another—they dared not say it aloud—"There goes the hero who defies the Duce."

It was the defiance of a man who, in the midst of all ugliness and evil, saw beauty and goodness at the heart of things. And he developed this fundamental idea—the beauty of goodness, the goodness of beauty—in a series of more than fifty books.

Yet he refused to refer to his philosophy as a systematic unit. He called it merely a loose collection of random observations. Let us look at some of these rare flowers of wisdom growing out of an agitated soul:

In his first book—*The Materialism of Karl Marx*—he pointed out that the Marxist theory of economics is neither good philosophy nor good science. The field of economics is not a battleground between the classes and the masses, capital and labor, the seller and the buyer, the rich and the poor. It is much more important than that. Economics is a theory of human values—the very substance and vitality of life.

Indeed, Croce substituted the word *vitality* for *economics*. The transaction between buyer and seller is an exchange of goods and good will. It involves the universal choice between egoism and altruism, dishonesty and honesty, suspicion and trust. The scientific principle of economics, therefore, is co-extensive with the vital philosophical problem of the good, the beautiful, the true. The economic adjustment of society will come about not through a violent struggle between class and class, but through a trustful understanding between man and man.

And thus Croce subordinated the material to the spiritual values of life. He made Utility the servant of Beauty. He translated the old Platonic idea of justice into a modern concept of economic and social harmony.

In Croce's philosophy, *economics* is to be regarded as a branch of *aesthetics*—the science of art—and of *ethics*—the study of morals.

Croce is perhaps at his best in his book entitled *Aesthetic*. Art, he believes, is the science of sciences. The other sciences—like chemistry, physics, and mathematics, for example—take us away from individual facts to universal abstractions. But art brings us back from universal abstractions to concrete persons, definite objects, and individual facts. (It would be interesting to know what Croce would have said about the "science" of the so-called ultra-modern artists, with their incongruous mishmash of tendentious abstractions that are neither fish nor flesh nor red herring.)

The creation of art, declared Croce, is the ability to produce images. "Art is the product of the imagination surveying the world. It does not qualify objects, it does not define them; it feels and presents them—nothing more." The basis of all thought is imagination; hence the basis of all science is art. Leonardo, perhaps the greatest artist-scientist in history, was aware of this fact. We must first imagine, he said, before we can think or act. "The minds of men of genius are most active in invention when they are doing the least external work." They re-create the world in the workshop of their imagination before they reproduce it in words and figures and colors and tones. Michelangelo, too, was aware of this idea. "One paints with the brain before he can paint with the hands."

Croce incorporated this doctrine into the very essence of his philosophy. "When we have mastered the internal word, when we have vividly and clearly conceived a painting or a statue, when we have found a musical theme, expression is born and is complete. Nothing more is needed. If we open our mouth, and speak or sing . . . if our hands strike the keyboard of the pianoforte, if we take up pencil or chisel or brush . . . what we are doing then is to execute laboriously and outwardly what we have already executed briefly and rapidly within."

As for those of us who have not the talent to create, we can cultivate the ability to understand—"to bring ourselves into harmony with the music of the world." In our financial transactions as well as in our artistic perceptions, we must learn to form the correct images of our individual relationship to our fellow men. Economic justice and aesthetic beauty are the result not only of the artist's genius, but of the layman's ability to conceive and to express the correct images of a consistent world.

A world consistent with economic justice, aesthetic beauty, and an ethical spirit of fair play. The important thing in life is not merely to conceive the right image, but to perform the right act. "It is only the spiritual act that can be regarded as beautiful, logical, useful and good." Though he frequently criticized the established religions of the day, Croce was at bottom a man of the deepest religious faith.

He expressed this faith most clearly in his essay, *Why We Cannot But Call Ourselves Christians*. Christianity, he observed, "has been the greatest revolution in history." For it has inspired humanity to a new way of life—from justice to mercy, from mercy to love. Christianity represents the spiritual aspect of democracy, for it emphasizes the equal dignity of all men.

It is true that as the Christian faith has advanced, "it has clothed itself in mummeries and myths." Yet, in spite of all this, it has retained its original truth. We must appreciate it for the purity it has preserved instead of blaming it for the infections to which it has succumbed. "We read Homer," he said, "not for his errors but for his truths."

And the true value of Christianity, of any great religion, is that it preserves a center of stability in the vortex of our human passions. Let us not criticize it for its rituals and its institutions. Even science and philosophy are not free of them. The system of laws and sacraments developed by the Church has helped to educate barbarian nations, to counteract the pessimistic philosophy of the Orient, and to emphasize the superiority of moral principles to political expediency.

Now and then, to be sure, corruption has crept into the Church —the Protestant as well as the Catholic. But the Church has always managed to get rid of its corruptions. And it lives on because it has a vital function in life. "An institution dies not for its incidental defects, but because it fails to satisfy a universal need."

And thus the churchmen sustain the order of the past, while the philosophers and the scientists are trying to devise a better order for the future. Don't destroy the old house before you have finished the new. "None can say whether another revelation or religion, of equal or higher rank, will light upon humanity in a future of which we now discern no glimmer." But unless and until such a revelation arrives, "we must live within the limits of Christianity."

So let there be an understanding between the guardians of order and the champions of progress. Instead of fighting against one another, let them unite as co-equal actors in the drama of life —supporting one another, giving one another their proper cue, and each retiring graciously into the wings when the turn comes for the other to hold the stage.

This harmony between order and progress, religion and philosophy, the stability of tradition and the mobility of transition— all this is but a part of the universal harmony that Croce hoped to see in the ethical relationship between man and man. Croce wrote a whole series of ethical essays based upon his personal observations of life. Adjust yourself to the logical world of reality, and don't live in an illogical world of fitful dreams. Are you frustrated, ill-treated, ill-employed? Don't jump from the frying pan of a temporary evil into the fire of a permanent hate. Do you think it would make you happy to see your enemy's accidental death? If so, you have not escaped from an enemy; you have merely weakened your will to face him and, if possible, to convert him into a friend.

Take another example of practical ethics. Everyone you love is destined to die. Should you steel yourself against the loss of your beloved, as Montaigne advises, by limiting your love? No, declares Croce. On the contrary, true love will accept the reality of the pain along with the spirituality of the joy. "True happiness is to be won by loving with such elevation of spirit as to attain the strength to stand up to grief"—the ability to "surpass the old love with an even greater new love."

The purpose of love, of all ethics, is to fortify the individual against his own weakness and to fit him as a well-adjusted character into a rational pattern of life.

IV

Croce was opposed to every sort of outbreak—Nazism, Fascism, Communism—that tended to destroy this fundamental pattern. To the end of his days he hated explosions and earthquakes. His interest lay not in the outbursts of war but in the intervals of peace. During the "irrational parenthesis" of Fascism he shaped the minds of men to a new government of reason. When Mussolini fell and Victor Emmanuel came back to the throne, Croce refused to truckle to him. The madness of Monarchism was as distasteful to him as the frenzy of Fascism. He was foremost among those who insisted upon the dethronement of the obstinate king.

But, throughout this political turmoil, Croce was determined upon a peaceful return to sanity. When Gentile was assassinated by the anti-Fascists, Croce expressed his horror at the violent death. "I had hoped, in memory of our early friendship, to insure his personal safety, and to guide him back to the studies which he had deserted."

Here we have Croce's philosophy in a nutshell. Turn your enemies into friends, and guide them back from their belligerence into the sensible ways of peace. Urged, upon the abdication of King Emmanuel, to become president of the new republic, Croce refused the honor. He was modestly aware of his limitations. "What Italy needs in this crisis is not a tired old philosopher but a vigorous and practical man of the world."

Yet the vigor of Croce's intellect remained undiminished to the end. At the age of eighty (in 1946) he began a series of lectures for postgraduate students—to repay him, as he said, for his enforced exile from the young generation during the Fascist regime. At eighty-four he was on the point of death from a cerebral hemorrhage. But he recovered for another two years of lecturing and writing and showing the way to a life of greater utility and beauty and faith. And when he died, his grateful countrymen, both young and old, flocked to the funeral of their beloved "Don Benedetto"—the man with the rugged face of a fighter and the sensitive eyes of a saint.

CHAPTER XXX

John Dewey—the Architect
of a Better World

[1859–1952]

IN A TRIBUTE to John Dewey on his seventieth birthday (1929), Professor Herbert W. Schneider, of Columbia University, told an interesting story. When ancient Greece was destroyed, said Professor Schneider, the gods departed from Mount Olympus in search of a better home. One of them, the great god Pan, wandered for several centuries until he finally landed on the summit of the Green Mountains in Vermont. There he found another god, Logos, who had preceded him to the New England mountaintops.

Here the two antagonistic divinities—the god of romance and the god of reason—settled down to a new life. But they moved into different parts of the mountains. One of them looked down upon the valleys of the East; and the other, upon those of the West. And whenever they met, they began to quarrel in a very ungodlike manner. For each of them insisted that his own point of view was the one true picture of the entire world.

But one day they decided that it took three gods to make a heaven and to measure the world. And so they descended from the mountains to seek for a third god who might reconcile their divergent points of view.

After much blundering through the woods and the valleys, the two gods finally landed in Burlington. And here they came to an important decision. Instead of searching for a third god—whom they might never find—they would both enter into the soul of a newborn child. "I fear," said Logos, the god of reason, "that this will be the ruin of two perfectly good gods."

"It may be," said Pan, the god of romance, "but it may also be the making of a very wise and decent human being."

And thus it was on October 20, 1859, in Burlington, Vermont, that John Dewey was born. A Yankee incarnation of romance and reason, paganism and propriety, fantasy and fact.

II

John Dewey was brought up in New England; he taught in the Middle West—at the universities of Minnesota, Michigan, and Chicago; he studied and lectured in Europe and in China; he absorbed the best thoughts of the ancient and the medieval world; and he finally reorganized the Department of Education at Columbia. And thus, from the mountaintop of his accumulated experience, he was able to see philosophy in its widest application. Philosophy, he said, is co-extensive with our entire human adventure in the wilderness of the world. It is not a calm contemplation, but an eager motion—a lifelong endeavor on the part of the individual to find the way. And every one of us must find his *own* way. There is no such thing as a safe and charted course for all of us to follow. The traditional roads of yesterday may be obsolete today. For time changes all things.

The keynote of Dewey's philosophy is to be found in the word *change*. In his Yankee outlook on life, philosophy has become transformed from a noun into a verb. It is *knowledge in action*. Philosophy, in short, is not the possession of cosmic ideas, but the motion of the mind to adjust the individual to his environment. And the adjustment must keep changing, just as the environment keeps changing, all the time.

Dewey's own life was a continual adjustment to changing conditions. The father of five mischievous children, he had to develop an ability to cope with all sorts of sudden emergencies. His study was right under the bathroom. One day, as he was trying to untangle a philosophical problem, he felt a trickle of water down his back. He hurried upstairs to find the bathtub transformed into an overflowing river filled with a fleet of toy sailboats. His little boy Freddie was trying desperately to shut off the water. As Dewey opened the door, Freddie shouted: "Don't argue, John—do something about it!"

"Don't argue—do something" may well serve as the summary of John Dewey's philosophy. It is a practical philosophy for America, an intellectual stimulus for pioneers. A philosophy of vigorous action and daring experiment. It was the aim of Professor Dewey to turn philosophy into a science—the science of dealing with individual facts instead of accepting general truths.

Indeed, declared Dewey, there is no such thing as a general truth. What is true for you may not be true for me. And what was true for me yesterday may not be true for me today. For all life is a kaleidoscope of shifting scenery—a constant readjustment between ever changing individuals and an ever changing world.

And it is the business of philosophy to teach us how to make this readjustment. Philosophy, in other words, is a continual process of learning. It was no accident that Dewey was a pioneer in modern education. Wisdom, he said, begins not in some postgraduate college seminar, but in the primary classroom. We must learn to educate our children in the fundamental principles of philosophy. That is to say, in the conscious activity of living harmoniously together. The school, he said, is not a preparation *for* life, but a part *of* life. A life of interdependence, of social co-operation for individual needs. A mutual responsibility to live, to let live, and to help live.

III

It was this social spirit of interdependence that motivated Dewey to practice, as well as to teach, his new philosophy. He not only wrote a number of books on education—"the greatest thinking on the subject since Plato's *Republic*"—but he founded, in

Chicago, a progressive school of "learning through activity." In this school the child, rather than the curriculum, became the center of attention. The teachers showed the pupils *what* to do and *how* to do it in a spirit of co-operative good fellowship. The main purpose of the school was to enable the child to develop a desire for individual initiative as well as a social instinct for fair play.

But this individual and social development must come from the child himself. It can not be imposed by the teacher. "Learning," maintained Dewey, "never can be got into the child from without. It involves organic assimilation starting from within." Knowledge, in other words, is not a piling up of facts, like sticks and stones into a building; it is a process of growth, like buds and branches into a tree. The purpose of education is to enable the child to further his own growth. The very word *education* means *a bringing out* of a person's potentialities.

This was the literal sense in which Dewey understood the word. "All the school can or need do for pupils," he said, "is to develop their ability to think."

To think, and not merely to accumulate data. And the function of thinking, said Dewey, is to solve present difficulties in the light of past experience. This active phase of knowledge is as important for the child as it is for the adult. For the school is "inherently a part of the total social process. . . . When the school introduces and trains each child of society into membership within such a little community, saturating him with the spirit of service and providing him with the instruments of effective self-direction, we shall have the best guaranty of a larger society which is worthy, lovely and harmonious."

And thus Dewey's system of education is to bring up—*by bringing out*—worthy citizens of a democratic society—self-reliant, social-minded, and free—men and women who have acquired knowledge, through action, for better living. Pupils in the School of Life who, while still maintaining the old-fashioned three R's, have added something far more important—the three H's. The practical education of the head, the hand, and the heart.

IV

Like most other mental pioneers, John Dewey had to fight his way through a wilderness of ridicule and misunderstanding and indifference and spite. He has been compared to "another Atlas struggling to lift a world" above the mists and the clouds. And he succeeded to a great extent. The old education is slowly giving way to the new. Many a modern school today can trace its inspiration to his daring thought. Movable desks, free action, mutual service, a conscious effort to meet the demands of a world in which every child has to play a part, a closer co-operation between principal and teacher and pupil and parents, and the realization on the part of educators that the school is a part of the social process of life—in short, the new school of learning through action, to replace the old school of stagnation through cramming—this, to a great extent, is the result of Dewey's philosophy of education.

And he has carried this philosophy out of the school into the larger world. For the school, as he has pointed out again and again, *is* a part of the world. All life is a school for learning through action. "Knowing is a part of doing." Even more than William James, John Dewey is the philosopher of American practicality. American philosophy, at its best, tries to find a degree of freedom for the individual within certain restraints conditioned by the needs of other individuals. A friendly society of give and take. This philosophy of the New World looks with historical interest, but not with blind devotion, upon the Old World philosophy of kings and subjects, masters and masses, rulers and ruled. The American individual is a free member of a society in which all the other members are equally free.

This idea of freedom based upon the practical demands of life —the philosophy of Pragmatism—did not begin with Dewey or even with William James. The word *pragmatism* was coined within recent times. But the idea dates back to pre-Revolutionary days. It is the very essence of Americanism. In 1750 Dr. Samuel

Johnson, the first president of King's College—now known as Columbia University—declared that philosophy should be considered "not as a system of curious and idle speculations, but as a *practical principle of discipline* firmly possessing the heart and incessantly exerting itself in life."

Today this pragmatic idea of philosophy as "thought translated into practical action" has found its way even into the comic strip. "The question, Hennessey," remarks Mr. Dooley, "is, Does it work? The jawing isn't worth a tinker's dam."

The question is—Does it work, in the school as well as in the larger sphere of life? And the only way to find out whether a thing works is to experiment. Let us accept the world not only as the museum of a dead past but as the laboratory of a living present. Let us learn to walk by a series of falls. The only way for philosophy as a factor in constructive living is the way of trial and error. "Better it is for philosophy to err in active participation in the living struggles and issues of its own age and times than to maintain an immune monastic impeccability. To try to escape from the snares and pitfalls of time by recourse to traditional problems and interests—rather than that, let the dead bury their own dead."

And thus Dewey has become the articulate voice of modern America. The voice of collective action and individual growth through fair play. The philosophical spirit of democracy. True democracy, said John Dewey, is "a life of free and enriching communion. . . . There is nothing so important in life as the free, unobstructed communication of ideas and experiences and their transmission from one to another, without any kind of restriction, censorship or intimidation."

Dewey insists upon the free communion of a people educated, from their very childhood, to a knowledge of their own rights and duties, and to an understanding of the rights and duties of their fellows. This is the function of a democratic government—the best *political* truth for us in America today. According to Dewey, we must remember, there is no such thing as *absolute* truth for all people at all times. There are only *relative* truths for different people at different times.

But to return to Dewey's democratic philosophy. Democracy, he believes, is "government by organized intelligence." It is our business to introduce into government a practice already established in science. "In spite of science's dependence for its development upon the free initiative, invention and enterprise of individual inquirers, the authority of science issues from and is based upon collective activity, co-operatively organized." The same idea should apply to social and political as to scientific development. We must learn to co-ordinate our individual *goals* into co-operative *goods*. We must have a free communication of ideas as a guide to collective security.

And thus democracy, the form of government based upon the wishes of the governed, freely expressed, is more than a political philosophy. It is a way of life—the lifelong activity of learning to live together. It is the only form of government in which the people can rule from within, instead of being ruled from without. Democracy recognizes the fact that "no man or limited set of men is wise enough or good enough to rule others without their consent." The wisdom of mankind is greater than that of any one man. The individuals of the submerged mass may know less than the individuals at the top—an argument often advanced in behalf of the undemocratic forms of government. But there is one thing that the rank and file of the people are in a position to know better than anybody else—"and that is, where the shoe pinches."

The composite vote of the people, therefore, is necessary for the understanding of their composite needs. Their "pooled and co-operative" experience alone is the proper source of information for their representative government. It is a false philosophy that a few favored men are endowed, either by birth or by wealth or even by education, with a superior ability to regulate the lives of their fellow men. Everybody best knows his own needs. And it is only through the free expression of these needs that some sort of co-ordinated union can be elaborated.

A union co-ordinated upon the basis of human equality. This, observes Dewey, does not mean that men have equal endowments. But it does mean that they have equal rights to impartial treatment under the law, and to equal votes and opportunities even though they may not be equally wise in the exercise of their votes or equally skillful in the grasping of their opportunities.

And there is another basic reason for the democratic ideal of government. This reason is the growing faith of humanity that every individual has something important to contribute to the welfare of all. It is the pooled strength of the individuals that makes for a united power, and the pooled intelligence of the individuals that makes for a united wisdom.

And thus democracy is the expression of an organized "free intelligence" for the functioning of an organized "freedom of action." This idea of freedom is not "the right of each individual to *do* as he pleases," but his right to *say* as he pleases—so that his vote may become an important part of the composite voice, and his interest an integrated element in the co-operative interests of all.

This sort of democracy, declares Dewey, is not as yet an accomplished fact; it is a goal toward which we are moving. What we have in America today is (a measure of) organized intelligence on a political, but not as yet on a social or on an economic level. We have public votes but private wealth, equality on Election Day but inequality on all the other days, organized production but chaotic distribution, too much for the few but too little for the many, reckless competition among individuals and pitiable submission among the masses. What we need if we are to realize our democratic ideal is "an intelligence, a sentiment and an individuality of a new type."

Today, declares Dewey, even the so-called "rugged individuals" are drifting aimlessly they know not whither. They may call themselves captains of industry, but they are not "captains of their own souls." They are unhappy because deep down in their hearts they know that there is no direction to their endeavors—that the fundamental human desire is not for private profit but for social warmth.

And so we have a society of "lost individuals." Our economic leaders have no emotional outlet for their spiritual energies. They are trying to "refind" themselves. They are blindly seeking to transform their economic individualism into a social and political collectivism. They want a government in which the mind—the only *creative* individuality in human existence—will find more important work to do than the monotonous multiplication of dollars and cents.

As for the rest of the public, they too are awaking from their submissive paralysis. Free speech, free education, and a free press are beginning to produce their effect. The wage earners are no longer tied to their machines. They find the time to square their shoulders and to look around. Caliban in the coal mines, no less than Plato's philosopher in the cave, is preparing to have a look at the green earth under the sun. And to demand a share of its fruits. We are all moving, not toward a republic ruled by a philosopher-king, but toward a democracy governed by thoughtful men.

A *collective* democracy. A government which, far from *hampering* the individual, will help him to *expand* to his fullest mental, moral, political, social, and spiritual stature.

For a healthy society, a healthy state, a healthy world, is based upon the "friendly interactions" of all the people—the vital interplay of their private interests to produce a common storehouse of well-being. *The Co-operative Commonwealth.*

In such a government, based upon the mutual regard of all for one and of one for all, there will be no need of lost individuals. For "if, in the long run, an individual remains lost, it is because he has chosen irresponsibility." On the other hand, the richest individual—and riches need not be counted in savings and stocks—will be the one with the deepest responsibility for social integration. Such a man will be the best citizen, and a model for all the other citizens, in the government of political freedom, social intelligence, financial co-operation, equal justice, and lasting peace. "Until that method . . . is adopted, we shall remain in a period of drift and unrest whose final outcome is likely to be force and counterforce, with temporary victory to the side possessed of the most machine guns."

And Dewey, true to his spirit of philosophy as vigorous action rather than as passive thought, threw himself fearlessly into various efforts to outlaw war and to establish a bond of good will among the governments of the world.

V

Dewey's philosophy of action applies not only to politics but to ethics as well. He would widen the scope of the Ten Commandments from the singular *thou* to the plural *you*—from the individual greed to the social need. We must transform our moral concepts, he observes, to include "everything which affects the values of human living." And these values, he adds, "are involved on the widest scale in social issues."

But the change from personal to social morality, he points out, "does *not* signify that morality becomes impersonal and collective; it remains and must remain personal in that social problems must be faced by individuals." The world, however, is becoming smaller; and by the same token, the conception of human neighborliness is becoming larger. It is the business of the individual nowadays to fit himself into this larger conception, to establish a peaceful partnership not only between himself and his own community, but between his own community and the rest of the world. The second world war has shown that the remotest islanders in the Pacific are within a day's journey of our own back yard. And their hopes, within a fraternal embracement of our own hopes. *Their* hunger is *our* hunger; *their* welfare, *our* welfare. We must work together for our individual goods and our common good. "For many individuals," explains Dewey, "it is not now a question of whether they individually will appropriate property belonging to another, but whether existing large-scale economic arrangements"—such as national monopolies or international cartels— "operate to effect an equitable distribution of property; and if not, what they as individuals shall do about it."

What we need, in other words, is "an interpenetration of interests"—a new kind of freedom "unlike that which the unconstrained economic liberty of individuals [and of nations] has produced and justified." We need a kind of individual (and national) freedom which is general and shared, and which has the backing and guidance of a social control intelligently organized for the general good.

But, Dewey warns us, this new freedom—this interdependence of individuals and nations—can not spring suddenly out of a violent revolution. It is a matter of slow growth. *Progressive change through rational growth*—this is the gist of Dewey's philosophy. The goal of our life's adventure is not sudden perfection, but "the ever-enduring process of perfecting, enduring, refining."

So don't be too eager to bring about the millennium in your own day. The way to Heaven is not to be found through dictatorship or war. Go slow, and watch your step. Experiment. Be cautious in eliminating the evil and adopting the good. Your judgment, you know, may sometimes be wrong. Don't jump too fast. Take a step at a time. Don't aim to possess the world. Try rather to make it a place that will be more willing to possess you. Seek the individual freedom that will prompt you to allow others to be free.

Individual freedom, for the collective building of a better world. In the School of Life, observes Dewey, we are slowly learning that there is a *rhythmic correlation* between the parts and the whole. The collective movement of the stars is a textbook for the collective life of mankind.

And the individual life must find its proper groove in the cosmic movement of the whole. Dewey found his own groove in a combination of philosophic vision and Yankee thrift. When he taught at Columbia, he lived on a Long Island farm and raised eggs and vegetables to sell to his neighbors. Some years he would earn enough money on his farm "to pay for his keep." One day a rich lady customer telephoned for a dozen eggs. Since the children were all at school, Dewey delivered the eggs himself. He rang the front door bell and was gruffly ordered to go around to the back door. A couple of weeks later, he gave a lecture to a group of the local blue bloods. As he stepped upon the platform, the lady customer exclaimed in an audible whisper: "Why, he's the perfect image of our egg-man!"

VI

He remained the "egg-man philosopher" of the practical life to the end of his days. At the age of eighty, he headed a commission to investigate the wholesale executions of the so-called "plotters against the Socialist Government" in Russia. His report proved that the trials which resulted in the executions had been a farce, and that Stalin was a ruthless tyrant.

The Communists attacked Dewey's report as "the vaporings of a senile mind." But Dewey disproved his "senility" by publishing, at eighty-one, his brilliant work on *Logic*—regarded by many of his followers as perhaps his most important book.

No less amazing than his mental power was his physical prowess. Having lost his first wife, he married a second time at eighty-seven. And a year later, the young-old couple had acquired two children—not their own, however, but adopted war refugees.

And at ninety, at a banquet held in his honor, he made one of the most energetic and forward-looking speeches of his entire career.

He was ninety-two when he died (in 1952)—surrounded as of old by admiring friends, playful children, and the serenity of wisdom to meet the final adventure of death as eagerly as he had met the exciting adventure of life.

Index

Acosta, Uriel, 156
Addison, Joseph, 177
Adeodatus, 96
Aesthetic, Croce's, 295–96
Aeschylus, 11, 39
Agassiz, Louis, 269
Alexander, Czar of Russia, 212
Alexander the Great, King: Aristotle's relationship with, 41–42; death of, 47, 65, 68; dialogue with Diogenes, 61–62; wars of, 45, 66–67
Alfadel, 107
American philosophy: Dewey's knowledge in action and educational theories, 301–11; James's pragmatism, 268–77; Thoreau's beliefs in Nature, 230–39
Amyntas, King, 39
Ananias, 79
Anarchism, Kropotkin's, 283
Anthony, Marc, 78
Antichrist, Nietzsche as, 241
Antipater, King, 47
Antisthenes, 57–58
Antoninus, Emperor, 87
Anytus, 20
Ares, 16
Aristocles. *See* Plato
Aristotle, 39–48: as Alexander's tutor, 40–42; ethics of, 47; Golden Mean philosophy, 44; Maimonides compared with, 108; peripatetic school of, 43–44; scientific research by, 42–43
Arouet, François Marie. *See* Voltaire
Asclepius, 28
Ashley, Lord, 147

Ataraxia, 69
Athens, Socrates' trial in, 18–28
Atomic theory, in Epicurean philosophy, 72
Augustine. *See* St. Augustine
Avidius Cassius, 87–88

Bacon, Francis, 135–44: admiration for Machiavelli, 121; extortion conviction, 135, 139–40; philosophy of, 140–43; political career of, 135–39; utopia in *New Atlantis,* 143; Voltaire's admiration of, 177
Beauty, Plato on, 32
Beethoven, Ludwig von, 204
Berlichingen, Götz von, 203
Berliner Monatsschrift, 198
Boleyn, Anne, 132
Borgia, Caesar, 114–15, 117, 119
Brandes, Georg, *quoted,* 175
Buckingham, Lord, 139–40
Buddha, 220
Business, pragmatism as philosophy of, 272–73

Caesar, Julius, 80
Callisthenes, 42
Candide, Voltaire's, 185–87
Carpenter, Edward, *quoted,* 267
Cavour, Count di, 291
Channing, Ellery, 232
Charity, Maimonides' eight degrees of, 110–11
Charles I, King of England, 145, 151
Charles II, King of England, 146, 147, 154
Châtelet, Marquise du, 179, 183

Chesterton, G. K., 174
China, Confucianism in, 49–56
Christ. *See* Jesus Christ
Christianity: basic beliefs of, in St. Paul's Epistles, 81–84; Comte's comment on, 229; Marcus Aurelius' persecution of, 89; Nietzsche's antagonism to, 241–42, 244–45; opposition to, 76; St. Augustine's conversion to, 95–103; St. Paul's conversion to, 77–81; Stoicism compared to, 94; Vivekananda's merger with Eastern religions, 253–54
Christian Socialism, 131
Church of England, 133
Cicero, Marcus, 78
Cleopatra, 78, 235
Columbus, Christopher, 124
Communist Revolution, 289
Comte, Auguste, 222–29: life of, 222–24; religion of Humanism founded by, 224–29
Condé, Prince de, 164
Condorcet, Marquis de, 223
Confessions, Rousseau's, 166, 173
Confessions, St. Augustine's, 98–99
Confucius, 49–56
Congreve, William, 177
Contractual consent, Locke's philosophy of, 148–52
Corinthians, First Epistle to the, 82–83
Couvreur, Adrienne le, 178
Critique of Practical Reason, The, Kant's, 194–98
Critique of Pure Reason, The, Kant's, 192–94
Crito, 27–28
Croce, Benedetto, 291–300: *Aesthetic,* 295–96; economic theories of, 295; opposition to Mussolini, 293–95; religion of, 297–99
Cromwell, Oliver, 145–46
Cromwell, Thomas, 121
Cynicism: of Diogenes, 57–65; influence on Marcus Aurelius, 87; philosophy of, 67
Cypris, 16

Dance of Life, The, Ellis's, 263–65
D'Annunzio, Gabriele, 293

Dante, 71
Darwin, Charles: Chinese beliefs akin to, 49; influence on Kropotkin, 286; precursors of, 15, 44, 73; Vivekananda adopts theories of, 254
Declaration of Independence, U.S., 150
de Gourmont, Remy, *quoted,* 66
de Medici, Lorenzo, 117
Democracy: Empedocles as father of, 12, 17; Locke's philosophy as forerunner of, 148–54; as "organized intelligence" of Dewey, 307–10
Democritus, 72
Descartes, René, 99
Dewey, Freddie, 302
Dewey, John, 301–11: anecdotes on, 301–3, 311–12; educational theories of, 303–4; ethics of, 310–11; knowledge in action philosophy, 302, 305–11
Dialogue of Comfort against Tribulation, A, More's, 133–34
Dictatorships: Machiavelli's *Prince* textbook for, 115–21; Nietzsche's Superman glorification of, 242–46
Diderot, Denis, 174
Diogenes, 57–65: anecdote on death of, 65; cynicism of, 57–60, 64; on liberty, 61–62; on security, 60–61; on simplicity, 62–64
Dionysius, King, 36–37, 40
Discourse on Inequality, Rousseau's, 169
Discourses, Machiavelli's, 115
Dishonesty, Machiavelli's cult of, 114–22
Domitian, Emperor, 90
Dooley, Mr., *quoted,* 306
Dreyfus, Albert, 277

Eckermann (zoologist), 287
Edison, Thomas, 265
Educational theories: of Dewey and the progressive movement, 303–4; of Plato in the *Republic,* 32–34
Egmont, Goethe's, 204
Einstein, Albert, 264
El-Adil, 104
Elective Affinities, Goethe's, 204

Elizabeth I, Queen of England, 136–38
Ellis, Edward, 257
Ellis, Havelock, 257–67: *Dance of Life* philosophy, 263–65; personal life, 257–59, 266–67; sex studies, 260–62
Emerson, Ralph Waldo: *quoted,* 205; and Thoreau, 237
Emerson, William, 232
Emile, Rousseau's, 170, 189–90
Empedocles, 11–18: death of, 11; Love vs. Strife theory, 14–17; philosophy of, 13–17
England, history of. *See* Great Britain, history of
English philosophers: Bacon, adventurer-politician, 135–44; Ellis and Dance of Life studies, 257–67; Locke and political philosophy, 145–55; More and Utopia, 123–34
Epictetus, 86, 89–94: beliefs, 90–94; *quoted* on Diogenes, 63; simplicity of, 89–91; Stoicism compared with Marcus Aurelius', 91–94
Epicurus, 66–75: atomic theory of, 72; Garden of, 68–74; philosophy of pleasure, 68–71
Epistles of St. Paul, 81–84
Erasmus, Desiderius, 123, 127
Essex, Earl of, 136–38
Eternal Peace, Kant's, 199–200
Eternity, St. Augustine's riddle of, 100–1
Ethics, Kropotkin's, 286, 290
Ethics, Spinoza's, 160
Evil, Machiavelli's cult of, 114–22
Evolution: Aristotle's theory of, 44; Chinese belief in, 49; Empedocles' theory of, 15; Epicurus' theory of, 73; Kropotkin's Mutual Aid theory of, 286–88
Ezekiel, *quoted,* 271

Fadiman, Clifton, 235
Faraday, Michael, 265
Fascism, Croce's opposition to, 293–95
Faust, Goethe's, 205–10
Faustina, Queen, 88

Ferdinand, King of Spain, 119
France, Anatole, 182
Franklin, Benjamin, 223
Frederick the Great, King of Prussia, 172, 183–84
Frederick William, King of Prussia, 198–99
French philosophers: Comte and Humanism, 222–29; Rousseau, 165–73; Voltaire, 174–88
Friendship, Epicurus on, 74–75

Gamaliel, 78
Gandhi, Mahatma, 233
Garden of Epicurus, 68–74
Garibaldi, Giuseppe, 291
Gentile, Giovanni, 293–94, 299
German philosophy: Goethe and romanticism, 201–11; Nietzsche and the Superman, 240–47; Schopenhauer and pessimism, 212–21
Giolitti, Giovanni, 293
God: Cynics as servants of, 64; as impartial power for good, in Rousseau's philosophy, 170–71; mystery of, St. Augustine on, 100; spiritual power of, Maimonides' faith in, 108–10; Trinity of, St. Paul on, 81–83; Vivekananda's interpretation of, 250–55
Goethe, Johann W., 96, 201–11: *Faust,* 205–10; novels, 203–4; personality, 201–2
Golden Mean, Aristotle's doctrine of, 45–47
Goodness, Plato on, 32
Gourmont, Remy de, 66
Government: Aristotle's theories of, 46–47; Bacon's belief in self-government, 143; Dewey's theory of organized intellect as directing, 307–10; Kropotkin's Mutual Aid theory of, 286–89; Locke's theory of contractual consent as, 148–54; Machiavelli's championship of dictatorships, 114–22; Nietzsche's Super-State theory of, 243–46; Plato's theories on, in the *Republic,* 32–37; Rousseau's social contract theory of, 167, 171–72
Great Britain, history of: Bacon's chancellorship under Elizabeth,

betrayal of Essex, 136–40; Bloodless Revolution of 1688, Locke's influence on, 145–55; Henry VIII's establishment of Church of England, More's opposition to, 132–33

Greek philosophers: Aristotle, 39–48; Diogenes, 57–65; Empedocles, 11–18; Epicurus, 66–75; Plato, 29–38; Socrates, 18–28

Guide for the Perplexed, Maimonides, 107

Gulliver's Travels, Swift's, 181

Hawthorne, Nathaniel, 231–32
Hedonists, 67
Hegesias, 67
Heine, Heinrich, *quoted,* 190, 197
Hemingway, Ernest, 212
Henry of Navarre, 175
Henry IV, King of France, 174
Henry VIII, King of England, 121, 126–28, 131–34
Hermias, 40
Hindu philosophy, 248–56
Hinton, James, 259
History of Western Philosophy, Russell's, 228
Hitler, Adolf: Machiavelli's influence on, 122; Nietzsche's influence on, 242–43, 245
Homer, 11, 297
Housman, A. E., 259
Humanism, 224–29
Humanitarianism, 226
Hume, David: host to Rousseau, 172; Kant's criticism of, 191, 193; *quoted,* 165
Hunt, William Morris, 269

Idols, false, in Baconian philosophy, 141–43
Imperturbability, Epicurean doctrine of, 69
Indian philosophy, 248–56
Inferno, Dante's, 71
Inge, Dean, *quoted,* 274
In Praise of Folly, Erasmus', 127
Italian philosophers: Croce, 291–300; Machiavelli, 114–22

James I, King of England, 138
James, Henry, 269

James, William, 268–77: personal life, 268–72, 276–77; Pragmatism of, 272–76, 305; religious views, 274–75

Jeans, Sir James, 101

Jesus Christ: Confucius compared with, 52; Kant quoted on, 198; Nietzsche's antagonism to, 241; Ramakrishna compared with, 250, 251–52; St. Paul's vision of, 77; Shaw quoted on, 56. *See also* Christianity

Jewish philosophers: Maimonides, 104–13; Spinoza, 156–64

Joan (Richard the Lion-Hearted's sister), 104

John the Baptist, 241
Johnson, Samuel, 305–6
Jonson, Ben, 139
Jules-Bois, *quoted,* 256
Justice, Plato on, 32, 34–37

Kali, 250
Kant, Immanuel, 189–200: *Critique of Practical Reason,* 194–98; *Critique of Pure Reason,* 192–94; religious beliefs, 197–98, 200; Rousseau's influence on, 189–91; Schopenhauer's admiration of, 220

Karl August, Prince, 204, 210
Katherine of Aragon, 132
Kropotkin, Peter, 278–90: anarchism of, 283; Mutual Aid theory of government and Nature, 285–89; Siberian service, 280–82

Labriola, 292
La Critica, Croce's, 293
Lampe (Kant's servant), 50–1
Lavoisier, Antoine, 223
Lees, Edith, 261
Leibniz, Gottfried, 185
le Vasseur, Thérèse, 167
Liberty, Diogenes on, 61–62
Life in Nature, Hinton's, 259
Life of Aristotle, Fuller's, 43
Light, The, Maimonides', 107
l'Ingénu, Voltaire's, 180
Littré, Maximilien, 229
Locke, John, 145–55: Kant's criticism of, 191, 193; personal life,

145–48, 154–55; political philosophy, 148–54, 171
Logic, Dewey's, 311
Logos, 301–2
Louis XIV, King of France, 146, 164, 174
Louis XV, King of France, 175, 183
Louis XVI, King of France, 175
Lucretius, 70
Lycurgus, 91

Macaulay, Thomas B., 121
Machiavelli, Nicolo, 114–22: influence of, 121–22, 141; personal life, 114–16; political doctrines in the *Prince,* 115–21, 131
Marcus Aurelius, 86–89, 91–94: career as emperor, 86–89; *Meditations,* 87; philosophy of, 91–94; Stoicism of, compared with Epictetus', 91–94
Margaret, Princess of England, 126
Maimonides, Moses, 104–13: *Guide for the Perplexed,* 107; *The Light,* 107; medical career, 107, 111–13; philosophy of, 107–11; wanderings of, 105–6
Marx, Karl, 31, 292, 295
Materialism of Karl Marx, The, Croce's, 295
"May Day Riots," 127
Mazzini, Giuseppe, 291
Medici, Lorenzo de, 117
Meditations, Marcus Aurelius', 87
Meletus, 23
Mennonites, 160
Meyer, Dr., 164
Michelangelo, 296
Micromégas, Voltaire's, 181–82
Mill, John Stuart, 229
Montaigne, Michel de, 298
More, Sir Thomas, 123–34: *Dialogue of Comfort against Tribulation,* 133–34; legal career, 126–27; philosophical romance, *Utopia,* 128–31; and Henry VIII, 126–27, 131–33
Morton, Archbishop, 124
Mumford, Lewis, *quoted,* 274
Mussolini, Benito: Croce's opposition to, 293–95; Machiavelli's influence on, 122; Nietzsche's influence on, 242, 245
Mutual Aid: a Factor in Evolution, Kropotkin's, 286

Napoleon, 212, 226: Machiavelli's influence on, 122; Nietzsche's admiration of, 244, 246
Nature: Ellis on beauties of, in *The Dance of Life,* 263–67; Kropotkin's theory of Mutual Aid in, 286–89; as material, in Epicurus' philosophy, 72–73; Schopenhauer's cynical views on, 216–18; Thoreau's belief in simple life of, 232–38
Nero, Emperor, 85
New Atlantis, Bacon's, 143
New Héloise, The, Rousseau's, 170
New Spirit, The, Ellis's, 261
Newton, Isaac, 177
Nicholas, Czar of Russia, 278
Nietzsche, Friedrich, 240–7: insanity, 246–47; Machiavelli's influence on, 121–22; philosophy of the Superman, 115, 240, 243–46; *Thus Spake Zarathustra,* 242–43
Nihilism, Kropotkin's, 281, 283
Nordau, Max, *quoted,* 246
Norfolk, Duke of, 133

Olympias, Queen, 41
On the Improvement of the Mind, Spinoza's, 160
On the Nature of Things, Lucretius', 70
Oriental philosophies: Confucianism of China, 49–56; Vedanta of India, 248–56

Pan, 301–2
Pantheism, Spinoza's, 161
Parsifal, Wagner's, 242
Pascal, Blaise, 198
Paul of Tarsus. *See* St. Paul
Pepys, Samuel, *quoted,* 146
Peripatetic school, 43–44
Pessimists, 167
Peterson, Houston, *quoted,* 263
Petrarch, Francesco, 218
Philip, King of Macedonia, 39–41
Philosophers: Aristotle, 39–48; Ba-

con, 135–44; Comte, 222–29; Confucius, 49–56; Croce, 291–300; Dewey, 301–11; Diogenes, 57–65; Ellis, 257–67; Empedocles, 11–18; Epictetus, 86, 89–94; Epicurus, 66–75; Goethe, 201–11; James, 268–77; Kant, 189–200; Kropotkin, 278–90; Locke, 145–55; Machiavelli, 114–22; Maimonides, 104–13; Marcus Aurelius, 86–89, 91–94; More, 123–34; Nietzsche, 240–47; Plato, 29–38; Rousseau, 165–73; St. Augustine, 95–103; St. Paul, 76–85; Schopenhauer, 212–21; Socrates, 18–28; Spinoza, 156–64; Thoreau, 230–39; Vivekananda, 248–56; Voltaire, 174–88

Philosophical Letters, Voltaire's, 177–78

Philosophies: Confucianism, 49–56; Cynicism, 57–65, 67, 87; Epicureanism, 66–75; Hedonism, 67; Humanism, 224–29; Pessimism, 67; and poetry, 11–12; Pragmatism, 272–76; and religion, 11–12; Skepticism, 67; Stoicism, 86–94; Vedanta, 248–56

Plato, 29–38: Academy of, 32, 40; Dionysius invites to establish Republic in Sicily, 36–37; observation of Spartan government, 30–31; *quoted,* 11; *Republic* of, 32–37, 303; Socrates' influence on, 29–30; sold into slavery, 37; and song, 50

Pleasure, Epicurean philosophy of, 66–75

Poetry, and philosophy, 11–12

Political theories: of Aristotle, 46–47; Bacon's self-government in *New Atlantis,* 143; Dewey's democracy directed by organized intelligence, 307–10; Kropotkin's anarchism, then Mutual Aid beliefs, 286–89; Locke's contractual consent philosophy, 148–54; Machiavelli's statecraft of oppression, 114–22; Nietzsche's "Super-State," exploitation of masses for the Super class, 243–46; of Plato, in the *Republic,* 32–37; Rous-

seau's social contract beliefs, 167, 171–72

Polo, Marco, 282

Pope, Alexander: *quoted* on Bacon, 137; and Voltaire, 177

Positivism, Comte's, 224–29

Pragmatism: in American life, 305–6; of Dewey, 305–6; of William James, 272–76

Prince, The, Machiavelli's, 115–21, 131

Prometheus, 63

Proudhon, Pierre, 283

Psychology of Jingoism, The, James's, 277

Ramakrishna, 248, 250–2

Relativity, of time, 99–100, 101–2

Religions: Christianity, 81–84, 95–103; Confucianism, 49–56; Humanism of Comte, 222–29; and philosophy, 11–12; Rousseau's "religion of the heart," 170–1; Vivekanada's universal Fellowship of Faith, 248–56

Renaissance, 124

Renan, Ernest, *quoted,* 164

Renouvier, Charles, 269

Republic, Plato's, 32–37, 303

Richard the Lion-Hearted, King of England, 104, 113

Robespierre, Maximilien, 212

Rohan, Chevalier de, 175–76

Roman philosophers: Epictetus, 86, 89–94; Marcus Aurelius, 86–89, 91–94

Romans, Epistle to the, 82

Rousseau, Jean Jacques, 165–73: *Confessions,* 166, 173; influence on Kant, 189–90; personal life, 165–67, 172–73; philosophy, 168–72; religious beliefs, 170–1; *Social Contract,* 170–2

Russell, Bertrand: neglect of Comte, 228; *quoted* on Revolution of 1688, 145; *quoted* on Rousseau, 172; *quoted* on St. Augustine, 99

Russia: Kropotkin's rebellion against social order of, 278–90; Nietzsche's comment on as possible "Super-State," 245

St. Albans, Viscount. *See* Bacon, Francis

St. Augustine, 95–103: *Confessions,* 98–99; conversion, 98–99; on eternity, 100; on mystery of God, 100; philosophy, 99–103; sinful youth, 95–98; time theories, 101–3

St. Francis, 105

St. Paul, 76–85: changes name from Saul, 80; conversion, 77, 79; Epistles of, 81–84; influence on St. Augustine, 99; Maimonides compared with, 108; missionary journeys, 80–1; Socrates compared with, 27; Stoicism in doctrines of, 94

Saint-Simon, Laude de, 223

Saladin, 104, 107, 113

Sanskrit, 249

Santayana, George, *quoted,* 70, 72

Sarkar, S. L., 255

Saul of Tarsus. *See* St. Paul

Savonarola, 114

Schneider, Herbert W., 301

Schools: Aristotle's peripatetic, 43–44; Dewey's progressive, 304; Plato's Academy, 32, 40

Schopenhauer, Arthur, 212–21: Comte contemporary of, 222; cynicism of, 216–18; influence on Nietzsche, 241; pessimistic philosophy, 213, 215–21; *quoted* on Kant, 194; recluse life, 214–15

Science, Aristotle's studies of, 43

Security, Diogenes's views on, 60–1

Seneca, 85

Sermon on the Mount, 51

Sex, Havelock Ellis's studies of, 26, 260–2

Shaftesbury, Earl of, 147

Shakespeare, William, 135, 161, 193

Shaw, George Bernard, *quoted,* 56, 131

Siberia, Kropotkin's experiences in, 280–2

Simplicity, Diogenes's views on, 62–64

Skepticism, 67

Social Contract, The, Rousseau's, 17, 170–2

Socialism, Christian, 131

Socrates, 18–28: Antisthenes disciple of, 57–58; death of, 27–28, 31; influence on Marcus Aurelius, 87; Plato disciple of, 29–30; submission to Athenian justice, 62; trial of, 18–25

Soderini, 116

Sorrows of Werther, The, Goethe's, 203

Sparta, Plato's study of, 30–1

Spaventas family, 291

Spinoza, Benedict, 156–64: cast out by Jews, 158–59; pantheism of, 161; philosophy of, 160–3; St. Augustine's influence on, 99

Stalin, Josef, 212

Statecraft, Machiavelli on, 116–21

Stein, Gertrude, 271–72

Stella, Goethe's, 204

Stoicism, 86–94: double appeal of, 92; of Epictetus, 89–94; of Marcus Aurelius, 86–89, 91–94; similarity to Christianity, 94

Studies in the Psychology of Sex, Ellis's, 261–62

Sully, Duc de, 175, 176

Superman, Nietzsche's glorification of, 240, 243–46

Swift, Jonathan, 177, 181

Tarsus, St. Paul's childhood in, 78

Teng Shih, 50

Thales, 136

Thoreau, Henry David, 230–9: Diogenes compared with, 63; life at Walden Pond, 232–36; Nature cult, 233–36, 238; philosophical creed, 233–37

Thus Spake Zarathustra, Nietzsche's, 242–43

Time: relativity theory of, 99–102; St. Augustine's theories on, 101–2

Time Machine, The, Wells's, 18

Timon of Athens, 214

Tolstoy, Leo: disciple of Thoreau, 233; St. Augustine compared to, 95

Treatise on Politics, A, Spinoza's, 160

Treatise on Religion and the State, A, Spinoza's, 160

Trotsky, Leon, 212

Turgenev, Ivan, 281
Twain, Mark, 182

United States, philosophy in. *See*
  American philosophers
Unzelmann (actor), 215
Utopia, Sir Thomas More's, 128–31
Utopias: Bacon's *New Atlantis,* 143;
  More's *Utopia,* 128–31; Plato's
  Republic, 32–37

Van den Ende, 158
Vaux, Clotilde de, 224
Vedanta philosophy, 248–56
Vercellis, Madame de, 166
Victor Emmanuel, King of Italy,
  299
Vivekananda, 248–56: American
  missions, 248–49, 253–55; Rama-
  krishna's disciple, 248, 250–2;
  universal religion of, 248, 252–55
Voltaire, 174–88: *Candide,* 185–87;
  English exile, 176–78; influence
  on Comte, 223; life at Cirey, 179–
  83; life at Ferney, 184–85; *Philo-*

sophical Letters, 177–78; quarrels
  with Rousseau, 169; rational faith
  of, 185

Wagner, Richard, 246
Walden, Thoreau's, 232–33, 238
War: Machiavelli's views on, 121;
  Nietzsche's views on, 241–43
Warens, Madame de, 166
Wells, H. G., 18
Whitman, Walt: Goethe compared
  to, 211; *quoted,* 69
*Why We Cannot But Call Ourselves
  Christians,* Croce's, 297
Wilhelm I, Kaiser, 122
Wilhelm Meister, Goethe's, 204
William of Orange, King of Eng-
  land, 154
Wolsey, Cardinal, 129
World as Will and Idea, The,
  Schopenhauer's, 212, 215
Wright, J. H., 249

Zadig, Voltaire's, 180–1
Zarathustra, 242–43